The Structure of Behavior

THE STRUCTURE
OF BEHAVIOR

by Maurice Merleau-Ponty

Translated by ALDEN L. FISHER

BEACON PRESS   BOSTON

CONTENTS

Contents

TRANSLATOR'S PREFACE

Il ne me souvient pas qu'une mort ait consterné davantage. Dans l'instant, nous avons perçu qu'une dimension de la vérité nous était retirée, qu'une expression du vrai, longuement attendue, ne serait jamais dite.
Alphonse De Waelhens
Les Temps Modernes, 1961

The premature death (May 1961) of the author of this book undoubtedly came as a grave shock to the whole of the philosophical and intellectual world. That the English translation of his first published work—which undertaking he so graciously placed in my hands, and the progress of which he followed with such interest, encouragement and warmth—did not appear in his lifetime is a matter of very deep regret to me. This completed task, then—with all its defects—is respectfully dedicated to the memory of Professor Maurice Merleau-Ponty.

Few philosophers have outlined as rich a philosophy of language as did the author of this book, nor consequently have understood so well the difficulties—perhaps even the impossibility—of truly faithful translation. Awareness of this constituted both a support and a burden in completing this work: the first, because it provided some consolation for the inadequacy; the second, because it emphasized the problems at hand. Among the many particular decisions involved in the attempt to translate a difficult and nuanced philosophical text, there is one guiding choice which must be made: that between a wholly literal rendition of the original at the expense of style in the second language, and a free rendition which bows completely to the literary demands of the latter. The present translation does not pretend in the least to have achieved the proper balance between these two poles. But, while some concessions to the requirement of readability were obviously necessary, the primary goal has been to communicate the subtle thought of the author as accurately as possible;

ix

hence the option for the more literal and less elegant rendering has been taken when this seemed necessary to preserve the idea.

In this connection, the use of certain technical terms should be given some preliminary clarification. Throughout the book, when the author refers to "critical thought" (*la pensée criticiste*), problems and solutions in the "critical" tradition, etc., the term "critical" has reference to the philosophical tradition initiated by Kant (but not necessarily to all of Kant's own thought; cf. p. 248, n. 41) and represented, especially in this book, by the idealism of a philosopher such as Brunschvicg. As exemplified in the introduction, the author's use of the terms: "realistic," "realism," "realistic analyses or thinking," and frequently the word "real" itself, refers for the most part to a reductive realism typical of certain trends in modern (not necessarily contemporary) scientific thought and characterized by partitive analysis and the tendency to consider the resulting scientific constructs and scientific view of the world as representative or even descriptive of the ontologically real. "Realism" also occasionally refers to the naive realism of common sense or of science; only in the last chapter do the expressions have specific reference to any of the classical forms of philosophical realism—and then it is usually a question of the realism of the late scholasticism to which Descartes reacted. Likewise, the expression "causal thinking" is most frequently taken in the sense of a mechanistic action of a part on a part—although the meaning is again somewhat enlarged in the last part of the book.

As is well known, the French term *"conscience"* has many shades of meaning—from simple awareness to explicit consciousness, the all-embracing sphere of the mental, and finally simply the mind itself. With few exceptions the word "consciousness" has been retained in English in order to preserve some of the flexibility and continuity of the French expression; the context usually provides ample clarification of the particular shade of meaning in question. The term *"l'esprit"* has been consistently translated as "mind," as well as the term *"l'intelligence." "Spirituelle"* and its derivatives have been translated as "mental" or "rational," depending on the context; *"psychique"* has been translated as "mental" or "psychological," again depending on the context. Reference to the order of life or to vital activity—preserved in the English—has a restricted meaning in this work, referring to the biological or vegetative sphere. When several English equivalents exist for technical terms, the more neutral expression, the one less closely associated with a particular theoretical frame of reference, was usually chosen. Finally, in the original, certain portions of the text appear in reduced type; these sections are not quotations but by and large represent concise presentations and summarizations of the findings of science which are relevant to the author's discussion but do not form an integral part of the main line of philosophical reasoning. For this reason the present translation (based on the Second French Edition which was revised and amplified by the author) has retained this format. With these few indications, it is hoped that the general context itself will allow the reader to follow the author's precise meaning in any given case.

It is with pleasure and genuine appreciation that certain obligations are acknowledged. First and foremost, this work could not have been completed without the generous and unfailing assistance of my wife, whose efforts extend from the most thankless mechanical details to a careful critical reading of the final draft, and whose help was invaluable at all levels; to her, I am most grateful. I am also indebted to many friends and colleagues at Saint Louis University and the University of Louvain for advice and encouragement; among these persons, I am particularly grateful to the Reverend H. L. Van Breda, O.F.M., and Alphonse De Waelhens for their assistance in the initial stages of the project, and to James Collins and John Higgins for their valuable assistance with certain technical problems. Nevertheless, the usual disclaimer that all the mistakes and inadequacies of this work are completely and solely the responsibility of the translator must apply with special force in this instance.

ALDEN L. FISHER
Saint Louis University

Foreword

Maurice Merleau-Ponty died on May 4, 1961, having lectured for eight years as the successor of Bergson and Gilson in the chair of philosophy at the Collège de France. It is hard for those of us who were acquainted with him and who heard him speak during his extraordinarily active and productive career to realize that his life is over. But his highly original and perceptive works are still accessible. I am glad that this relatively early work, first published in 1942, is being made available to English and American readers and that other of his works will soon become available in English language editions.[1] I welcome this opportunity to make a few comments on the present work's general significance, and on its relevance to English and American philosophy at the present time.

Like other European philosophers of his time, Merleau-Ponty was thoroughly trained in the discipline of phenomenology, in the literature of which he had read widely and deeply. He carefully studied the writings of Husserl, not only the published works but also the later unpublished manuscripts at Louvain, becoming deeply interested in the development of Husserl's thought, the direction in which it had been moving. The new vistas opened by this reading of Husserl challenged Merleau-Ponty and beckoned him onward. He devoted his professional life to the disciplined exploration of these vistas.

Although Merleau-Ponty must be regarded as a phenomenological thinker, he never accepted any position before thinking it through for himself, and without trying to develop it further. From this book, the English language reader can get a sense of phenomenology, not as it was in the time of Husserl, but as a distinctive style of philosophizing, living and working in our own time. It may

1. *The Phenomenology of Perception,* translated by Colin Smith, has been published by Routledge and Kegan Paul, London, 1962. The Northwestern University Press will soon publish translations of Merleau-Ponty's *Éloge de la Philosophie, Sens et non-sens,* and *Signes.*

be true, as our author held, that Husserl's thought was already developing in the direction which Merleau-Ponty himself gave to phenomenological thought. But the present study of human behavior contains existential elements that are not found in any of Husserl's published works. Merleau-Ponty is not interested in an abstract, worldless consciousness but in that of historical man as he is engaged and existing in the world.

For many years closely associated with Sartre and often stimulated by Sartrian insights, he nevertheless subjects them to a searching criticism, as is evident from this volume, and sharply rejects the ontological dualism of the *en soi* versus the *pour soi,* which he recognizes as coming from Cartesian sources. There is no question that Merleau-Ponty was also affected by his reading of Heidegger's book, *Sein und Zeit,* in the 1920's, and the penetrating description of being-in-the-world which he found there. But he was certainly unaffected by the *Seinsmystik* which underlies this work, by its lack of any serious concern for contemporary science, and by its neglect of perception and the human body. One cannot imagine Heidegger engaging in the careful study and criticism of Gestalt and Freudian psychology with which this work begins.

The French thinker is just as clear as Heidegger that the world in which we exist cannot be reduced to the objective variables and functional relationships which physical science reveals. The life-world has a meaningful structure of its own, which must be approached in a very different way if it is not to be radically reduced and distorted. But the perspectives of physical and biological science also reveal distinctive orders and structures which the philosopher needs to understand. In a way that reminds us of Scheler, Merleau-Ponty shows, without accepting any traces of vitalism, how a higher order is founded on a lower and in a sense contains it, but at the same time takes it over and integrates it into new structures which cannot be explained by those that are taken over. The philosopher, it is true, is chiefly concerned with the life-world and its overarching structures. But in order to explore it properly, he needs to understand how it is contrasted with, and how it is related to, the more abstract, subordinate orders. Hence instead of peremptorily dismissing them, the author of this work devotes half of his pages to a disciplined study of physical and biological approaches to human behavior, showing how science itself, at critical junctures in its procedure, is led by the facts themselves to take over uncritically assumptions about the life-world which it is in no position, with its more restricted methods, to examine carefully and critically.

There is a widespread impression in this country that phenomenology is merely an empty method with no firmly established results, and that it has been used by a variety of different authors as a plausible pretext for "justifying" their radically different metaphysical views. A careful reading of Merleau-Ponty's work will show the falsity of these opinions. The task of exploring the human life-world as it is lived, which was inaugurated by Husserl—though only just begun—has already arrived at results which have been inter-subjectively confirmed and which have, in a sense, become common property. Thus Merleau-Ponty has taken over from Husserl the general conception of the phenomenological method and the well-known analysis of perception through profiles (*Abschattungen*); from Sartre, with important qualifications, the notion of consciousness as involving negation and distance; from Heidegger many aspects of his analysis of man as being-in-the-world; and from Scheler the notion of structural levels. But he has rejected Husserl's notion of the transcendental ego, Sartre's metaphysical dualism of the *en soi* and the *pour soi,* Heidegger's hypostatization of *Sein,* and Scheler's metaphysical pantheism. He has given himself to the careful study of the works of other phenomenologists, but this study has always been critical. He has rejected their errors, but has recaptured and rethought their insights, using them to support and to develop original insights of his own. It is out of this patient winnowing process of mutual stimulation and criticism that lasting truths are gradually achieved. In his life and in his works, Merleau-Ponty has shown us how an independent philosopher can creatively cooperate with his philosophical and scientific colleagues in a great task that is still unfinished—the disciplined exploration of the structures of the life-world.

Social scientists will be interested in his selection of behavior (*comportement*) as a central category, because of its neutrality with respect to the traditional distinction between mind and body. Human behavior is neither a series of blind reactions to external "stimuli," nor the projection of acts which are motivated by the pure ideas of a disembodied, worldless mind. It is neither exclusively subjective nor exclusively objective, but a dialectical interchange between man and the world, which cannot be adequately expressed in traditional causal terms. It is a circular dialectic in which the independent beings of the life-field, already selected by the structure of the human body, exert a further selective operation on this body's acts. It is out of this dialectical interchange that human meanings emerge. These meanings are neither passively assimilated from an external, cosmic order that is already fixed and established, as the realists have imagined, nor constructed *de novo* by a creative mind, as the idealists have supposed. As he reads through this whole account of the dialectic of human behavior, the American reader will be reminded, at many points, of the social behaviorism of the American philosopher, George H. Mead.

Merleau-Ponty's account of the lived body is marked by a high degree of both perceptiveness and originality. This body, as I live it from the inside, is quite different from the objective body which is observed, though each perspective is legitimate and the two overlap at certain vital points, which introduces an essential ambiguity into the whole situation of man. He is both a being among other beings in the world, and at the same time an originating source of the whole world order in which he exists. Merleau-Ponty is not satisfied with his thorough criticism and rejection of Cartesian dualism. Modern analytic philosophers would, of course, accept this. He is also concerned with working out a new way of understanding the lived body which will avoid the extremes of an objective behaviorism, on the one hand, and a vitalistic psychism, on the other. He emphatically denies that what was called the soul is a separate, vital force exerting a peculiar, non-physical power of its own. This is merely an over-correction of physicalism. The Aristotelian view that I am related to my body as the pilot to the ship is unacceptable. If I thought of my body in this way, I would not call it *mine*. Furthermore, I do not use my body as an instrument. It is better to say that I *am* my body. My meanings are found in the structures of its behavior, and it is the center of the world in which I exist.

The French philosopher not only rejects Cartesian dualism and in many painstaking analyses suggests a viable alternative; he is also interested in describing the experiences of fatigue and sickness, where the body seems to become a mere inert and unresponsive object and where dualism seems to find genuine, empirical support. Clinical psychologists and psychiatrists will be interested in Merleau-Ponty's criticism of certain causal aspects of Freudian theory, and in his suggestive interpretations of certain complexes as rigid pieces of behavior that are not integrated in a coherent and flexible field of meaning.

Indeed, we find in the disintegrated consciousness an illustration of psycho-physical parallelism, where conscious states run parallel to isolated bodily occurrences. In such sickness, this isolated body may causally affect my perception, so that what I perceive may lie like a "subjective" veil between me and the real things and persons around me in the world.

But the soul and the body of the integrated person are not allowed to fall apart in this way. This person's body does not act as a separate cause to introduce distortions into his perceptions, for it is now understood and endowed with meaning, as El Greco took over his astigmatism, gave it a new meaning, and turned it into a necessary expression of his being. A disintegrated consciousness may be parallel to an isolated cycle of physical events. But true consciousness is parallel to the world. Our worlds of meaning, however, are constantly falling apart; our unity is never automatically guaranteed. We maintain some modicum of human integrity only at the cost of constant struggle and reinterpretation.

At a time when the artificiality of many classical problems has been clearly recognized, English and American philosophers, whatever their point of view may be, will be interested in the way in which the phenomenological thinking of this book cuts through the traditional oppositions between realism and idealism, body and soul, sense and reason, and subjectivism and objectivism. Not merely by dogmatic pronouncements or sweeping generaliaztions, but by careful, phenomenological description and analysis, Merleau-Ponty works out a new way between and beyond these traditional extremes. This way leads him into the human life-world, the original world we perceive, in which we exist and face death. Past thinkers have, of course, been dimly aware of this original "pre-conceptual" world. They have assumed it and taken it for granted. But with a few noteworthy exceptions, such as Augustine, Pascal, and Kierkegaard, they have never subjected it to careful, disciplined investigation. On the contrary, for the most part, both in ancient and modern times, they have disparaged it as confused, ephemeral, and subjective. And in a certain way, from a certain abstract point of view, these adjectives are justified, for this world is extraordinarily rich and far-reaching; it is through and through temporal and historical; and finally it is centered in our own existence, which we live through from the inside. But because it is not open to the special and more abstract methods of the different sciences, we need not infer that it is a mere chaos closed to any method whatsoever.

The work of Merleau-Ponty shows that it is open to disciplined exploration and analysis by the methods of phenomenology. The application of these methods has already shown that philosophy can become something more than a mere appendage to the triumphant advance of the natural sciences without abandoning itself to unbridled speculation and the irresponsible expression of individual opinion. There are world facts of another order which it is in a position to describe, and interpretations of another kind which it is in a position to work out and confirm. From such investigations, if they are carried on in a careful and disciplined way, we may now follow Merleau-Ponty in hoping for a new style of philosophizing, and a revival of philosophy itself in all its various levels and branches.

This book is a significant contribution to the disciplined study of human behavior. It should be of interest not only to philosophers, but to anthropologists, sociologists, clinical psychiatrists, and, indeed, to anyone seriously concerned with the foundations of the human disciplines.

JOHN WILD

Evanston, Illinois
1962

Chairman, Department of Philosophy
Northwestern University

A PHILOSOPHY OF
THE AMBIGUOUS

Contemporary philosophical doctrines willingly reiterate that being-in-the-world constitutes the definition of man (if the idea of definition be applicable to man at all). But this thesis manifestly requires that man's existence itself be conceived outside the alternative of the for-itself (*pour-soi*) and the in-itself (*en-soi*). If man is a thing *or* pure consciousness, he ceases to be in the world (*être au monde*). For a thing *coexists* with other things; it does not transcend them, since it has no horizon. However, the world is not in things, but at the horizon of things. And, conversely, pure consciousness is only a gaze which unfolds everything before it—without implications, obstacles or ambiguities—and the conception of which is rebellious to the very idea of resistance or involvement which constitutes for us the prototypal-experience of the real.

It must be admitted, nevertheless, that the authors most resolved to equate existence and being-in-the-world have most frequently neglected or avoided describing for us this mixture which is human consciousness. Heidegger always situates himself at a level of complexity which permits imagining that the problem which concerns us here is resolved. For it is at the level of perception and the sensible that this problem must receive its decisive treatment. But the projects which, according to *Being and Time,* engender the intelligibility of the real for us already presuppose that the subject of daily existence raises his arm, since he hammers and builds; that he directs his gaze, since he consults his watch; that he orients himself, since he drives an automobile. That a human existent can accomplish these different tasks raises no difficulty once his capacity to act and move his body, once his faculty of perceiving, have been judged "evident." Tracking down the "evidences" of common sense is a never-ending task; and the reader of Heidegger realizes too late that the minute acuity manifested by the author in the description of the world which we project has had as a counterpart a total negligence of the world which for us is "always-already-there."

And it is indeed in this latter that arises the paradoxical structure of a conscious existence, of an existence which becomes thing while hovering over the thing. If a project and an interpretation of the real are possible for me, it is because I am a partisan of this real in a radical sense. But in *Being and Time* one does not find thirty lines concerning the problem of perception; one does not find ten concerning that of the body.

The case of Sartre is even more strange. *Being and Nothingness* indeed contains, in addition to a very detailed critique of sensation and of the psychological in general, a systematic study of corporeity as fundamental modality of being-in-the-world. It is Sartre who introduced into contemporary existentialism the distinction—of major importance—between the body for-me and my body for-others, without which the whole problematic of the body shades into confusion and remains defenseless against the attacks of positivism. With regard to the theses put forward by Sartre concerning the nature of corporeity itself—conceived essentially as a dialectic opposing the body-as-instrument (in a very particular sense) to the body-as-given-in-bare-fact *(corps facticité)*—they appear to be exceptionally fruitful and capable of finally allowing us to understand how existing consciousness can be an inherence and a project at the same time. What is unfortunate is that it is difficult to see how these theses can be understood and accepted as soon as one situates oneself, as one must, in the general framework of Sartrian ontology. For this ontology precisely underscores with an unrelenting tenacity the opposition—no longer dialectical this time, but radically irreconcilable—between the in-itself and the for-itself. Thus the Cartesian dualism of thinking substance and extended substance is restored in its essence. To say that it is restored, moreover, is too weak; in reality, an aggravation is involved since thought and extension in Descartes, although they are without common determination, are nevertheless unified to a certain extent in virtue of the fact that both are conceived as substances. Thus they are in like manner subsistent in themselves and in like manner relative to the creative action of God. Sartre will object, it is true, that this double analogy would have revealed itself to be illusory if Descartes had taken the care to make its signification explicit. Perhaps; but this would be to plead guilty. Let us take a closer look. Consciousness, we are told, is a nothingness of being (*néant d'être*) which unfolds itself in the nihilation of being (*néantisation de l'étant*).[1] The definition of knowledge is not perceptibly different: "in this ek-static relation which is constitutive of the internal negation and of knowledge, it is the in-itself 'in person' which is the concrete pole in its plenitude, and the for-itself is nothing other than the emptiness in which the in-itself is detached." [2]

The consequences of this for the problem which concerns us are important. They reveal a glaring discrepancy between the metaphysical doctrine of Sartre and the givens described by the phenomenology of the same author. For how is it possible, if consciousness and knowledge are defined in the same manner, to maintain henceforth that there is no identity between them, that "not all consciousness is knowledge"? [3] But it is precisely such an identification, phenomenologically untenable as Sartre himself admits, which will render both perception and the body incomprehensible. In conformity with what has just been said, the first is reduced to that presence of the thing which is both immediate and distanced [4] of which sight provides the prototypal-structure: "To perceive red as the color of this notebook is to reflect [back oneself] as internal negation of that quality. That is, the apprehension of quality is not a 'fulfillment' (*Erfüllung*) as Husserl makes it, but the giving form to an emptiness as a determined emptiness *of* that quality. In this sense quality is a presence perpetually out of reach. . . . We shall best account for the original phenomenon of perception by insisting on the fact that the relation of the quality to us is that of absolute proximity—it 'is there,' it haunts us—without either giving or refusing itself; but we must add that this proximity implies a distance. It is what is immediately out of reach, what, by definition refers us to ourselves as to an emptiness." [5]

But if perception testifies to a presence of the thing—*clearly laid out before us without equivocation or mystery*—if it has the crystalline transparency of a gaze which the for-itself poses on the in-itself, it is no longer distinguishable in the least from any other type of knowledge: "There is only intuitive knowledge." [6] It seems, then, that we return to the intuition of classical rationalism; and all its difficulties in justifying the original meaning and bearing of perception are found again. We have even lost the right of getting more or less out of trouble, as Descartes and Spinoza did, by calling perception a confused idea. Once the for-itself and the in-itself are radically separated, once consciousness becomes a spectator without consistency in its own right, the die is cast: such a consciousness will know or not know, but it cannot know in several ways or be related to the in-itself in an ambiguous fashion. As soon as it knows, it pierces through; as soon as it speaks, everything is said at once. Doubtless consciousness parcels out its negations and is not, by means of knowledge, negation of the whole of the in-itself in one moment. But the qualities which it perceives are perceived absolutely. Consciousness is not in the world because it is not involved in what it perceives and does not collaborate in its perception. But precisely this collaboration and this involvement are what give to sensible knowledge a character of constant and intrinsic incompletion, a necessity of being perspectival and of being accomplished from a point of view —all traits which Sartre, the phenomenologist, has very clearly seen, but which his metaphysics does not justify. Doubtless he saves and even underscores the immediate character of realism by his doctrine; but he never succeeds in explaining that the thing—immediately present—is nevertheless only given to us in a way which is both evident and sibylline: for the perceived, indubitable inasmuch as perceived, always awaits the reception of its full meaning from a subsequent exploration which, in turn, delineates a new horizon of potentialities. In Sartre, the metaphysician, the diverse views of the same object succeed each other only because consciousness had decided it in that way, in conformity with an arbitrarily invoked necessity of its own structure; this partiality, this successive and ambiguous character of perception, does not follow from the nature itself of the contact which puts consciousness and the thing at grips with each other. For Sartre, consciousness parcels out a knowledge which it could just as well exhaust all at once simply because an exhaustive look (perfectly possible or even required in principle) would solidify consciousness into a thing, would congeal it into the in-itself and would, by that very fact, destroy it.[7] Sartre recognizes a dialectic of perception, not because this dialectic would be inherent in the very grasp which we can have on things, but because there would be no life of consciousness without it. But it can be seen that this life is not assured in principle; it is invoked and posited rather than included in the phenomenon of perception itself.

The same difficulties arise when Sartre attempts to harmonize his phenomenology of the body and his metaphysics. The descriptions—as original as they are true—which he gives of the body can be accepted without objection. But one never succeeds in *understanding* them. At first glance, however, Sartre's explanations seem clear, coherent and truly capable of providing an answer to the problem. Not possessing being in itself, the for-itself can only exist as the nihilation of a facticity. This latter is precisely the body proper.[8] We can also understand that this facticity—which, in a sense, defines our situation—being inseparable from a project by which it is recovered and interpreted, is illuminated (to employ a Heideggerian term) in terms of this project itself. Thus the facticity, the body or the past show themselves to be variable according to the meaning which our projection accords them. All this lays itself open to no immediate objection. But the situation is no longer the same as soon as one tries to distinguish in the in-itself what does and what does not arise from the body. For then we end up with the thesis—paradoxical, to say the least—that, since all knowledge is constituted by the nihilation of an in-itself, everything known is integrated into our facticity, becomes our body. Sartre sometimes accepts this consequence of his doctrine and, in a certain way, it is not unjustifiable.[9] For if the for-itself affirms itself by arising as a nihilation of the total being (*étant*), this total being is the facticity which it nihilates and therefore, according to the definition just enunciated, is the body itself. Nevertheless, the problem involves another aspect which, because of its phenomenological givens, is much less easy. For phenomenology—including that of Sartre—as a matter of fact reveals a facticity *which is mine* in a sense which is much more profound and much more radical. It is the facticity which, at an almost inaccessible limit, is revealed to us by suffering and nausea. Let us quote Sartre: when we envisage the body in this way, "for us it is simply a matter of the way in which consciousness *exists* its contingency; it is *the very texture of consciousness*[10] insofar as it surpasses this texture toward its own possibilities; it is the manner in which consciousness *exists* spontaneously and in the non-thetic mode, that which it *constitutes* thetically but implicitly as point of view on the world. This may be pure grief, but it may also be a mood, an affective, non-thetic tonality, the pure agreeable, the pure disagreeable. In a general way, it is anything which is called *coenesthesia*. This 'coenesthesia' rarely appears without being surpassed toward the world by a transcendent project on the part of the for-itself; as such it can only be studied with difficulty in isolation. Yet there exist some privileged experiences in which it can be grasped in its purity, in particular in what we call 'physical' pain." [11] The meaning of this text is clear and, as difficult as it may be to reconcile it with certain fundamental theses of Sartrian metaphysics, we could not pretend to forget it under this pretext. For it claims the rights of an incontestable experience which, short of renouncing the status of phenomenologist, must be maintained with regard to and against every metaphysical presupposition.

It cannot be denied therefore that consciousness or the for-itself, even though ontologically nothingness of being, exists nevertheless in the mode of inherence or, to say it another way, that it is encrusted in some in-itself and in this way carves out a facticity *of its own*. Doubtless this brute facticity of our body is not easily brought to light because it is normally recovered in a project which renders it both significative and mundane ("this pain comes from a stomach ulcer, *is* my ulcer") and because, in this form, it is no longer anything but an element or a facet of the general organization of the real—an organization which I elaborate necessarily by the very fact that I exist. But, ultimately and in principle, a facticity which is both pure and purely mine can be discerned. Let us advise a reading of *La Nausée* to him who doubts it. But how is such a facticity conceivable if there is no complicity of nature between the in-itself and the for-itself? Why is it that it does not merge with the whole of my past and of the objects which I have known (as well as the body according to the first meaning described)? If it is true that the for-itself exhausts itself in being nihilating distance and if every experience is the nihilation of that which we are not, why is it that every experience—as pure facticity and exclusive of any valuation by the project—does not weigh with the same heaviness? Or rather, how are we to understand that a facticity can weigh at all? For, though it is true that whether or not I give in to a pain—one minute, one second, or one tenth of a second later—always depends upon me, it is also true that pain oppresses me.

In other words, if the for-itself is only the distance of a gaze without being, it is difficult to understand—a facticity being admitted —why everything is not facticity for it to the same extent, why there is, even within *my* experience, a facticity which is *mine* in a radical sense and a facticity which is one only in a relative sense. It is of little importance that this difference is in actual fact isolable only with difficulty; it is sufficient that it be recognized in principle to see being-in-the-world take on a new dimension for which the absolute duality of the in-itself and the for-itself *could not account or rather which it makes impossible.* We will conclude therefore that this duality compromises being-in-the-world, or at least that it confers a meaning upon it which is inadequate in relation to the description. The same impoverishment or, if you wish, the same weakness would be noted, moreover, with respect to the Sartrian notion of freedom—at least at the level of explicitation to which the author has developed it in his published works.

The difficulties which have just been raised with respect to Heidegger and Sartre are the very ones from which the reflection of M. Merleau-Ponty is born. His whole endeavor tends toward the elaboration of a doctrine of the involved consciousness. For the first time an existential philosophy is affirmed in which the ultimate mode of being of the for-itself does not manifest itself, in spite of contrary intentions and descriptions, to be that of a consciousness-as-witness. This is the fundamental thesis which, at different levels, is defended by *The Structure of Behavior* and the *Phénoménologie de la perception.*[12] In the final analysis it is still the same conception which is found again in the various articles in which this author has outlined his philosophy of history and his interpretation of Marxism.[13] It is true that in these last works the Hegelian influence becomes more apparent. But—and this has not been sufficiently noted —there is no contradiction between such an existentialism and the deeper inspiration which animated Hegel, above all the Hegel of the *Phenomenology of Mind.*[14] The anti-Hegelian protestations of a Kirkegaard and a Jaspers or the somewhat scornful attitude of a Husserl with regard to any dialectical philosophy have too long maintained serious equivocations concerning the point. Here again it is appropriate to make the necessary distinctions.

The first task which confronts us is to clarify exactly the difference of point of view brought to light by *The Structure of Behavior* and the *Phénoménologie de la perception.* For one could wonder what necessity impelled the author to write two books whose subject is, in one sense at least, the same. If it is true, as M. Merleau-Ponty maintains, that the natural experience of man situates him from the beginning in a world of *things* and consists for him in orienting himself among them and taking a stand, to describe man's behavior

and his perception of things is to devote oneself to the same object.
According to this aspect, the author's second book would simply be
more complete than the first since, in the prolongation of perception
itself, he endeavors to bring to light what such a doctrine implies
concerning the natural reflection (which we are opposing to the
scientific and, if need be, metaphysical reflection of man) and the
mundane temporality and freedom of the subject. Will it be said
that *The Structure of Behavior* is above all a negative work which
attempts to show the inanity or the inadequacy of the answers to the
problem of our behavior which are contributed by laboratory psychology—and this in spite of the facts which it has itself discovered
and underlined? But this would be to restrict outrageously the scope
of this book in which the position which constitutes the heart of
M. Merleau Ponty's ideas is already formally enunciated and to forget
that his second work also comprises a very important critical part,
directed this time against the intellectualist psychology of the great
classical rationalists and their epigones: Descartes, Spinoza, Leibnitz,
Lachelier, Lagneau and Alain. The real distinction seems to us to
reside rather in the type of experience described. The *Phénoménologie de la perception* establishes itself without hesitation on the plane
of natural and ingenuous experience which the Husserl of the final
period had already described. If the work appeals very frequently
and often very ingeniously to the data provided by laboratory
psychology or psychopathology, it is with the aim of clarifying or of
preparing the interpretation of natural experience—alone in question. On the contrary, *The Structure of Behavior* accepts another
debate. It takes hold of the image which is traced of us—in colors
which are not always harmonious—by the principal schools of experimental psychology (above all Gestalt psychology and behaviorism) and devotes itself to proving that the facts and the materials
gathered together by this science are sufficient to contradict each of
the interpretative doctrines to which behaviorism and Gestalt psychology have implicitly or explicitly resorted. *The Structure of Behavior* is situated, therefore, not at the level of natural experience,
but at that of scientific experience, and undertakes to prove that this
experience itself—that is, the ensemble of facts which, brought to
light by scientific investigation, constitutes behavior—is not comprehensible within the ontological perspectives which science spontaneously adopts.[15] One succeeds in obtaining a coherent view of behavior only if it is interpreted with the help of a conception which

places no more credit in the hypothesis of a behavior-as-thing than that of a behavior-as-manifestation of a pure mind. From this it must be concluded that the notion of an involved-consciousness, such as will be revealed later by the description of natural or ingenuous experience, is found to be already implied, indeed imposed, by the interpretative critique of scientific experience. Nevertheless, the thesis of *The Structure of Behavior* remains in fact subordinated to that of the *Phénoménologie de la perception*, as the experience of the scientist remains subordinated, in its origin, to the everyday experience which it has the responsibility of explicating and without which it would not be. "To return to things themselves is to return to the world which is prior to knowledge, of which knowledge always *speaks* and with regard to which every determination is abstract, signative and dependent, as is geography with regard to the landscape where we first learned what is a forest, a prairie or a river."[16]

However, it seems to us to be preferable to begin by reading *The Structure of Behavior*. It is the order which the author himself wished[17] and one cannot abandon it without serious reasons. Far from there being such reasons, there are others on the contrary which impel us to accept his invitation. For access to the conception defended by the author is hardly easy and, although it does not jar a certain spontaneous feeling of our being, it goes directly counter to what modern philosophy has taught us to *think* concerning this being. In order to understand him correctly, therefore, it is well not to neglect certain detours and to be persuaded ahead of time that, concerning the problem of perception and its prolongations, the solutions of the modern tradition are decrepit. Moreover, instead of penetrating immediately to the heart of an arduous and disconcerting doctrine, we would do better to experience first why all the paths traced by a certain history are impasses; then, perhaps, little by little and progressively we will see another light emerge from these failures.

These few explanations guard us from a serious misunderstanding. It consists in alleging, as a critic of M. Merleau-Ponty once did in our presence, that this philosophy, since it is careful throughout to support itself with the facts brought to light by progress in psychology, would be solidary with present-day science and destined to stand or fall with it, that is, already condemned at this moment in a certain sense. This position constitutes an absolute misreading and, for that matter, most of the objections which have been raised against M. Mer-leau-Ponty's doctrine in certain circles draw their inspiration from an idea which is exactly the contrary (and equally false), since they reproach him with having rendered science valueless or impossible. Let us observe that this alleged enslavement of the philosophy which concerns us here to any experimental science whatsoever (biology, physiology, psychology) does not have the slightest appearance of justification. If M. Merleau-Ponty unstintingly collates and examines the facts given us by scientific experimentation or psychiatry, it is with the single aim of making the ontological frames of reference—generally implicit—in which they are presented literally fly to pieces. This does not mean that the author wants to impose the tasks or responsibilities of the metaphysician upon the scientist. It simply signifies that for this philosophy, the scientist—as any man—spon-taneously thinks in terms of an ontology—and that, in the present circumstances, this ontology—which seems self-evident because of a long habituation—is in radical opposition to the views which natural and ingenuous experience—in which all scientific experience is rooted—seems to impose when we undertake to understand it with-out prejudice.[18]

ALPHONSE DE WAELHENS
University of Louvain

NOTES

1. "The being of consciousness qua consciousness is to exist *at a distance from itself* as a presence to itself, and this empty distance which being carries in its being is Nothingness." *Being and Nothingness,* tr. by H. E. Barnes, New York, Philosophical Library, 1956, p. 78 (*L'Être et le Néant,* Paris, Gallimard, 1943, p. 120)
2. *B.N.,* p. 177 (*E.N.,* p. 225). Or again and more clearly: ". . . knowledge . . . is confused with the ek-static being of the for-itself." *B.N.,* p. 216 (*E.N.,* p. 268)
3. *B.N.,* p. lii (*E.N.,* p. 18)
4. This signifies simply that the for-itself, not being a thing, cannot be at a distance from the thing; but, on the other hand, since perception is a perpetual affirmation that one is the thing in not being it, that the ontological distance of the for-itself to the thing always remains infinite.
5. *B.N.,* p. 187 (*E.N.,* pp. 236-237)
6. *B.N.,* p. 172 (*E.N.,* p. 220)
7. Cf. *B.N.,* pp. 182, 183 (*E.N.,* pp. 231, 232)
8. Cf. *B.N.,* p. 309 (*E.N.,* p. 371). We are limiting ourselves here to considering the ontological explanations of corporeity, not its phenomenological description.
9. ". . . on the other hand the body is identified with the whole world . . ." *B.N.,* p. 309 (*E.N.,* p. 372)
10. Underlined by us
11. *B.N.,* p. 331 (*E.N.,* p. 396)
12. Paris, Gallimard, 1945 (New ed., 1949)
13. These articles have been gathered into two volumes: *Humanisme et Terreur,* Paris, Gallimard, 1947, and *Sens et non-sens,* Paris, Nagel, 1948.
14. "There is an existentialism of Hegel in this sense that, for him, man is not a consciousness which possesses its own thoughts clearly from the beginning, but a life given to itself which seeks to understand itself. The whole of the *Phenomenology of Mind* describes this effort which man puts forth to recover himself." Merleau-Ponty, "L'Existentialisme chez Hegel," *Sens et non-sens,* p. 130
15. The scientist cannot make the rejoinder here that he thinks without ontological background. To believe that one is not doing metaphysics or to want to abstain from doing it is always to imply an ontology, but an unexamined one—just as governments run by "technicians" do not make political policy, but never fail to have one—and often the worst of all.
16. *Phénoménologie de la perception,* Part III: "All knowing is established in horizons opened by perception," p. 240; "The numerical determinations of science are schematically patterned upon a constitution of the world which is already made before them," p. 348.
17. Three years separated the publication of these two books.
18. "All the sciences situate themselves in a 'complete' and real world without realizing that perceptual experience is constituting with respect to this world." *The Structure of Behavior,* p. 219.

The Structure of Behavior

INTRODUCTION

Our goal is to understand the relations between consciousness and nature: organic, psychological or even social. By nature we understand here a multiplicity of events external to each other and bound together by relations of causality.

With respect to physical nature, critical thought brings a well-known solution to this problem: reflection reveals that physical analysis is not a decomposition into real elements and that causality in its actual meaning is not a productive operation. There is then no physical nature in the sense we have just given to this word; there is nothing in the world which is foreign to the mind. The world is the ensemble of objective relations borne by consciousness. It can be said that physics, in its development, justifies *de facto* this philosophy. One sees it employing mechanical, dynamic or even psychological models indifferently, as if, liberated from ontological pretensions, it were indifferent to the classical antimonies of mechanism and dynamism which imply a nature in itself.

The situation is not the same in biology. In fact the discussions concerning mechanism and vitalism remain open. The reason for this is probably that analysis of the physico-mathematical type progresses very slowly in this area and, consequently, that our picture of the organism is still for the most part that of a material mass *partes extra partes*. Under these conditions biological thought most frequently remains realistic, either by juxtaposing separated mechanisms or by subordinating them to an entelechy.

As for psychology, critical thought leaves it no other resource than to be in part an "analytical psychology" [1] which would discover judgment present everywhere in a way parallel to analytical geometry, and for the rest, a study of certain bodily mechanisms. To the extent that it has attempted to be a natural science, psychology has remained faithful to realism and to causal thinking. At the beginning of the century, materialism made the "mental" a particular sector of the real world: among events existing in themselves (*en soi*),

some of them in the brain also had the property of existing for themselves (*pour soi*). The counter mentalistic thesis posited consciousness as a productive cause or as a thing: first it was the realism of
"states of consciousness" bound together by causal relations, a second
world parallel and analogous to the "physical world" following the
Humean tradition; then, in a more refined psychology, it was the
realism of "mental energy" which substituted a multiplicity of fusion
and interpenetration, a flowing reality, for the disconnected mental
facts. But consciousness remained the analogue of a force. This was
clearly seen when it was a question of explaining its action on the
body and when, without being able to eliminate it, the necessary
"creation of energy" was reduced to a minimum:[2] the universe of
physics was indeed taken as a reality in itself in which consciousness
was made to appear as a second reality. Among psychologists consciousness was distinguished from beings of nature as one thing
from another thing, by a certain number of *characteristics*. The
mental fact, it was said, *is* unextended, known all at once. More
recently the doctrine of Freud applies metaphors of energy to consciousness and accounts for conduct by the interaction of forces or
tendencies.

Thus, among contemporary thinkers in France, there exist side
by side a philosophy, on the one hand, which makes of every nature
an objective unity constituted vis-à-vis consciousness and, on the
other, sciences which treat the organism and consciousness as two
orders of reality and, in their reciprocal relation, as "effects" and as
"causes." Is the solution to be found in a pure and simple return to
critical thought? And once the criticism of realistic analysis and causal
thinking has been made, is there nothing justified in the naturalism
of science—nothing which, "understood" and transposed, ought to
find a place in a transcendental philosophy?

We will come to these questions by starting "from below" and
by an analysis of the notion of behavior. This notion seems important
to us because, taken in itself, it is neutral with respect to the classical
distinctions between the "mental" and the "physiological" and thus
can give us the opportunity of defining them anew.[3] It is known
that in Watson, following the classical antinomy, the negation of
consciousness as "internal reality" is made to the benefit of physiology; behavior is reduced to the sum of reflexes and conditioned
reflexes between which no intrinsic connection is admitted. But precisely this atomistic interpretation fails even at the level of the theory

of the reflex (Chapter I) and all the more so in the psychology—
even the objective psychology—of higher levels of behavior (Chapter
II), as Gestalt theory has clearly shown. By going through behaviorism, however, one gains at least in being able to introduce consciousness, not as psychological reality or as cause, but as structure. It will
remain for us to investigate (Chapter III) the meaning and the mode
of existence of these structures.

I. REFLEX BEHAVIOR

Introduction

The scientific analysis of behavior was defined first in opposition to the givens of naive consciousness. If I am in a dark room and a luminous spot appears on the wall and moves along it, I would say that it has "attracted" my attention, that I have turned my eyes "toward" it and that in all its movements it "pulls" my regard along with it. Grasped from the inside, my behavior appears as directed, as gifted with an intention and a meaning. Science seems to demand that we reject these characteristics as appearances under which a reality of another kind must be discovered. It will be said that seen light is "only in us." It covers a vibratory movement, which movement is never given to consciousness. Let us call the qualitative appearance, "phenomenal light"; the vibratory movement, "real light." Since the real light is never perceived, it could not present itself as a *goal* toward which my behavior is directed. It can only be conceptualized as a cause which acts on my organism. The phenomenal light was a force of attraction, the real light is a *vis a tergo*. This reversal immediately poses a series of questions.

From the moment that light is defined as a physical agent which makes an impression on my retina, one no longer has the right to consider the characteristics which belong to phenomenal light as given in the former. The stimulus which we call "spot of light" is decomposed, for scientific analysis, into as many partial processes as there are distinct anatomical elements on my retina. In the same way, if one treats it as a reality beyond my consciousness, the enduring action of the luminous spot on my eyes is resolved into an indefinite succession of physical facts; with each moment of time it must be renewed, as the Cartesian idea of continuous creation expresses it so well. Again in the same way, the movement of my eyes which fixate the luminous spot posed no problem to naive con-

7

sciousness because this movement was guided by a goal. But now there is no longer any *terminus ad quem*; if my eyes oscillate in such a way that the luminous spot comes to be reflected in the center of my retina, it is in the antecedent causes or conditions of the movement that one must find the sufficient reason for this adaptation. There must be devices at the point of the retina where the luminous spot is first formed, which appropriately regulate the amplitude and the direction of my fixation reflex. One would say then that each place on the retina has a determined "spatial value," that is, that it is united by pre-established nerve circuits to certain motor muscles such that the light, in touching it, only has to release a mechanism which is ready to function. Finally, if the luminous spot moves and my eye follows it, I must here again understand the phenomenon without introducing into it anything which resembles an *intention*.

On my retina, considered not as just any kind of screen, but as a receptor or rather as an ensemble of discontinuous receptors, there is not properly speaking a movement of light. A wave is not an individual except for the man who regards it and sees it advancing toward him; in the sea it is nothing but the successive vertical rising of portions of the water without any horizontal transference of matter. In the same way the "movement" of the luminous wave on my retina is not a physiological reality. The retina registers only a successive excitation of points across which the wave passes. In each of these, acting on a distinct nerve element, it can evoke a fixation reflex similar to that described above; it is because of this that my eye seems to "follow" the light. In reality its movement is the integration of a series of partial adaptations, just as walking is reducible to a succession of recovered falls. To generalize, physical agents cannot affect the organism by their properties of *form*, such as movement, rhythm and spatial arrangement. The spatial or temporal form of a physical event is not registered on the receptor; it leaves no other trace there than a series of stimulations external to each other. It is only by their punctual properties that excitants can act. Thus, as soon as one ceases to place confidence in the immediate givens of consciousness and tries to construct a scientific representation of the organism, it seems that one is led to the classical theory of the reflex—that is, to decomposing the excitation and the reaction into a multitude of partial processes which are external to each other in time as well as in space. The adaptation of the response to the situation would be explained by pre-established correlations (often

conceived as anatomical structures) between certain organs or receptor apparatuses and certain effector muscles. The simplest nerve
functioning is nothing other than the setting in motion of a very
large number of autonomous circuits. The reflex would be, one could
say, a "longitudinal" phenomenon. It is the action of a defined physical or chemical agent on a locally defined receptor which evokes a
defined response by means of a defined pathway.

In this linear series of physical and physiological events the
stimulus has the dignity of a cause, in the empirical sense of a constant and unconditioned antecedent; and the organism is passive
because it limits itself to executing what is prescribed for it by the
place of the excitation and the nerve circuits which originate there.
Common sense believes that one turns one's eyes "in order to see."
Not only is this "prospective activity"[1] banished to the anthropomorphic data of internal observation, but it does not even exist
except as an effect of the reflex mechanism. Not only does spatial
perception not guide the fixation movement of my eyes, but it must
even be said to be the result of it. I perceive the position of the spot
because my body has responded to it by adapted reflexes.[2] In the
scientific study of behavior, one must reject every notion of intention
or utility or value as subjective because they have no foundation in
things and are not intrinsic determinations of them. If I am hungry
and, absorbed in my work, I extend my hand toward a piece of fruit
placed near me by chance and lift it to my mouth, the piece of fruit
does not act as an object invested with a certain value; what releases
my motor reaction is an ensemble of colors and lights, a physical
and chemical stimulus. If, because I was inattentive, I put my hand
on one side of the "goal," a second attempt at prehension should
not be related to some permanent intention but explained simply by
the permanence of the causes which had evoked the first. If behavior
seems intentional, it is because it is regulated by certain pre-established nerve pathways in such a way that in fact I obtain satisfaction.
The "normal" activity of an organism is only the functioning of this
apparatus constructed by nature; there are no genuine norms; there
are only effects. The classical theory of the reflex and the methods
of realistic analysis and causal explanation, of which the reflex theory
is only an application, alone seem capable of constituting an objective and scientific representation of behavior. The object of science
is defined by the mutual exteriority of parts and processes.

But it is a fact that contemporary physiology has gone beyond the classical theory of the reflex. Is it sufficient to amend it or ought one to change methods? Might mechanistic science have missed the definition of objectivity? Might the cleavage between the subjective and the objective have been badly made; might the opposition between a universe of science—entirely outside of self—and a universe of consciousness—defined by the total presence of self to self—be untenable? And if realistic analysis fails, will biology find its method in an ideal analysis of the physico-mathematical type, in Spinozistic intellection? Or might not value and signification be intrinsic determinations of the organism which would only be accessible to a new mode of "comprehension"?

The Classical Conception of the Reflex and Its Auxiliary Hypotheses

If the order in the reflex[3]—that is, the adaptation of the response to the stimulus and the coordination of partial movements in the total gesture—is assured by pre-established connections from the sensible surface to the effector muscles, the classical conception puts considerations of topography in a position of primary importance; the place of the excitation should decide the reaction; the stimulus should act by those of its properties which can modify the anatomical elements taken one by one; the nerve circuit should be isolated since the reflex, if it were not guided in this manner, could not be adapted to the stimulus as it is in fact. But it has long been known that the reflex thus defined is very rarely observable.

THE "STIMULUS"

The stimulus often acts much less by its elementary properties than by its spatial arrangement, its rhythm, and the rhythm of its intensities. More generally, it happens very frequently that the effect of a complex stimulus is not foreseeable on the basis of the elements which compose it.

Reactions comparable to those which the excitation of the receptors evokes are never obtained by the excitation of the nerve trunks. It has been possible to show in frogs and in baby mammals (Sherrington) that the excitation of the posterior roots evoke contractions at the level of the muscles which depend on the corresponding anterior roots: this reaction which is metemarized, segmental, and completely lacking in biological significance at this degree of organization, is not found when the behavior is regulated by the excitation of the receptors, doubtless this is because the latter—they themselves or their central projection—are disposed for registering the properties of form of the stimuli which, then, much more than the place and the nature of the excitant, would decide the reaction.[4] The same reason would explain the fact that typical reflexes can be rather limited in number: the "content" of the stimuli can vary without the released response itself varying if the former are of the same spatiotemporal form.[5] In case of competition of stimuli it is the form much more than the nature, the place or even the intensity of the excitation which determines the resulting reflex.[6] A painful excitation of the penis, even if it is weak, inhibits the reflex of erection. A simple touch immobilizes the spinal snake (Luchsinger), while stronger cutaneous excitations evoke very different responses. Five different reflex responses can be obtained by stimulating the ear of a cat depending on the structure of the excitant employed. The pinna of the ear flattens out when it is bent, but responds to tickling with a few rapid twitches. The character of the response is completely modified depending on the form of electrical excitation (faradic or galvanic) or its strength; for example, weak strengths evoke rhythmic responses; strong ones evoke tonic reflexes. A decerebrate cat [swallows] water as soon as it is placed in the pharynx; but water to which a few drops of alcohol has been added provokes a doubling-up response and movements of the tongue (Sherrington and Miller).

In the classical conception, this dependence of the reflex on the formal or global properties of the excitant could only be an appearance. To explain nerve functioning can only be to reduce the complex to the simple, to discover the constant elements of which behavior is constituted. Thus one would decompose the stimulus as well as the reaction until one encountered the "elementary processes" composed of a stimulus and a response which were always associated in experience. For example, the action of the scratching stimulus would be analyzed into as many partial actions as there are anatomically distinct tactile receptors in the ear. The twitching of the ear which responds to this excitant would be resolved in turn into a certain number of elementary contractions. In principle, to each part of the stimulus there should correspond a part of the reaction. And the same elementary sequences, combined differently, should constitute all the reflexes. The qualitative properties of the situation and those of the response—that which makes the difference for consciousness between scratching and bending the ear of the animal, between a twitching of this ear and a retraction movement—should, if the same receptors are really affected in both cases, be reducible to diverse combinations of the same stimuli and of the same elementary movements. It is absolutely excluded that an organic substrate could fulfill truly different functions in turn and that the reaction could change in *nature* because of a simple difference in the rhythm of excitations applied in turn to the same apparatuses. Yet the reflexes which we have just enumerated cannot be decomposed into elementary reactions. To cite only two examples, the action of water with a few drops of alcohol on the decerebrate cat cannot be understood in terms of the action of the pure water nor of that of the pure alcohol. On the other hand, water and alcohol do not constitute a chemical combination which could exercise a different action than that of the components. It is within the organism then that we will have to look for that which makes a complex stimulus something other than the sum of its elements. In the same way the inhibiting effect of a cutaneous contact on a spinal snake cannot be understood as a simple algebraic addition of the excitations which it provokes and of those which, on the other hand, provoked the crawling movement. If the most frequent observations are considered, there is no basis for treating the reactions which we will call qualitative as appearances, and the reactions which conform to the reflex theory as exclusively real.

These remarks do not introduce, with the notion of the form or totality of the stimulus, anything which implies a sort of mentalism in order for the stimulus to be registered. Attention has rightly been called to the fact that machines which are specially constructed for the receiving of forms are known in physics.[7] A keyboard is precisely an apparatus which permits the production of innumerable melodies, all different from each other depending on the order and the cadence of the impulses received; the extent to which the metaphor of the keyboard has been used in the physiology of the nerve centers is well known.[8] An automatic telephone is even more clearly an apparatus which responds only to excitants of a certain form and modifies its responses according to the spatial and temporal order of the stimuli. But do the constellations of excitants act on the organism as the fingers of the pianist act on the instrument? Nothing is ever produced in the piano itself but the separate movements of the hammers or the strings; it is in the motor system of the performer and in the nervous system of the auditor that the isolated physical phenomena, of which the piano is the seat, constitute a single global phenomenon. And it is there that the melody truly exists in its sequence and characteristic rhythm.

The organism cannot properly be compared to a keyboard on which the external stimuli would play and in which their proper form would be delineated for the simple reason that the organism contributes to the constitution of that form.[9] When my hand follows each effort of a struggling animal while holding an instrument for capturing it, it is clear that each of my movements responds to an external stimulation; but it is also clear that these stimulations could not be received without the movements by which I expose my receptors to their influence. ". . . The properties of the object and the intentions of the subject . . . are not only intermingled; they also constitute a new whole." [10] When the eye and the ear follow an animal in flight, it is impossible to say "which started first" in the exchange of stimuli and responses. Since all the movements of the organism are always conditioned by external influences, one can, if one wishes, readily treat behavior as an effect of the milieu. But in the same way, since all the stimulations which the organism receives have in turn been possible only by its preceding movements which have culminated in exposing the receptor organ to the external influences, one could also say that the behavior is the first cause of all the stimulations.

Thus the form of the excitant is created by the organism itself, by its proper manner of offering itself to actions from the outside. Doubtless, in order to be able to subsist, it must encounter a certain number of physical and chemical agents in its surroundings. But it is the organism itself—according to the proper nature of its receptors, the thresholds of its nerve centers and the movements of the organs—which chooses the stimuli in the physical world to which it will be sensitive.[11] "The environment (*Umwelt*) emerges from the world through the actualization or the being of the organism—[granted that] an organism can exist only if it succeeds in finding in the world an adequate environment." [12] This would be a keyboard which moves itself in such a way as to offer—and according to variable rhythms—such or such of its keys to the in itself monotonous action of an external hammer.

The model of the automatic telephone appears more satisfactory. Here indeed we find an apparatus which itself elaborates the stimuli.

In virtue of the devices installed in the automatic central, the same external action will have a variable effect according to the context of the preceding and following actions. An "O" marked on the automatic dial will have a different value depending on whether it comes at the beginning, as when I dial the exchange "Oberkampf," for example, or second, as in dialing "Botzaris." Here, as in the organism, it can be said that the excitant—that which puts the apparatus in operation and determines the nature of its responses—is not a sum of partial stimuli, because a sum is indifferent to the order of its factors; rather it is a constellation, an order, a whole, which gives its momentary meaning to each of the local excitations. The manipulation "B" always has the same immediate effect, but it exercises different functions at the automatic central depending on whether it precedes or follows the manipulation "O," just as the same painted panel takes on two qualitatively distinct aspects depending on whether I see a blue disc on a rose-colored ground or, on the contrary, a rose-colored ring in the middle of which would appear a blue ground. In the simple case of an automatic telephone constructed for a limited number of manipulations, or in that of an elementary reflex, the central organization of the excitations can itself be conceived as a functioning of pre-established devices: the first manipulation would have the effect of making accessible to subsequent ones only a certain keyboard where the latter would be registered.

We will have to examine whether, in reactions of a higher level, it is possible in the same way to make a distinct operation correspond to each stimulus, a visible device to each "factor," or even to relate the function to ideal variables which would be independent. Even at the level of the reflex, it is now certain that the interaction of the stimuli precludes considering nerve activity as a sum of "longitudinal" phenomena unfolding from the receptors to the effectors and that, as in the automatic central, "transverse phenomena" must be produced somewhere in the nervous system.[13]

These remarks relate not only to compound reflexes. Under the name of "combinations of reflexes," physiologists have long studied complex reactions which are not entirely foreseeable on the basis of the laws of the simple reflex. But it was with the hope of reducing them to these laws when the latter would have been more adequately determined. In fact, the least stimulus affects several anatomical elements of the receptors at the same time. Are not the laws of the "composition of reflexes" the laws of the reflex itself?[14] Since all of the reactions we know are reactions to a complex of stimuli, what is said of an elementary reaction is conjectural. We cannot even presume that what is functionally simple necessarily corresponds to what is anatomically simple. In fact, certain physiologists are led to reintroduce quality into the language of science.[15] In order to formulate the laws of the "composition of reflexes" Sherrington takes into consideration the biological value of stimuli: when two excitants are in competition it is the painful excitant, he says, which inhibits the other.[16] But since the classical conception to which he remains faithful requires that the reflex depend on a local device, and since the biological value of the stimulus which appears to be determining does not have adequate receptors, he posits specialized local terminations for the reception of painful excitants.[17] At the very moment that one is obliged to introduce value into the definition of stimulus one actualizes it, so to speak, in distinct receptors. In the theory of nerve functioning everything happens as if we were obliged to submit to the alternative of anthropomorphism or the anatomical conception of the reflex, when perhaps it is necessary to go beyond it. Before any systematic interpretation, the description of the *known facts* shows that the fate of an excitation is determined by its relation to the whole of the organic state and to the simultaneous or preceding excitations, and that the relations between the organism and its milieu are not relations of linear causality but of circular causality.

THE PLACE OF THE EXCITATION

It seems established that one cannot speak of an anatomically circumscribed receptor field for each excitant.

Sherrington has pointed out that the limits of the reflexogenic field for the scratch reaction vary with days and circumstances.[18] It can be added, with the intensity and frequency of the excitants.[19] The receptive field is strictly defined only under the artificial conditions of laboratory experiments or again in pathological conditions: it is only after transverse section of the medulla that the receptors of the ipsilateral extension reflex are invariable in man.[20] It is generally accepted that it is impossible to assign a fixed "spatial value" for each point of the retina and, consequently, that the "local sign" of each sensation (if one conserves this notion) is not a simple function of the position of the excitant on the retina. In considering perception here as a particular case of reaction, it is doubtless permissible to apply to the reflex theory what the physiology of the senses teaches us.[21] The excitation of the macula can give rise to localized sensations "in front," "to the right" or "to the left" depending on the position of the eye in relation to the orbit and of the head in relation to the body. In the same way the excitation of one receptor can evoke different reflexes and the excitation of two distinct points can give rise to the same reflex.[22]

Classical theory at first attempts to furnish an interpretation of these facts without abandoning its guiding concepts; accordingly it becomes necessary to suppose that each receptor is joined by pre-established connections to all the motor devices whose exercise it can control. The principle of "private" pathways—that is, each one destined to a special category of response—is maintained; the theoretician is satisfied with multiplying them. But one would have to go a long way in this direction, since observation shows that the same motor response can sometimes be released by orders distributed among the most diverse points of the organism. Since, on the other hand, there are five times as many afferent as efferent pathways, Sherrington admits that the centrifugal devices involve a "final common segment" in which the same nerve substrate can serve to release qualitatively different reactions. Does he not thereby abandon the classical conception of order which is explained by the solidarity of a specialized receptor and a specialized effector? If the same motor substrate can serve several functions, it is difficult to see what in principle would exclude the extension of this hypothesis to the afferent sector. Instead of corresponding to so many "private" circuits, the different reflexes would represent the various modes of functioning of the same nerve apparatus. We will not yet consider this alternative conception as established; but the classical theory of nerve functioning is led by the force of things to burden itself with auxiliary hypotheses which are almost in contradiction with it, just as the Ptolemaic system revealed its inadequacy by the large number of *ad hoc* suppositions which became necessary in order to make it accord with the facts.

THE REFLEX CIRCUIT

Is there a defined pathway, an isolated conduction process, when one passes from the excitation to the reaction? The distinction, introduced by Sherrington, of exteroceptivity, interoceptivity and proprioceptivity seems obvious at first. Nevertheless, Sherrington's own work and the observations of contemporary physiology doubtless would permit establishment of the fact that there is never any pure exteroceptive reflex, that is, one which needs only the intervention of an external stimulus in order to exist. All reflexes demand the con-currence of a multitude of conditions in the organism external to the reflex arc which have as much right as the "stimulus" to be called causes of the reaction. The same thing is taking place with regard to our knowledge of the organism as has been pointed out in regard to our knowledge of nature: one becomes accustomed to treating as "cause" the condition which we can most easily influence.[23] If one forgets to mention, among the antecedents of the reflex, those which are internal to the organism, it is because they are most frequently conjoined at the critical moment. But this relative constancy of intra-organic conditions itself raises a problem, since the reflex apparatus is neither anatomically nor functionally isolated, and thus the stability of the internal conditions cannot be maintained as given by a pre-established structure.

First, the reflex clearly seems to be under the influence of a series of chemical, secretory and vegetative conditions powerful enough to cancel, sometimes even to reverse, the expected effect of a certain stimulus. Extremely variable reactions are manifested by the excitation of the vagus or sympathetic nerves depending on the humoral state. Calcium, which ordinarily slows down the pulse, accelerates it in the case of an aortic insufficiency. Pilocarpine, normally an excitant of the vagus nerve, can become an excitant of the sympathetic nerves under certain conditions. Excitation of the vagus nerve accelerates the heartbeat following treatment with nicotine. The sensitivity to adrenalin varies considerably as a function of the secretion of the pituitary gland. In cholesterinemia the sensitizing action of adrenalin depends on the chemical milieu which should be neutral or acid, which is the equivalent of saying that the ionic state conditions the functioning of the autonomic nervous system. But this latter supposes further a certain equilibrium between the electrolyte and the colloidal particles, which in turn is bound up with the cell wall potential, which depends on a whole series of factors and finally on the state of the vegetative nervous system. Thus once again a veritable circular causality is involved here. But the animal system is itself dependent on the vegetative system. Section of the vagus modifies the chronaxie in the cortical fields. Pharmaco-dynamic action on the vegetative system modifies the chronaxie of the peripheral sense organs. Conversely, moreover, certain lesions of the brain which were observed after war injuries have

entailed modifications of blood pressure, pulse rate and pupillary innervation.[24]

To this first series of conditions must be added the cerebral and
cerebellar influences which, at least in man, probably intervene in all
reflexes. Nobody contests the existence of the phenomenon of "shock"
which, in the frog for example, after the crushing of internal organs or
the legs, interrupts or modifies all the reflexes.[25] It has long been known
that, in man, paying attention to a reflex is sometimes sufficient to inhibit
it. Fatigue or hypnosis modify the reflexes by attenuating or accentuating
them. The plantar flexion reflex of the toes evoked by stimulation of
the sole depends so much on cerebral conditions that the appearance of
dorsal extension reflex in place of a flexor movement is considered to be
a sign of a lesion of the pyramidal tracts (Babinski). Speaking generally,
it seems incontestable that the reflexes of a decerebrate animal are very
different from normal reflexes.[26] In certain octopi, after ablation of the
cerebral ganglia and a part of the central ganglia, the thresholds are raised
or, on the contrary, extremely lowered; the coordination of the movements of the arms is compromised; the prehension and consummatory
reflexes with regard to crabs are irregular.[27] Thus activities which are
called spinal depend on cerebral and cerebellar influences.

Authors are divided only when it is a question of interpreting
these facts. Often an explanation is sought which allows the conception of the reflex to be maintained by subordinating it merely to a
cerebral regulation and, initially, to a wholly negative control: that
the brain possesses a general power of inhibition would be accepted.
But the facts in no way force us to interpret the "shocks" which we
were discussing above as the releasing of inhibiting devices proper to
the brain, since a total inhibition is obtained just as well in the period
just following a spinal section (spinal shock). Might not shock then
be an alteration of functioning which is not localized anywhere and
which can originate in very different nerve regions? If this is accepted and since there does exist a cerebral shock, the intervention of
the brain in the reflex could not consist simply in authorizing or
prohibiting certain already established reactions—it should bring a
certain positive contribution to the very way in which the reactions
take place. In this regard the qualitative notion of "vigilance" (Head)
would be more satisfactory when it is a question of explaining reflex
insufficiencies in infections, fatigue and hypnosis. But this notion
only gives a description which is too far removed from behavior and
does not make the role of the brain sufficiently precise. Is it only a
question of a coordinating and integrating function? These notions

can designate the simple association of pre-established automatisms. The idea of integration or coordination and the idea of control or inhibition both imply that a hierarchical structure of two levels in the nervous system is accepted: a first degree composed of reflex arcs conforming to the classical type upon which would be superimposed a higher instance—coordinating centers or inhibiting devices—charged with governing the automatisms, with associating and disassociating them. It is this hierarchic conception which we would like to examine in an example where the notions both of integration and of control are thus found indirectly implied.

We recalled above that the plantar flexion reflex is replaced by an extension reflex of the digits in case of lesion of the pyramidal tracts. An explanation of this fact has been attempted by supposing that, in the normal subject, the extension reflex which is ready to function finds itself inhibited by the pyramidal excitations which, according to Sherrington, would favor the phasic medullar reflexes, of external origin, at the expense of the tonic and proprioceptive reflexes.[28] But this hypothesis is uncontrollable: the existence of a reflex device which can in no way be observed in the adult and normal subject is posited in order to explain its appearance in the affected subject by simple "escape from control" or liberation of the automatism. If one limited oneself to describing the effects of the sickness, it would be necessary to say that it brought with it a change of form in the reflex. The character and the structure of the response are modified depending on whether the entire nervous system or only a part of it is involved.

It is precisely this qualitative alteration of behavior that the classical reflex theory considers an appearance. It reduces it to the simple substitution of one pre-established circuit for another. Pathological behavior must be understood by subtraction from normal behavior; sickness is treated as a simple deficit or, in any case, as a negative phenomenon; what is desired is that there be really no *event* in the organism. The hypothesis of an extension reflex ready to function in the normal subject is evidently a *construction*. It entails a second one. If it is true that there exists in the normal subject a circuit capable of releasing the extension reflex, why this reflex is not produced must still be explained. It is supposed, therefore, that it is inhibited. The idea of inhibition is forged in order *to justify the absence of an arbitrarily posited extension reflex*. Here the idea is not introduced in order to render the fact itself intelligible but to mask a visible disagreement between theory and experience. It is therefore permissible to say that the purpose of the auxiliary hypotheses of control and inhibition is more to maintain the classical reflex theory than to make the nature of nerve activity understood positively. Perhaps the least contested idea of modern psychology is that the conduct of the diseased subject—as, moreover, that of the animal, the child or the "primitive"—cannot be understood by simple disaggregation of adult, healthy and civilized behavior. Physiological explanation must be united with psychological description.

Let us try therefore to make precise, with the example we have chosen, the qualitative transformation of nerve functioning which would be the essential element of illness. The extension reflex is encountered in peripheral paralysis, where the path which goes from the cortex to the pyramidal tracts and to the anterior horns is in no way involved and where, consequently, it is not possible to posit a liberation of the automatism. Many subjects who present the extension reflex in the normal position, cease to present it as soon as the knee is bent, as soon as one places them in a ventral position or even as soon as one has them execute certain head movements. If, as it seems, the extension reflex is conditioned by reversal of the chronaxies —those of the flexor muscles becoming higher than those of the extensor muscles, and extension easier than flexion—let us say that the relationship, normal or pathological, of these chronaxies is determined, not by some local inhibiting device, but by the nerve and motor situation in the whole of the organism.[29] It follows that the action of the brain on reflex activity is no longer the authorization given or refused by a higher instance to automatic or autonomous processes. At the same time that it loses its role of arbitrator between mechanisms which are ready to function, the brain, reintroduced into the nerve circuit, assumes a positive role in the very constitution of reflex responses. It is the brain which would make one mode of organization predominate over another, for example, flexion over extension.[30] Here one touches on the general problem of nerve localizations or of the relations between function and substrate in the nervous system. Initially, in the reflex theory as well as in that of central functioning, there was a tendency to assign, for each nerve element, a fragment of behavior which depended upon it: "verbal images" were localized; for each reflex movement a special device was sought. The facts have not permitted maintaining this realistic analysis of behavior into isolable fragments. More and more it was realized that the different nerve regions corresponded, not to real parts of behavior—to words, to such and such a reflex defined by its stimulus—but to certain types or to certain levels of activity: for example, to voluntary language as distinguished from automatic language, to flexion reflexes which, compared to extension reflexes, represent a finer adaptation, one of higher value. It is therefore a new kind of analysis, founded upon the biological meaning of behavior, which imposes itself at the same time on psychology and physiology.[31]

The effect of intervention of cerebral influences would be to reorganize behavior, to elevate it to a higher level of adaptation and life, and not merely to associate and disassociate pre-established devices. It is not a question here of an arbitrary construction: this hypothesis is molded on the facts while that of the classical conception obliges us to treat the Babinski reflex as an inhibition of inhibition. Moreover, it is in accord with other results of pathology. It presents the nervous system as a whole, not as an apparatus made up of two heterogeneous parts. But, speaking generally, the appearance of reason and that of the higher nervous system transforms the very parts of behavior which depend on the middle brain and appear the most instinctive. A dualism of simple subordination is impossible.[32]

The putting into play of a "reflex circuit" also depends on the simultaneous or preceding reactions. The fact has long been studied under the name of "composition of reflexes." In general, when a reaction is produced, all those which other stimuli could provoke at the same moment turn out to be inhibited; and when two antagonistic reflexes enter into competition in this way there is no compromise; only one of the two is achieved.[33] Everything happens as if the nervous system could not do two things at once. This fact clearly necessitates the establishment of transverse relations between nerve circuits. But in many authors they remain of the same type as the longitudinal relations of the classic conception: the organism plays no positive role in the elaboration of stimuli. Such is the meaning of the notions of inhibition or of reciprocal innervation introduced by Sherrington. The nerve processes which govern the contraction of the flexors would automatically provoke the inhibition of the extensors and vice versa. But here again the mode of liason posited between the nerve circuits is not sufficiently flexible. According to Goldstein, what appears to be a reciprocal inhibition is observed only if one employs electrical stimulation on muscles severed from their insertions. Except for that of a strong movement, natural innervation does not follow this rigid law. As soon as it is a question of fine movements of the hand, or even of grasping movements, a simultaneous innervation of the antagonistic reflexes is observed, the distribution of which depends on the goal to be obtained and on the type of movement to be executed.

Thus, it is not what happens at the level of the flexors which determines what happens at the level of the extensors, or inversely; but these two partial processes appear as aspects of a global phenomenon which must still be described.[34] More generally, it seems necessary to raise questions concerning the value of the notion of antagonism; for example, it has been possible to contest the view that vegetative life consists in an equilibrium between sympathetic and parasympathetic excitations.[35] In order not to multiply hypotheses unnecessarily, one would have to define a conception of nerve functioning which renders intelligible at the same time and by the same principle the reciprocal exclusion of reflexes and the varied collaboration of the nerve circuits within each one of them. If it were accepted that each reflex presupposes an elaboration of stimuli in which the whole nervous system is involved, one would understand rather well that it cannot "do two things at once" without the need of positing any special mechanism of inhibition. As to the regulated distribution of the motor excitations, it would find its explanation in precisely this same elaboration of stimuli which would be the proper function of the nervous system. Besides, if one wants to posit a pre-established device in order to take into account each of the influences which acts on the reflex, it would be necessary to multiply them beyond all measure; the effector organs themselves would have to be joined to the center by afferent conductors especially charged with the determination of the impending reflex, since observation shows that this latter is a function of the initial situation of the very muscles in which it is completed.

The same stimulation on the arm of a starfish evokes a movement toward the stimulated side if the arm is extended on a horizontal plane and, in contrast, a uniform movement toward the tautest side if the arm is hanging down.[36] In man, a blow under the kneecap provokes a reaction of extension if the leg involved is crossed over the other, a reaction of flexion if it is passively extended. The extract of the pituitary evokes inverse reactions of the uterus depending on whether a woman is pregnant or not. The excitation of the vagus nerve has opposite effects depending on whether the cardia is contracted or dilated at the moment considered.[37]

Should we posit special inhibitory devices here again which prevent a certain reflex depending on the state of the terminal organ? But they are required only by the postulates of the classical method. The functioning of the organism is analyzed by proceeding from the periphery to the center; nerve phenomena are conceived on the model of discrete stimulations which are received at the surface of the organism; the discontinuity of these sensory terminations is extended into the interior of the nervous system, so much so that the functioning is finally represented as a mosaic of autonomous processes which interfere with and correct each other. Because one has begun by positing the existence of predetermined reflex arcs, when it is observed that our responses vary with the state of the muscles which the responses *are going* to bring into play, it is necessary to add supplementary orders to the normal devices which can inhibit them at the crucial moment. But what would one think of a physicist who, with each new observation, was obliged to add to his theory something like a safeguarding clause which would change its application? What is true is that, as a figure owes its characteristic appearance to the ground from which it emerges, each movement supposes positive and negative conditions in the whole of the nervous system,[38] but these conditions should not be thought of as separate, as if they were added to already prepared reactions and modified them at the last moment. It would be more in conformity with the facts to consider the central nervous system as the place in which a total "image" of the organism is elaborated and in which the local state of each part is expressed—in a way which must still be made precise. It is this image of the whole which would govern the distribution of the motor influxes, which would immediately give them the organization to which the least of our gestures gives witness and which would distribute the excitation between the flexors and the extensors, the state of the terminal organs being taken into account.

The same hypothesis would account for a final fact which we must discuss: the dependence of each reflex on those which have preceded it (Sherrington).

It has been observed that a given reflex is often followed by an inverse movement and this phenomenon is designated by the significant terms: sometimes, "strike-back";[39] sometimes, "successive induction."[40]

The temporal development of reactions and the influence of prior effects are still more visible in the phenomena of irradiation (Sherrington) and of reflex reversal. An excitant applied to a receptor for a long time and with a growing intensity provokes fuller and fuller reactions, to the point where the entire organism may finally collaborate in them.[41] According to the classical interpretation, if responses vary for the same excitant—contraction of the flexors of a leg, then of the extensors of the opposite leg, to the exclusion of the ipsilateral extensors and of the contralateral flexors—it is because the same excitation is diffused over the receptor and successively affects nerve areas more and more removed from the point originally touched. But this interpretation conforms poorly with the facts. Among the five laws which Sherrington formulates on the basis of his study of irradiation in the excitation of nerve roots, we indeed find a law of "spatial proximity" which makes the functional relation between the afferent and efferent roots depend on distance; but the second law establishes that, even for the weakest excitants, the motor discharge is distributed over several segments and thus that the motor roots are not functional unities; the third, that each one of the motor apparatuses demands not only a certain quantity of excitant, but further an excitant of a certain nature. (Strychnine has precisely the effect of rendering the extensor commands sensitive to the same agents which stimulate the flexors.)[42]

Therefore it is probable that, from the moment of the weakest excitation, certain muscular, and consequently nerve, groupings are completely at work.[43] Each wave, even the smallest, clearly seems to run through the whole system: as observation procedures are improved more distant effects are observed for each excitation; and we have said that the ablation of such nerve regions modifies all the reflexes.[44] In the phenomenon of irradiation, since the basic excitation is carried in all the circuits, additional excitation cannot simply have the effect of bringing about the intervention of new ones whose commands would be more removed from the point stimulated at the origin. Doubtless it provokes a redistribution of excitations and of inhibitions, a "reordination of the state of the whole" "as the blow which one gives to a kaleidoscope."[45] The great merit of Sherrington is to have generalized the idea of inhibition, to have understood that all reflexes comprise excitations and inhibitions in variable proportions. It is the distribution of these inhibiting actions and excitants which varies as the stimulation con-

tinues and becomes more intense.[46] In this sense inhibition appears
to be a particular case of collaboration. On the other hand, since it
is rare that the stimulation of a certain muscular region is accompanied in the others by inhibition pure and simple, one cannot hold
the law of all or nothing as established in the functioning of the
motor nerve elements: each one of them appears capable of functioning in different ways according to what is prescribed at the given
moment by the global situation of the system.

These conclusions would be confirmed if, instead of studying
the not very favorable case of rachidian excitations, we described the
effects of certain cutaneous stimulations, in particular on the most
mobile parts of the body. With an increasing stimulation of the
concha of the ear in a cat one obtains in turn: movements of the
neck and of the front ipsilateral paw, movements of the back ipsilateral paw, contractions of the muscles of the tail and of the torso,
movements of the contralateral back paw and movements of the
front contralateral leg. Thus the pretended irradiation mixes sym-
metric and asymmetric reflexes, short or long, and does not invade
the motor devices in the order in which they are anatomically placed.

But if the law of spatial proximity does not come into play,
then what law can be brought to light by these observations? Just
as in the instance above where the excitation, after influencing the
flexors of one leg, contracted the extensors of the other leg as if in
order not to render impossible the upright position of the animal,
so here "the fundamental forms of the movement of walking are
what determine the character of the reflex much more than the
spatial diffusion in the nerve substance."[47] While the stimulus increases in a continuous manner, the organism does not respond by
movements which would express a continuous diffusion of excitation
through pre-established circuits: the excitation is elaborated in such
a way that at each notable increase it is translated in the motor apparatuses by new movements and is distributed among them in such
a way as to release a gesture endowed with biological meaning. This
discontinuous change of form in the configuration of reflex motor
excitations, the appearance in nerve functioning of a new type of
order no longer founded on the permanence of certain circuits[48]
but created in each movement by the proper activity of the nervous
system and according to the vital exigencies of the organism: these
are the facts which, in Sherrington's own observations, go beyond
the older conception of the reflex, to which nevertheless he remains

committed.[49] If it is possible to find a law of behavior, that law could not connect the observed reactions directly to certain local devices; the former depend upon the total state of the nervous system and on the active interventions which are necessary for the conservation of the organism. How is this dependence of the parts with respect to the whole to be understood? One does not refute finalism by ignoring the facts from which it argues, but by understanding them better than it does.

The dependence of the reflex with respect to those which have preceded it is again visible in the facts of reflex reversal. Here it is a question of a borderline case of threshold phenomena. Weber's law would show that the same stimulus may or may not evoke a response in the organism depending on whether it intervenes after a series of other excitations, or whether, on the contrary, it finds the nervous system in a state of repose. In reflex reversal the same stimulus evokes not only discontinuous but also inverse reactions. But it is not difficult to find physical models for these phenomena. An equal increase of the pressure exerted on a gas produces different effects depending on whether or not the gas happens to be near the maximum pressure at the temperature of the experiment. In physics as in the natural sciences the formula: "the same causes produce the same effects" is equivocal. But the fact that there exist "thresholds" in physics would only support a mechanistic physiology if the physical interpretation were necessarily mechanistic. The classical theory of the reflex understands the phenomenon of "thresholds" as a substitution of circuits: the reflex paths are accessible to an excitation only of a determinate intensity, and when the accumulated excitations go beyond the threshold assigned to one of them, they are carried over another circuit. The discontinuity of the effects is explained by the anatomical discontinuity of the substrate and by the absolute properties of the elements. The theoreticians of the reflex seem to believe that this mode of explanation is the only one which is "scientific."

Physics shows that there is nothing to this. Whatever the present direction of the theory of changes of state, no physicist believes that the fate of science is tied to a mechanistic interpretation which would treat the passage from a gaseous state to a liquid state as a concretion of quasi-solid parts, pre-existent in the gas, and which would reduce the apparent discontinuity of the phenomenon by positing particles endowed with invariable properties. It does happen that modern physics takes into consideration discontinuous and in a certain sense anatomical structures, but most often it integrates them into fields of force.[50] And in no case does it believe itself forced to choose between the ontological affirmations: continuous or discontinuous, force or extension. If physiology wishes to draw its inspiration from physics, it should in turn go beyond the prejudice of realistic analysis.

No reason of principle, no exigency of the scientific method obliges us, then, to interpret Weber's law in the language of the older reflex theory, that is, to consider the thresholds of different nerve apparatuses as defined once and for all by their proper structure. As for the facts, it is known that central lesions or merely fatigue often have the effect of elevating or lowering the reflex thresholds, more generally, of rendering them labile. The thresholds would be functions therefore of the general state of the nervous system. Small quantities of adrenalin lower blood pressure the more the tonus in the muscles of the blood vessels is elevated (Cannon). But if the action of adrenalin occurs while the stomach muscles are relaxed, it will have, on the contrary, a tonic effect (Kroetz). Outside of any preconceived hypothesis, this fact would be exactly described by saying that the nerve apparatus, in which each efficacious excitation provokes a rupture of equilibrium, becomes insensitive to external interventions beyond certain intensities. If they continue to be produced it reacts in such a way that in fact they provoke, not an increase, but on the contrary a diminution of the general state of excitation. Since the thresholds themselves are not invariable characteristics of certain nerve apparatuses, nothing warrants translating this description into the language of physiological atomism; nothing justifies supposing, for example, that the tonic reflex attributed in its own right to certain apparatuses is produced only below a certain threshold fixed once and for all and that, once this threshold is attained, the excitation diffuses automatically into another apparatus charged with the inverse reflex. What prescribes its momentary threshold to the tonic apparatus (if one wishes to posit one) is the general state of the nervous system; what closes this apparatus and contrariwise assigns a chronaxie to the antagonistic device such that it is in turn affected by the excitation is again the activity of the central nervous system.

Even in supposing that each typical reaction is tied to a distinct apparatus, one cannot avoid the hypothesis of a central elaboration in which the vital necessities of the organism are in fact expressed. Everything happens as if it oscillated around a preferred state of excitation which it is the law of our reflexes to maintain and which prescribes to each stimulus its effect. But from this point of view, reflex reversal, instead of being "reduced" to Weber's law, could give it a signification which was not at first perceived in it.[51] When the organism, in the presence of an additional stimulus, limits itself to deferring it instead of reversing the reflex, this resistance to new excitation should not be interpreted as a simple phenomenon of inertia. Here again, if certain excitations remain subliminal, it is because the nervous system elaborates them in such a way that the state of equilibrium is not modified (Koffka's law of leveling). When the additional excitation continues to increase, it finally ceases to be any longer compatible with the state in which the system maintained itself until then. The equilibrium is then reorganized at another level of excitation, higher than that which would be required by the present stimulus (Koffka's law of emphasis), and in which the organism will maintain itself for an appreciable time while the stimulus continues to increase.[52] Thus the excitation will never be the passive registering of an external action, but an elaboration of these influences which in fact submits them to the descriptive norms of the organism.[53]

THE REACTION

Even if there existed specific stimuli, receptors and nerve pathways, they would not of themselves be able to explain the adaptation of the reflex to the stimulus, since the movement to be executed in each case depends upon the initial position of the members, which is variable. In a scratch reflex the muscular contractions necessary to bring my hand to the point stimulated are very different depending on whether my hand happens to be extended initially toward the right or toward the left. Is it imagined that there are as many pre-established circuits at the point scratched as there are possible initial positions for my hand? One would still not understand how the influx chooses, among the open pathways, precisely that one which will evoke the appropriate movement in the situation considered. And Sherrington has shown that an adapted movement is possible in this case without a proprioceptive message coming from the moved member, which fact precludes our imagining a series of corrections based on proprioceptive indications which the center would bring to the initial movement. Thus it must be that "the reflex carries within itself the condition(s) of a correct localization movement." [54] From where does it get them, since they are not immediately given with the local stimulation?

This immediate adaptation of our reflexes does not merely take place with regard to the space occupied by our body. External space is reached by them with the same assurance. If a blindfolded subject backs up a certain distance and is then asked to go over the same distance again going forward, he succeeds in doing so, whether by walking straight ahead or sideways, whether with small steps or big ones. What is it that regulates or governs his movement in this case?[55] How is its physiological substrate to be represented? It cannot be a question of visual control, since the eyes of the subject are blindfolded. Watson has shown more generally that movement cannot be guided by the reproduction of exteroceptive stimulations. Will it be said that the first movement leaves behind kinesthetic traces which will serve as a guide for the second? But Lashley has established that rats, after ablation of the cerebellum, remain capable of correctly traversing a labyrinth which they have "learned," which at least precludes considering kinesthetic images as the only directing principle of movement.[56] Moreover, in the example we have taken, the work executed in the preparatory experiments and the work requested in the critical experiment are, considered element by element, incommensurable since the direction of walking has been reversed and the size of the steps has been modified.

In cases of this kind authors who have provided themselves, in the reflex theory, with inadequate bodily explanatory principles are tempted to make "intelligence" intervene. But, aside from the fact that this does not eliminate the necessity of defining the bodily instruments of the movement, an intelligent response is very unlikely either in the present example or in infantile learning. If, while I am pointing to an object with my right hand, I am blindfolded and asked to designate it with my left hand or with my head,[57] I succeed in doing so without judgment: intelligence, if it intervened, would in this case have to accomplish an extremely long task, and one which I do not even suspect before having reflected on it. It would be necessary to determine the position of my right arm in relation to a system of coordinates and to calculate the position that my left arm should occupy in relation to the same system in order to designate the direction of the same object. In fact, I possess the conclusions without the premises being given anywhere. I execute the proposed task without knowing what I am doing, just as habits acquired by one group of muscles can be transferred immediately to another: my handwriting on the blackboard resembles my handwriting on paper although the muscles concerned in each case are not the same. There is something *general* in our reflex responses which precisely permits these effector substitutions. When the blindfolded subject backs up a certain number of steps, this movement must be registered in the centers, not in the form of an imprint of the muscular contractions which have been actually produced, but in the global form of a certain "space traversed" which is immediately translatable into steps of another size and differently directed.

What regulates our motor reactions in a decisive manner is this general factor which is not necessarily tied to any of the materials of behavior. ". . . [L]ike man, animals know how to move themselves in an area of space which is not given to them in perception and without possessing signs which indicate the 'way'." [58] Thus, animals and men react to space in an adapted manner even in the absence of adequate actual or recent stimuli. "This space is bound up with the animal's own body as a part of its flesh. When the animal moves itself in this space to which it is adapted, a melody of spatial characteristics is unfolded in a continuous manner and is played in the different sensory domains." [59] Science must conceive of a physiological representation for this "intention of movement" [60] which is "first given as a nucleus from which the totality of the movement is subsequently differentiated." [61] In its functioning the body cannot be defined as a blind mechanism, a mosaic of causally independent sequences.

With the physiologists, we have attempted to discover adequate stimuli, specific receptors and invariable reflex arcs for a given reaction—that is, instead of classifying the facts, we have presented them, at the risk of some repetition, in the order in which they present themselves to an investigation based on the classical postulates. But these repetitions are significant: to the extent that one tries to make the notions of stimulus, receptor and reflex arc more precise one sees them merge into each other; the reflex ceases to be a series of events juxtaposed in the body and one ends up with a problem which we would like to formulate in summarizing the preceding pages. The adequate *stimulus* cannot be defined in itself and independently of the organism; it is not a physical reality, it is a physiological or biological reality. That which necessarily releases a certain reflex response is not a physico-chemical agent; it is a certain form of excitation of which the physico-chemical agent is the occasion rather than the cause. It is for this reason that physiologists do not succeed in eliminating terms from their definition of stimulus which already designate a response of the organism, as when they speak of painful stimuli. For the excitation itself is already a response, not an effect imported from outside the organism; it is the first act of its proper functioning.

The notion of stimulus refers back to the original activity by which the organism takes in excitations which are locally and temporally dispersed over its receptors and gives a bodily existence to those beings of reason such as the rhythm, the figure, the relations of intensity and, in a word, the global form of local stimuli. The punctual excitations not being decisive, the *place of the excitation* could not be any more so—which the lability of the receptor fields confirms. Thus the same partial stimulus can give rise to variable effects and the same nerve element can function in a qualitatively different manner according to what is prescribed by the constellation of stimuli and by the elaboration to which it gives rise beyond the discontinuous sensory terminations. Could not this elaboration be conceived in such a way that the reflex schema remains valid in principle? It would be sufficient to suppose that central activity intervenes by closing certain circuits and directing excitation toward other circuits established in advance (inhibition, control). However, the classical conception is maintained only if the regulation is localized in certain devices comparable to reflex arcs. But it does not seem to be exclusively bound up with cerebral activity (there are the facts of the "liberation of the automatism" even in the absence of any lesion of the cerebro-spinal paths—cases of total inhibition where cerebral activity is not directly concerned); nor does it seem explicable moreover in each place by automatic devices of association or disjunction (reciprocal inhibition, successive induction). Depending on the case, each part of the nervous system can in turn appear to be inhibiting and inhibited. One could say of inhibition what has been said of coordination: its center is everywhere and nowhere.[62]

In the final analysis inhibition and control do not explain nerve functioning. They themselves presuppose a process which regulates their distribution. The higher systems to which the facts force us to subordinate the reflex need themselves to be explained, and for the same reasons for which they were introduced. It becomes necessary to renounce conceiving of nerve activity in its most essential character, not only as restricted to certain determined pathways, but even as a choice between several pre-established pathways. One is brought back to the idea of an innervation of the whole, which is itself capable of distributing the excitation and of constituting the reflex paths entirely by itself. The metaphor of a switching station is not applicable since one cannot find out where it should be situated, since it would be a station which receives its instructions from convoys which it is charged to direct and which improvises the pathways and the switches according to their indications. The stimuli do not come to the sensory surfaces and, according to Descartes' comparison, pull the strings which command the muscles involved in the response; there are no "strings"; and, even when it is stable, as in the plantar flexion reflex in the normal subject, the stimulus-response relation is mediated by complex interactions within the nervous system. In the same way the different movements which compose a reaction are not linked together by a material connection prior to this reaction. But, given a certain stimulus, where does the relative stability of its responses come from if everything depends upon everything in the organism? How is it that there are typical reactions, that there are even "reactions" and not inefficacious convulsions? If order cannot be based on pre-established anatomical structures, from where does the coherence of our reactions and their adaptation to the stimulus come?

This problem has been posed by Sherrington in regard to the facts of irradiation. He has seen clearly that in this case a biological order—that of the movements of walking—is substituted for the mechanical order of the anatomical connections. Thus, he admits that the classical reflex is an abstraction. But by this he merely means that the simple reflex circuits are in fact complicated and masked by the intervention of higher systems, by integration. He still feels that he can account for behavior by a combination of reflex liaisons; it is only a question of multiplying them; it is with a sum of abstractions that he tries to reconstruct the concrete. For him, the difference between the traditional schema and actual nerve activity is only the difference between the simple and the complex.[63] Sherrington's entire work shows that the order—the adaptation of the response to the stimulus and of the mutual adaptation of the parts of the response—cannot be explained by the autonomy of pre-established nerve pathways. But the inhibitions and the control devices which are superimposed on the simple reflex arcs are themselves conceived after the model of the reflex arc. These new circuits, as we have seen, are no more autonomous than the first and will in turn be susceptible to all sorts of interferences. Thus, the control itself will have to be submitted to a higher regulation; so it is not yet at this level that one will find the pure reflex. But the same reasoning will have to be reinitiated indefinitely; and the solution will always be deferred, never furnished, until the moment when a principle which *constitutes* the order instead of undergoing it has been introduced into nerve functioning. It is paradoxical to conserve the notion of the reflex arc theoretically without being able to apply it anywhere in fact. As in all the particular questions which we have mentioned, in his general conception of nerve functioning Sherrington seeks to save the principles of classical physiology. His categories are not made for the phenomena which he himself has brought to light.

The Interpretation of the Reflex in Gestalt Theory

Let us consider once again the ocular fixation reflex which has already served us in defining the classical conception of nerve functioning.[64] Even though it is admitted that the first movements of fixation are imperfect and that these must be subsequently ameliorated, either by learning or by maturation of the nerve apparatuses, their reflex character is not generally contested since it has been possible to observe them in the first days of life. To say that these movements are reflexes is to say, as we have seen, that the points of the retina touched by the light rays must be in central connection with motor nerves which are capable of bringing the luminous impression over the macula by making the eye move back and forth.[65] But this system of connections which would link up each fiber of the optic nerve to motor devices is still not sufficient. Let us suppose as a matter of fact that a subject's eye which is fixated on A moves toward A^1 and that then, without any movement of the head, it moves toward B. Point B is reflected on the retina in the same place as point A was reflected before, since both serve in turn as the point of fixation for the eye; and when the subject's eye is fixated on B, point B^1 is reflected at the very place A^1 was reflected

$$A^1 \quad \cdot \qquad\qquad B^1 \quad \cdot$$

$$A \quad \cdot \qquad\qquad B \quad \cdot$$

when the eye fixated A. Thus the same place on the retina is stimulated in turn by the two luminous points, A^1 and B^1. And yet the muscular contractions to be produced in order to pass respectively from A to A^1 and from B to B^1 are very different. If we want to use the language of pre-established connections, it would be necessary then to suppose that each fiber of the optic nerve is linked up not only with one motor device, but also with all those which it may have to put into action according to the position of the eye in the orbit.[66]

It can be seen to what complicated devices the hypothesis of anatomical structures leads. And one is still not sure that it does not contradict itself. For, having admitted that each point of the retina possesses all the required connections, it remains to be seen what directs the excitation toward the appropriate path in each particular case. The local luminous impression is evidently not sufficient for this since it is the same, in the above figure, when it is a question of fixating B^1 and when it is a question of fixating A^1. Thus, it must be admitted that the fixation reflex is determined concurrently by local retinal impressions and by proprioceptive excitations which express to the center the position of the eye at the beginning. How is the intervention of these regulating excitations to be conceived? An extremely complex shunting mechanism would be necessary for this.

Would it not be simpler to admit that the movement of fixation results, not from the addition of two series of excitations, but from a total process in which the portion of retinal excitations and that of the proprioceptive stimulations are indiscernable? What would recommend the hypothesis of pre-established anatomical connections between certain points of the sensory surface and certain motor apparatuses to the physiologist could only be the blind correspondence sometimes observed between the place of excitation and the motor effect. But here we encounter a case in which, the place of the excitation and also the functional effect remaining constant, the intermediary phenomena or, if one can speak this way, the instruments of the reflex are nevertheless different. Thus nothing compels us to conserve the hypothesis of pre-established connections in this case or to treat the retinal impressions and the proprioceptive stimulations as components really distinct from the total excitation.

But how then ought the relationship between the motor reaction and the constellation of stimuli which condition it be represented? What troubles and compromises anatomical conceptions is that they cannot easily introduce a regulation of the reflex either by the situation to which it responds or by its proper effects. "Now instinctive and even most of reflexive activity appears to be highly adapted; the animal does what is good for it in its environment. But from the point of view of this theory this adaptiveness is not a property of these actions themselves, but is instead a mere impression which they give to the onlooker. The actions are not determined in any way by the instrinsic nature of the situation, but altogether by these pre-existing bond-devices. The situation enters only as an agency which turns the key, presses the button, makes the machine go. But, like a true machine, the animal can only act according to the system of pre-established bonds, whether such an action be adequate to the circumstances or not. The relationship between situation and response is consequently purely contingent." [67]

The classical physiology of the reflex demands that function be only a product or result of existing structures; in short, it denies it any proper and objective reality: it is nothing but a human manner of designating the effects of the mechanism. But can scientific research be subjected to this ban? "It would be a hopeless task for the biologist to explain a structure, the marvelous complexity of which would assure an appropriate function, without the service of this function in guiding its development." [68] In order for vital movements to have immediately the rightness and the flexibility which are so striking in them, or at least for them to be able to correct themselves by experience, motor innervation must be regulated at each moment and, in each case, account must be taken of the particularities of the situation. ". . . [T]he innervation of muscles required in writing even a portion of a letter involves a wide range of variability, according as we write large or small characters, quickly or slowly, energetically or easily, with this or that position of the arm, to the right or to the left, above or below on the paper." [69] But all these regulations are executed instantaneously. Where can their origin be located if not in the afferent processes which prepare the motor reaction? It has been shown [70] that a baby holding a pencil in its hand puts it back in its mouth six times successively even if it was pushed away in a different direction each time. Thus at each moment the position of the arm, expressed at the center by proprioceptivity, is sufficient without learning to regulate the direction and amplitude of the motor reaction. Thus the receptive motor part of the nervous system must cease to be conceived as independent apparatuses, the structure of which would be established before they enter into relationship. "It has been customary to consider the reflex arc as composed of a centripetal and a centrifugal branch, these being regarded as independent parts, while the characteristic feature of the apparatus was the *connection* that exists between them." [71]

The facts suggest, on the contrary, that the sensorium and motorium function as parts of a single organ. It is known, for example, that it is very difficult to fixate an object in a landscape illuminated by daylight for very long and, on the other hand, that a luminous spot in the dark exercises something like a power of attraction on the eye which it is difficult to overcome. Again it is known that the reflex movements of our eyes are most often made in accordance with the contours of the objects perceived and, finally, that the eye always places itself in such a way that it receives the richest possible stimulations from the object looked at.[72] Everything takes place as if a law of the maximum regulated the movements of our eyes, as if at each moment these movements were what they should be in order to realize certain situations of preferred equilibrium toward which the forces which are at work in the sensible sector tend. If, in the dark, a luminous spot appears in a marginal zone, everything takes place as if the equilibrium of the sensory-motor system were broken up; from this results a state of tension resolved by the fixation movement which brings the luminous spot to the functional center of the retina. Thus the motor devices appear as the means of re-establishing an equilibrium, the conditions of which are given in the sensory sector of the nervous system; and the movements appear as the external expression of this reorganization of the field of excitations comparable to the settling of objects in a receptacle under the action of the weight. If a vertical line is presented to each of the eyes in a stereoscope in such a way that, for a normal degree of convergence, the two lines appear as parallel and very close to each other, the subject soon sees them fused into a single line. This is because our eyes have adopted, without our knowing it, a degree of convergence such that the retinal image of the two vertical lines is formed on the corresponding meridians.

Everything takes place as if the physiological processes which correspond to each of the retinal impressions exercised upon each other, in the visual center, a sort of attraction which would be translated in the motor region by movements oriented in the direction of these forces. "An examination of the situation from the standpoint of physics seems to show that such a thing might really occur . . . In the equilibrium distribution of process the field is still full of stresses which are for the moment in balance, but represent a store of energy. So in vision there seems to be stress tending to bring the two parallels together. In physics, if such a field is functionally connected with movable parts, amongst whose movements some definite form of motion would release the still existing stresses of the field, this movement will immediately occur, produced by the energy of those stresses. These only *'waited,'* as it were, for an opportunity to let their energy work, for instance influencing movable parts in the direction of a better equilibrium. The better equilibrium in physics lies always in the direction of those stresses which tend to produce some change, but which in our physiological case *cannot do it directly in the field.* If possible, then, they will do it by a detour influencing the muscles of the eyes as movable parts in the direction of release of their energy. There is nothing supernatural in such an orderly physical process, no process with or without detour can ever produce changes which are not directed toward a more stable equilibrium of the whole system. We have only to adopt this view for the case of the optical part of the brain and its nervous connection with the muscles of the eyeballs in order to have a new explanation of fixation movements . . ." [73]

A liquid which tends to a balanced distribution, in passing into a vase which communicates with the one in which it is contained, can use indirect paths if the more direct ones are obstructed; in the same manner the reflex could be produced through substitute nerve pathways if for some reason the habitual pathways are not usable. But even this comparison is not exact, for the liquid which seeks its equilibrium in the communicating vases follows pre-established paths. At the most one could suppose that the obstruction of the most direct paths, by causing the liquid to rise above the ordinary level, releases the openings of substitute paths, which are ready to begin functioning, by means of an automatic device. It is in another sense that the reflex would be relatively independent of the substrates in which it is ordinarily realized. For, as a drop of water submitted to external forces realizes a new distribution of elements and a global form which brings back the equilibrium by means of the reciprocal action of its internal forces, so reflex activity would be capable of improvising approximate substitutions which, without ever being the exact equivalent of the reaction which has become impossible, would maintain the threatened function in the organism. An almost constant functional result would then be obtained by variable "means" and it would be correct to say that it is the function which permits us to understand the organism. Thus, when they are inborn, anatomical structures should be considered as topographical conditions of the original functional development, modifiable by the functioning itself and thus comparable to the electrode which governs the phenomenon of electrolysis but is altered by it in return; when they are acquired, they should be considered the result of the most habitual functioning; thus anatomy should be considered as a stage in the development of physiology. Finally, if it were established that the nerve processes in each situation always tend to re-establish certain states of preferred equilibrium, these latter would represent the objective values of the organism and one would have the right to classify behavior as ordered or disordered, significant or insignificant, with respect to them. These denominations, far from being extrinsic and anthropomorphic, would belong to the living being as such.

But these consequences have been verified with regard to the fixation reflex by Marina's already old transplantation experiments.[74] If, in a monkey, the internal muscles of the eyeballs are connected with the nerve fibers which ordinarily govern the external muscles and these latter, on the other hand, with the nerve fibers which habitually govern the former, when the animal is placed in a dark room it turns its eyes correctly toward a luminous spot which appears, for example, at the right. Whatever the instrument of this adaptation, it is clear that it would not be comprehensible if the anatomical devices were decisive, if a regulator process of the type described above did not enter in to assure the adaptation of functioning after the exchange of the neuro-muscular insertions.

Koehler's hypothesis is applicable not only to the fixation reflex. One would introduce it just as readily in seeking to explain how the hand is moved when it goes to grasp a seen object or when it carries a touched object to the mouth. In these cases as in the preceding one, the visual or tactile impression, combined with the central representations of the position of the members and of the body, should itself regulate the motor reaction, since, as has been observed,[75] if a child tries to seize an object it does not look at its hand but at the object; if it tries to carry an object which it holds in its hand to its mouth, it never has to locate the position of its mouth with the other hand. One would also account for reflex movements of the head toward a source of sound by means of the same kind of explanation. It is known (Katz) that the only thing which intervenes in this reaction, when it is reflexive, is the interval of time which separates the arrival of the sound to the right ear and the left; moreover, the subject is not aware of this interval as such. Thus it is to be presumed that here again the nerve processes released by the two sound stimulations tend toward a state of equilibrium in which the two lines of waves are simultaneous and evoke the orientation movements capable of procuring this result.[76]

It has long been known that the dung beetle, after the amputation of one or several phalanges, is capable of continuing its walk immediately. But the movements of the stump which remains and those of the whole body are not a simple perseveration of those of normal walking; they represent a new mode of locomotion, a solution of the unexpected problem posed by the amputation. Moreover, this reorganization of the functioning of an organ (*Umstellung*) is not produced unless it is rendered necessary by the nature of the surface: on a rough surface where the member, even though shortened, can find points of application, the normal process of walking is conserved; it is abandoned when the animal comes upon a smooth surface. Thus, the reorganization of the functioning is not released automatically by the removal of one or several phalanges as would happen if a pre-established emergency device were involved; it is accomplished only through the pressure of external conditions, and we are led to believe that it is improvised, like the fixation reflex above, by forces which are at work in the afferent sector of the nervous system. Trendelenburg's experiments confirm this.

An animal, incapable of seizing its food with its right member after the partial excision of the appropriate cerebral region, recovers the use of it after amputation of the left member which had been substituted for the first. If at this time the excision of the centers which govern the right member is completed, the animal remains capable of utilizing it when the situation makes it imperative, for example, when the food is located outside of the cage. It is scarcely possible to posit a new emergency device corresponding to each of the phases of this experiment, for which devices the situation of the moment would be the adequate stimulus; the hypothesis that there is an entirely novel distribution of innervations for each phase, governed by the situation itself, is in much better agreement with the character of the phenomenon.

Moreover, functional reorganization, as well as the putting into effect of substitute actions (*Ersatzleistungen*) in which a member or an organ takes upon itself the function of another, takes place in a characteristic manner only if a vital interest is at stake and not if a "made to order" act is involved. Which is to say that it represents the means of a return to equilibrium for the whole nervous system and not the releasing of a local anatomical device. But functional reorganization and substitute actions remain elementary nerve phenomena which do not achieve the flexibility of reactions which are called conscious: they do not appear in a dog, a crab or a starfish as long as the member is only immobilized instead of being amputated. In these cases the activity is completely employed in efforts at liberation which gradually degenerate into disordered behavior. In man, on the contrary, useful "detours" will be produced without deliberation if the member is absolutely immobilized. These facts are essential for us, therefore, because they bring to light a directed activity between blind mechanism and intelligent behavior which is not accounted for by classical mechanism and intellectualism.[77]

But vision in persons with hemianopsia[78] furnishes the best example of a nerve activity directed toward functional equilibrium. If the retinal sectors which remain capable of evoking luminous sensations in a person with hemianopsia are determined by measuring the perimeter of vision, it is observed that he now has the use of only two half retinas; consequently one would expect that his field of vision would correspond to half of the normal field of vision, right or left according to the case, with a zone of clear peripheral vision. In reality this is not the case at all: the subject has the impression of seeing poorly, but not of being reduced to half a visual field. The organism has adapted itself to the situation created by the illness by reorganizing the functions of the eye. The eyeballs have oscillated in much a way as to present a part of the retina which is intact to the luminous excitations, whether they come from the right or the left; in other words, the preserved retinal sector has established itself in a central position in the orbit instead of remaining affected, as before the illness, by the reception of light rays coming from one half of the field. But the reorganization of muscular functioning, which is comparable to what we encountered in the fixation reflex, would be of no effect if it were not accompanied by a redistribution of functions in the retinal and calcarine elements which certainly seem to correspond point for point to the latter.

It is known that in a normal subject the different regions of the retina are far from being equivalent with regard to visual acuity, color perception and spatial perception. Since certain "peripheral" retinal elements in normal vision have now become "central" and inversely, a systematic permutation of functions must indeed have been produced between them. In particular the old fovea, pushed back to the periphery, has lost its privilege of clear vision and has been replaced by a "pseudo-fovea" situated in the center of the zone which is now sensitive. Fuch's measures show that the visual acuity of the pseudo-fovea is superior to that of the anatomical fovea by $1/6$, $1/4$ or even $1/2$. The luminous excitations that it receives are localized by the subject as "in front" of him. Finally, all the colors are perceived by the new fovea even if it is situated in a retinal region which in a normal subject is blind to red and green.

If we adhere to the classical conceptions which relate the perceptual functions of each point of the retina to its anatomical structure—for example, to the proportion of cones and rods which are located there—the functional reorganization in hemianopsia is not comprehensible. It becomes so only if the properties of each retinal point are assigned to it, not according to established local devices, but according to a flexible process of distribution comparable to the division of forces in a drop of oil suspended in water. Moreover a series of experiments[79] gives support to this hypothesis.

If a subject fixates a spot marked on the side of a screen upon which letters are projected, the objective distance from the fixation point to the letter which appears the clearest varies only slightly whether the subject is placed at one or two meters from the screen, and it is about equal to the distance from the clearest letter to the periphery of the field. Thus the place of clearest vision would not correspond to a retinal element established once and for all; it would be situated at each moment in the center of the actually perceived visual field and this latter would in no way coincide with the sector of the world which is objectively projected on the retina. If the size of the letters on the screen is varied, it is observed that the objective distance from the fixation point to the point of clearest vision, and consequently the objective size of the field encompassed by our perception, increases with the dimension of the projected letters. The influence of the characteristics of the object perceived on the objective size of the visual field is much more considerable than that of the strictly anatomical conditions, as is proved by a third series of experiments. If the dimensions of the letters and the distance of the subject from the screen are varied proportionally and at the same time, even though under these conditions the angle from which each letter is seen remains constant, it is discovered that, for the largest letters, the distance from the fixation point to the letter which appears the clearest is objectively greater, and therefore the area of the perceived visual field is also greater. It seems then that *the quantity of space encompassed by our perception and the place of the zone of clear vision in the phenomenal field express certain modes of organization of the sensory field related to the characteristics of the objects presented to the eye much more than the geometrical projection of objects on the retina, and depend upon certain laws of equilibrium proper to the nervous system much more than upon anatomical structures.*

". . . [T]he contribution of any part of the retina to the total performance changes according to the task with which the organism is confronted; and according to the kind of adjustment which a specific situation requires." [80] It is not *because* an object is projected on the macula that it is perceived as situated in front of us or that it is seen distinctly; rather, the inverse must be said: that the macula is the region of the retina where objects perceived as frontal and in clear vision are most often projected; and these characteristics in turn come to the phenomenal objects from the situation occupied by the physiological processes which correspond to them in the constellation of perceptual processes of the moment and from the relations of equilibrium which are established between both of these according to the general schema of Koehler. *Most frequently* the effect of these relations is to make the object whose image is formed in the center of the sensitive zone appear in clear vision and in a frontal situation. [81] Certain specific properties of the subsequent physiological processes should correspond to these phenomenal characteristics known by consciousness.[82] One can understand that the tissues are modified by them and that this would be why appropriate organs are created by the function, why a pseudo-fovea is constituted on the healthy half retina of a hemianopic. It is too early to extend this explanation to anatomical structures which until now have been considered to be inborn.[83] But a regulation by function must be accepted with regard to acquired localizations. As long as recognition of objects is not rendered impossible—for example, in the case of hemiamblyopia— no functional reorganization is produced.[84] It occurs on the other hand, and without the patient's knowing it, as soon as this essential function is eliminated.

Since our least conscious reactions are never isolable within the whole of nervous activity, since they seem guided in each case by the internal and external situation itself and capable, up to a certain point, of adapting themselves to that which is particular to it, it is no longer possible to maintain the sharp distinctions between "reflex" activities and "instinctive" or "intelligent" activities which the classical conceptions established theoretically. An opposition cannot be set up between a blind automatism and an intentional activity whose relations with the former would moreover remain obscure. Nevertheless, the classical conception of the reflex was founded on a certain number of observations which must be taken into account. For all degrees do exist in the organization and integration of behavior. Just as a series of conductors within which electrical charges are distributed according to a law of equilibrium can be joined by very small wires without constituting a single physical system, so nervous activity can be subdivided into partial groupings and articulated in distinct processes whose mutual influence is negligible.

If everything really depended upon everything else, in the organism as well as in nature, there would be no laws and no science. Koehler's whole-processes admit of an interior cleavage, and Gestalt theory stands at an equal distance from a philosophy of simple coordination (*Und-Verbindungen*) and a romantic conception of the absolute unity of nature.[85] But it attempts to distinguish true analysis, which follows the natural articulations of the phenomena, from one which treats them all as things, that is, as wholes gifted with absolute properties, and which does not respect the partial structures in which they are integrated. The reflex as it is defined in the classical conception does not represent the normal activity of the animal, but the reaction obtained from an organism when it is subjected to working as it were by means of detached parts, to responding not to complex *situations* but to isolated *stimuli*. Which is to say that it corresponds to the behavior of a sick organism—the primary effect of lesions being to break up the functional continuity of nerve tissues—and to "laboratory behavior" where the animal is placed in an anthropomorphic situation since, instead of having to deal with those natural unities which events or baits are, it is restricted to certain discriminations; it must react to certain physical and chemical agents which have a separate existence only in human science.[86] Every organic reaction supposes a global elaboration of the excitations which confers properties on each one of them that it would not have singly.

It is not surprising that, even in the laboratory, so few pure reflexes are found. Reactions which conform to the classical definition—that is to say, constant for a given excitant—have been able to be discovered only when there is an immediate relation of receptor and effector, only when a reaction of auto-regulation of organs is involved (Goldstein's *Eigenreflexe*) and where these latter are working for themselves, so to speak. The form of these reactions is characteristic: it always involves a movement of simple orientation with regard to the excitant, at the very most a movement of application and of grasping. In this way the organism obtains a neutralization of dangerous excitants and the constant reflex would thus be a "catastrophic" reaction which appears in "borderline situations," [87] comparable if one likes to the monotonous reactions of flight in human pathology. When classical physiology tried to obtain constant reflexes in the laboratory, inverse reactions for an identical stimulus or the same response for different stimuli were sometimes observed. The pseudo-constancy of the reflex which was considered normal and the caprices which seem in contradiction with it are in reality two different aspects of an identical functional anomaly. It is because the reactions are not solidly "centered" in the global activity of the organism that they can present this monotony in spite of modifications of the stimulus; and if, inversely, one reaction can suddenly be substituted for another while the stimulus remains constant, it is because neither one is integrated into a dynamic whole which would demand this and only this reaction.[88]

The pathology of higher behavior is also acquainted with this alternation of stereotypes and of "no-matter-who-ism" (Piaget), which likewise expresses the impotence of the subject to master a situation. As soon as physiology tried to analyze less rudimentary modes of adaptation—no longer simple auto-regulations of organs (*Eigenreflexe*), but reactions which resolve a problem posed by the milieu (*Fremdreflexe*); no longer simple compensatory processes, but true actions (in this sense even the scratch "reflex" is a true action)— it discovered neither the consistency nor, moreover, the extreme lability of the preceding reactions. What is observed, especially if the animal is placed in a natural situation, is another sort of consistency and another sort of variations. If I catch my toe on a root while walking, the flexor muscles of the foot are suddenly relaxed and the organism reacts by accentuating this relaxation, which will liberate my foot. If, on the other hand, I miss my step while coming down a mountain and my heel strikes the ground sharply before the sole of the foot, the flexor muscles are once again relaxed suddenly, but the organism reacts instantly by a contraction. It is a question here of responses which "result from the holistic utilization of stimuli, which vary when the stimuli appear in different total situations, or to put it differently, when they have a different meaning for the organism." [89] Here the variation of the response in the presence of analogous stimuli is related to the meaning of the situations in which they appear and, inversely, it can happen that situations which appear different if they are analyzed in terms of physical and chemical stimuli provoke analogous reactions. Laboratory reflexes resemble the movements of a man who walks in the dark and whose tactile organs, feet and legs function in isolation, as it were. [90]

This functioning by separated parts represents a late acquisition in animal ontogenesis. Reflexes properly so called are found only in the adult salamander; the embryo executes movements of the ensemble, global and undifferentiated movements of swimming. [91] It may even be that pure reflexes will be most easily found in man because man is perhaps alone in being able to abandon this or that part of his body separately to the influences of the milieu. When the pupillary reflex is examined in a human subject it could be said that the subject lends his eye to the experimenter; then and only then is a reaction observed which is approximately constant for a given stimulus; this regularity will not be discovered in the vital use of vision. [92] Thus the reflex—effect of a pathological disassociation characteristic not of the fundamental activity of the living being but of the experimental apparatus which we use for studying it, or a luxury activity developing late in ontogenesis as well as in phylogenesis— cannot be considered as a constituent element of animal behavior except by an anthropomorphic illusion.[93] But neither is the reflex an abstraction, and in this respect Sherrington is mistaken: the reflex exists; it represents a very special case of behavior, observable under certain determined conditions. But it is not the principal object of physiology; *it is not by means of it that the remainder can be understood*. Not every reaction obtained by investigating a sick organism or one under artificial conditions in the laboratory can be considered a *biological reality*. The object of biology is to grasp that which makes a living being a living being, that is, not—according to the realist postulate common to both mechanism and vitalism—the superposition of elementary reflexes or the intervention of a "vital force," but an indecomposable structure of behavior. It is by means of ordered reactions that we can understand the automatic reactions as degradations. Just as anatomy refers back to physiology, physiology refers back to biology. "The forms of movement of the reflexes are the marionettes of life . . . , the images of movements which an organism accomplishes when it stands upright, walks, fights, flies, takes and eats, in play and in reproduction." [94]

Conclusion

In summary, the critique of reflex theory and the analysis of a few examples show that we should consider the afferent sector of the nervous system as a field of forces which express concurrently the intraorganic state and the influence of external agents; these forces tend to balance themselves according to certain modes of preferred distribution and to obtain movements from the mobile parts of the body which are proper to this effect. These movements, as they are executed, provoke modifications in the state of the afferent system which in their turn evoke new movements. This dynamic and circular process would assure the flexible regulation which is needed in order to account for effective behavior.

We have given, following Koehler, several physical models and in particular an electrical model of this process. Koehler has been reproached for these "adventuresome physiological hypotheses." This is because they were not taken in the sense in which he understands them. He does not think that a few analogies are sufficient to be able to reduce nerve functioning to a process of electrical distribution. He submits the hypothesis to the judgment of experience and it is not to this model in particular that he adheres. It happens that there do exist "physical systems" whose properties are similar to those which we have recognized in the nervous system: these systems evolve to a state of privileged equilibrium and there is a circular dependence among local phenomena.[95b] If the character of a physical system in general [96] were granted, for example, to the visual sector of the nervous system, the fixation reflex as we have described it would be accounted for.

It is not a question of risking one hypothesis among others, but of introducing a new category, the category of "form," which, having its application in the inorganic as well as the organic domain, would permit bringing to light the "transverse functions" in the nervous system of which Wertheimer speaks[97] and whose existence is confirmed by experience without a vitalist hypothesis. For the "forms," and in particular the physical systems, are defined as total processes whose properties are not the sum of those which the isolated parts would possess.[98] More precisely they are defined as total processes which may be indiscernible from each other while their "parts," compared to each other, differ in absolute size; in other words the systems are defined as transposable wholes.[99] We will say that there is form whenever the properties of a system are modified by every change brought about in a single one of its parts and, on the contrary, are conserved when they all change while maintaining the same relationship among themselves. These definitions are applicable to nerve phenomena since, as we have just seen, each part of a reaction cannot be related to a partial condition, and since there is reciprocal action and internal connection among the afferent excitations on the one hand, the motor influxes on the other, and finally between both of these systems. Whatever the fate of Koehler's models, the analogy upon which they are founded exists and we can consider it as established. We must still investigate what it is which constitutes the distinctive character of physical forms and determine whether the reduction of "physiological forms" to "physical forms" can be accepted in principle.

But is it really necessary to introduce a new category in order to understand nerve phenomena? Gestalt theory justifies the notion of "form" by a criticism of the "anatomical" spirit in physiology. Would not the necessity of this notion be much less evident in a "functional" physiology which bases the nerve pathways on momentary connections such as those which are established, without regard for topography, between resonators (Schiff, P. Weiss) or between synchronized neurons (L. Lapicque)? Lapicque has posed the problem of order, as did Sherrington himself,[100] with respect to the phenomenon of irradiation. If the excitation, overflowing one member, tends, without regard for the proximity of motor commands, toward the one which functions in collaboration with the first in the life of the animal, there is no longer anything mysterious in this "choice": it is *because* certain paths are momentarily[101] synchronized that they alone are open to the excitation.

But the problem is only displaced. Now it is a question of knowing how the appropriate synchronizations are assured in the organism. According to Lapicque they depend upon peripheral and central factors. The position of the members can provoke, with a redistribution of chronaxies, the inversion of the reflex. A first movement executed or, contrariwise, obstacles opposed to this movement, can give rise by the same means to a "complete permutation of the muscles put into play." [102] All the same it is probable that these relations, just as those which are involved in irradiation, are not rigid and do not escape the "domination" [103] of the brain centers once and for all. But the shunting power of these centers is in turn not an absolute power. The author considers the ensemble of nerve conductors as a "functional system." [104] The brain is composed of neurons which, like all the others, can change chronaxie under the action of neighboring neurons and thus progressively under the influence of the periphery. Thus the chronaxie of the cortical motor centers will be variable. It can be modified by the heating, cooling or electrical excitation of the part of the body which projects into the zone under consideration. Quite variable chronaxic values have been found (Cardot) for the same center from one time to another depending in particular upon the pneumogastric nerve and the thyroid apparatus. Thus the distribution of chronaxies and the organization of nerve pathways depend upon the encephalon: the action by which the encephalon distributes the chronaxies is itself only an effect of certain peripheral or vegetative influences and in this sense results from prior synchronizations. "The power of shunting by modification of chronaxie which we attribute to the brain is not an anthropomorphic imagination dissimulated behind the mechanism which we posit as the instrument of this power. This power should result automatically from the mechanism itself when studies of this kind have made sufficient progress." [105] But if the distribution of chronaxies and the organization of nerve pathways depend in this way on multiple conditions which are at the same time internal and external to the organism—if the center refers back to the periphery and the periphery back to the center—it is necessary to pose to Lapicque the question which he himself posed to Sherrington.

What the chronaxie explains is the integration, the fact that the "ensemble of nerve commands is capable of making all the muscles of the body react under excitation from the most diverse points of the periphery." [106] It is still necessary to understand how, among all these systems of possible liaisons, only those which have a biological value are ordinarily realized, how this circuit of causes and effects results in "a movement" and not in "convulsive spasms without efficacy," to use Lapicque's terms.[107] The theory of the chronaxie brings to light, as the proper function of the nervous system, the *organization* of new pathways at each moment. By this very fact it only makes more apparent what remains to be explained. In order to assure a distribution of chronaxies which produces movements and not spasms, we can no longer count on any anatomical structure, on any stable apparatus or on any autonomous center. Not being guided by any topography and being subjected, on the other hand, to indefinitely variable conditions, how are we to understand that this distribution determines relatively stable typical actions, perceptions of constant objects, movements in which each partial excitation takes into account, so to speak, simultaneous and subsequent excitations, and finally actions molded, as it were, by the situations which evoke them?

But problems of "order" can be rejected as anthropomorphic. If Gestalt theory is not "vitalist," it would nevertheless introduce anthropomorphism and finality into physics as well as into physiology by the very fact that it projects human norms into phenomena and supposes "directed" or "ordered" processes. It is clearly evident that, in speaking of a response "adapted" to the stimulus or of a succession of "coherent" movements, we are expressing relationships conceived by our mind, a comparison made by the mind between the "meaning" of the stimulus and that of the reaction, between the "total meaning" of the response and the partial movements which compose it. These relationships of meaning by which we define order result precisely from our own organization. Thus they have no need to be explained by distinct principles. If order is defined in a formal way, by simple statistical frequency, the existence in every organism of "preferred behavior"—that is, more frequent than we would have expected from considering the external and internal conditions of behavior one by one—this fact also demands no special explanation. For "frequency" is still an observation of our mind; in things there are only singular events which must be accounted for each time by particular causes. Thus there is no reason for asking what guides the chronaxic mechanism and orients it toward "ordered" movements. When such movements are produced, it is because the necessary conditions for them are united. As long as illness or emotion, with their "reactions of disorganization," do not appear, it is because they are not possible under the given conditions. And if the ordered behavior is maintained, it is because it alone is possible.

It is useless to posit a "shunting power" "hidden behind" the cerebral mechanisms by which ordered behavior is realized; and the problem of order has no meaning if we make it a second problem of causality. Is this to say that, not being a cause, the "shunting power" is an effect or, again as Lapicque says, an "anatomical result" of the mechanism itself? The functioning of the nervous system could, in a rather advanced state of science, be reconstructed piece by piece proceding from one local phenomenon to another. Chronaxic analysis could be combined with a synthesis. But this real synthesis is inconceivable. If we start with the image which chronaxic analysis gives of nerve functioning as if it were a reality existing in itself, we find chronaxies of subordination which depend upon each other without term and without break; and each one, at the moment considered, presupposes all the others which in turn presuppose it.

The genesis of the whole by composition of the parts is fictitious. It arbitrarily breaks the chain of reciprocal determinations. The case is not the same as that of a thermostat in which *one* variation of internal temperature presupposes *one* position of the regulating valve which itself presupposes *one* state of internal temperature without *the same* phenomenon ever being at the same time conditioning and conditioned with respect to *the same* phenomenon. On the contrary, each chronaxie is but one aspect of the total process; it is by abstraction that it is treated as a local event. In the nervous system there are only global events. Even when a sector of the system seems to function "only for its own sake"—when, for example, important variations in thermal or interoceptive excitations leave the eye-blinking reflex approximately intact—the conception of the chronaxie shows that this isolation is functional, that it rests on a certain number of chronaxic disjunctions and must be integrated with the constellation of chronaxies in the ensemble of the system. The unity of nerve functioning is an objective characteristic of that functioning, as is more particularly that unity of reciprocal determinations which distinguishes it from simply circular phenomena. To conceive of it "as a result," that is, to derive it from the multiplicity of local phenomena in which it is immanent, is to break up this unity. By this very procedure, moreover, the return to an external "principle of order" is rendered inevitable, as is expressed in Lapicque himself by the term: *"domination"* of the encephalic centers. Once the chronaxic analysis has been made, the image of nerve functioning which it gives cannot then be posited as something in itself (*en soi*) or separated from the process by which the chronaxies mutually determine each other. It is this auto-distribution which is expressed by the notion of form. It is not a question of a second causality which would intervene to correct the mechanism: it is to the theory of coordinating centers that this objection can be made.

The notion of form does nothing other than express the descriptive properties of certain natural wholes. It is true that it renders possible the use of a finalistic vocabulary. But this possibility itself is rooted in the nature of the nerve phenomena; it expresses the type of unity which they achieve. "Preferred" behavior defines the organism just as objectively as chronaxic analysis can define it if, as is necessary, we renounce mechanistic realism along with finalistic realism, that is, if we renounce all the forms of causal thought.

II. HIGHER FORMS
OF BEHAVIOR

Pavlov's Reflexology and Its Postulates

The analysis of perceptual behavior was initially developed as the complement and extension of the reflex theory.[1] The problem which Pavlov posed for himself was to discover how the organism can enter into relationship with a much richer and more extended milieu than that which acts immediately on its sensory endings in the form of physical and chemical stimulations. But this extension of the milieu is obtained by transferring the power of the natural excitants to new stimuli: it is only a question of multiplying the commands which our inborn reactions depend upon and, in particular, of grouping them into chains of automatic reactions. It is always by the summation of the proprioceptive and exteroceptive stimuli present at each moment (the powers which conditioning delegates to them being taken into account) that one proposes to understand behavior. The essence of nerve activity remains the same: it is a process which can be broken down into real parts.[2]

Since the "situation" remains a mosaic of physical and chemical excitants and since the new connections result from the *de facto* contiguities which are encountered there, they will be initially established without choice and in all directions; for Pavlov, development will consist in a series of compensated errors, as does learning for psychological empiricism. Every stimulus which acts on the organism conjointly with an unconditioned stimulus tends to take upon itself the reflexogenic power of the latter.[3] From this would result the syncretic appearance of infantile and animal reactions. For some time a conditioned excitant could even communicate something of its power to any excitant, even to one which had never been associated with the absolute excitant. But this first law is not sufficient to explain the adjustment of our behavior to the essential aspects of a situation. A selection must be made among the possible conditioned excitants and the reflex must be focused.[4] Thus we are led to conceive of a counter-force which enters in to correct the effects of irradiation and to prevent just any stimulus from provoking just any one of the reactions with which it has been associated. Thus in Pavlov it is inhibition which will be conceived as a positive process capable of compensating for the disordered effects of irradiation.

Take, for example, a sound S[5] which has never been associated with powdered meat and which is presented several times along with a luminous excitant L which has become the conditioned stimulus of gastric secretion. Initially it acquires a weak reflexogenic power by irradiation but soon loses it: a stimulus associated with a conditioned stimulus becomes inhibiting when the latter is not joined to the absolute excitant (conditioned inhibition). Moreover the sound, like any new stimulus which is introduced in a customary situation, already possessed an inhibiting power (external inhibition) from the moment of its first occurrence. The effects of conditioned inhibition, which are of particular interest to us, are decisive: the sound, having become inhibiting by conditioned inhibition, ends up by completely restraining the reflex and no gastric secretion is any longer observed when the light and the sound are presented together. If the ticking of a metronome is added to this group of excitants and the new grouping associated with powdered meat, a gastric secretion is obtained, but it is weak and only half as much as the luminous excitant produced by itself at the beginning of the experiment. This is because the new excitant M has, as such, an inhibiting action (external inhibition) which will influence the stimulating power of L just as much as the inhibiting power of S. Restraint of the restraint, M should in this sense augment the reflexogenic power of the group L + S if it did not at the same time diminish that of L, as is shown by a controlled experiment in which, associated with the light alone, M is sufficient to reduce the gastric secretion which the former is capable of evoking. But if we continue to associate the three excitants together with the meat powder we finally obtain the following results, where the numbers indicate the number of drops of saliva collected:

$$L = 10 \quad L + M = 10 \quad L + S + M = 10$$
$$M = 4 \quad S + M = 4$$
$$S = 0 \quad L + S = 0$$

If we want to interpret this result within the system of concepts defined by Pavlov we would have to say that S, when it is joined to M, no longer exercises an inhibiting influence and that M, often associated with the meat powder along with L + S, has in this way acquired a certain reflexogenic power. From this we get the results: M = 4, S + M = 4. But on the other hand, joined to L, which is a very good excitant, S recovers an inhibiting power which it no longer manifested (L + S = 0). Thus everything happens as if the excitant M played a role which is not foreseen by the laws formulated up to this point—as if its presence suddenly modified the power of S to such an extent that, although S + L is inefficacious, M + S + L produces ten drops of saliva. It does not appear that the effects of a group of stimuli can be treated as the algebraic sum of the effects of each one of them taken separately. It is here that Pavlov invokes "a sort of nerve equilibrium, the nature of which cannot be made any more precise." [6] It is true that we have not yet brought into play a third law which, if it proves to be one, might make it possible to fill the gaps between theory and experience. Until now the stimulating or inhibiting power has not depended upon the nervous system itself but only on the associations achieved in the experiment, that is in short, on the course of physical nature. Pavlov also brings into play "transverse functions" although in the completely mechanical form, it is true, of "reciprocal induction." [7] Every excitation in a point of the cortex provokes an inhibition in the neighboring regions, and inversely, this new law has the effect of accentuating the delimitation of stimulated and inhibited zones in the cortex and compensates in this way for the effects of the first two.[8]

The fact that Pavlov is forced to correct one law with another at each step doubtless proves that he has not discovered the central point of view by means of which all the facts could be coordinated. Excitant L being defined as a conditioned stimulus of the secretion, excitant S as a conditioned inhibition, and finally excitant M as a conditioned counter-inhibition, the reaction provoked by the group L + S + M ought to be composed of a real synthesis based on the properties of each one of them. But we have just seen that this explanation leaves a residue. Associated with M, the excitant S loses its inhibiting power; but it conserves it when associated with L. Thus, in the two "situations", L + S and S + M, the stimulus S does not play the same role; in other words, they are not two wholes in which one could discover a common element S. But at this point we realize that the description of behavior with which Pavlov started is already a theory.[9] There is an initial presupposition that the processes in the organism which would be released by each of the elementary stimuli are contained in the complex excitation as real parts or again that each partial stimulus possesses its own efficacy. It is because of this postulate that, if L is a positive conditioned excitant when presented alone, one will suppose that its proper power remains the same when it is joined to S. Since the new grouping produces no secretion, a positive inhibiting power will have to be attributed to S. But when L + S enters into a larger grouping, the same realistic postulate will necessitate our retaining for the group L + S the inhibiting power which it has alone. Correlatively, the third term of the new group will be conceived as a counter-inhibitor since the group S + L + M produces a secretion.

The idea of inhibition understood as a positive process—and with it the difficulties which we have just indicated—becomes inevitable only by the assumed necessity of treating a total excitation as the sum of the excitations which would be produced by each of the partial stimuli. But Pavlov himself cannot adhere to this principle and we have seen him invoke a law of nerve equilibrium which he in no way explicates in order to explain the effects of the group M + S. Thus, he himself indicates the direction in which his analysis should be modified. A given objective stimulus produces different effects in the organism depending on whether it acts alone or along with this or that other stimulus. If L provokes a certain reaction of the organism, there is no need to posit an inhibiting power in S in order to explain that L + S do not produce it. L + S is not reflexogenic because the adjunction of S is not a simple or even an algebraic addition for the organism. The preceding stimulus S is not left subsisting; a new situation of which S is no longer a part is substituted for it. In the same way the group L + S + M can become reflexogenic by association with the meat powder without this property being transmitted to the group L + S which is *qualitatively* different for the organism.[10] Thus, the genuine stimulus is the ensemble as such.[11]

It has been possible to give a conditioned power to a constellation of excitants each of which remains inhibiting when taken separately. The series: light–high pitched sound–low pitched sound–contact, can be reflexogenic, while the series: light–low pitched sound–high pitched sound–contact, is not. One can obtain a reaction for two successive sounds of the same pitch and unequal intensity going from the less to the more intense while the same sounds in the inverse order produce no effect. The reaction persists if the absolute tone of these sounds is modified provided the difference of their intensities is maintained constant.[12] An early work[13] has shown that an octopus, after having acquired a positive reaction to a large receptacle in which it finds its food and apparently an inhibition to a smaller receptacle presented at the same time as the first, nevertheless visits the smaller one when it is presented alone. The genuine excitant of conditioned reactions is neither a sound nor an object considered as individuals, nor an assemblage of sounds or objects considered as groups which are both individual and confused, but rather the temporal distribution of sounds, their melodic sequence, the relations of the size of objects and, in general, the precise structure of the situation.

Far from being a faithful description of behavior, the theory of conditioned reflexes is a construction inspired by the atomistic postulates of realistic analysis. It carries over into organic activity the modes of cleavage which are appropriate to a universe of things and in no way represents the necessary instrument of a scientific investigation.[14] One can easily date these postulates: they belong to a bygone period of physiology and psychology. We would find them again—Pavlov himself draws this parallel[15]—if we attempted to analyze perception from within. Psychologists such as Helmholtz, dealing with the constancy of the apparent size of objects, supposed that an unconscious conclusion allowed us to discover the true size behind the image whose size varies with the distance. Pavlov suggests that retinal excitations evoked by the same object at different distances have become the conditioned stimuli of motor reactions of palpation executed when the object is within touching distance. The mode of thinking in the two cases is the same. One begins by supposing that individual images of different dimensions are given "in" consciousness or that physiological processes with no common measure are given in the organism for each perception of an object whose distance varies. And the problem is then to find the means of unifying these mental or physiological individuals in an intellectual operation or in some associative connection. But the question would not be posed in this way and these solutions would not have to be considered had we not begun by treating respectively the "mental images" of the same object or the physiological processes which it elicits in the nervous system as so many separated realities—if structure had been chosen as the guiding concept in psychology and physiology and not the atom.[16]

It may seem astonishing that Pavlov, determined to found a science of behavior and, in order to remain close to the facts, to accept only physiological explanations,[17] should have introduced the postulates of the old psychology into his research. This is because in reality physiological explanation cannot be direct in Pavlov or anywhere else. As far as Pavlov is concerned, the arbitrariness of his physiological schemata is not so apparent in the simple example which served us in describing them. But it becomes so when we confront them with certain complex levels of behavior to which Pavlov himself attempted to apply them.

He observes astonishing behavior in dogs submitted to repeated experiments.[18] As soon as the apparatus which permits the gathering of the secretions is put in place the animal falls into a state comparable to hypnosis. Presented with a conditioned stimulus, the dog responds by the ordinary secretory reactions but, on the other hand, the motor reactions do not take place. Presented with the unconditioned excitant (the morsel of meat), the animal does not react in the ordinary way: sometimes the salivary secretion is normal but the movements of mastication are not produced; sometimes, on the contrary, the dog eats the food but the salivary secretion is delayed for ten or twenty seconds. Let us examine the explanation which Pavlov gives of this last case. For him, the setting up of the conditioned reflex consists in a connection which is established between the cortical center which receives the conditioned stimulus, the one which governs the movements of mastication, and a subcortical center on which the alimentary secretions depend. Thus this behavioral disorder will be designated as a "disassociation of the motor and secretory reactions." No attempt is made to resituate this disorder in its biological context in order to discover a general alteration of behavior through these different symptoms.[19] The observed attitudes will be interpreted by saying that the secretory center is inhibited while the motor center is not. But this elective inhibition is itself in need of explanation. From this follow two hypotheses which we have no other reason for assuming: first, Pavlov posits a general inhibition of the brain which, starting from the points corresponding to the artificial conditioned reflexes, has been extended to the subcortical center which governs the salivary secretions and to the cortical motor-analyzers. After having introduced a total inhibition which is not revealed by observation, Pavlov suggests that the sight of the meat initially leaves the inhibition of the secretory center intact and surmounts that of the motor center which, he says, is more mobile than the other. This greater mobility is posited because of the demands of the situation. When he brings it into play, Pavlov *does not explain* the phenomenon; he only names it; he only describes in anatomical and physiological terms a disinhibition which is itself posited and "transcribes a process which is problematic in itself into a language still more problematic."[20] In speaking just now of the biological context of these disorders we alluded to the negativistic attitudes which Pavlov also described, but for which he seeks a separate explanation: the dog, in a state of hypnosis, turns its head away when the morsel of meat is offered to it on the first, second or even the third presentation. As soon as the food is taken away, however, it turns its head in the direction of the platter and follows it with its eyes. In the most favorable cases, it finally opens and closes its mouth with great difficulty and the inhibition disappears. In order to explain these attitudes Pavlov will bring into play a complicated system of excitations, inhibitions, and disinhibitions. He begins by defining the state of hypnosis or inhibition as a "paradoxical" phase in which the thresholds of the cerebral cells are lowered, so much so that a strong stimulus then acts like a too-powerful stimulus and provokes an inhibition. He suggests, on the other hand, that the motor center concerned in the reactions includes a positive innervation point which releases the movements toward the meat and a negative innervation point which, on the contrary, governs the movements of abduction. Once these hypotheses are made, the negativistic attitudes will be explained in the following manner: the visual excitations provoked by the meat terminate according to the established conditionings at the positive innervation point but they find it in a paradoxical state and thus evoke an inhibition there. In conformity with the law of reciprocal induction, the inhibition of the positive point evokes an inhibition of the negative point. The animal turns away from the meat. When the experimenter withdraws the meat the positive point, strongly inhibited until then, will of itself pass into a state of excitation in conformity with the law of internal reciprocal induction. In the same way the negative point stimulated during the first phase passes into a state of inhibition and tends to evoke the excitation of the positive point by reciprocal induction. Doubly stimulated, the latter will initially evoke movements toward the meat when it is withdrawn and, after two or three presentations, will evoke the normal motor reflex, at which point the negativistic attitude comes to an end.

These examples bring to light the distance which exists between the observable behavior and the anatomical-physiological hypothesis by which one tries to account for them. If the term *conditioned reflex* has any meaning, it should designate a relatively stable reaction linked with certain stimuli. The observation of animals reveals, however, that the reactions are variable and can be disassociated or even reversed. But with the notions of inhibition and reciprocal induction Pavlov provided himself with the principles which allow him to stop up all the cracks in the theory as well as to construct an explanation that leaves the notion of conditioned reflex intact.[21] The mechanisms of excitation, inhibition and disinhibition which he invokes necessarily appear as expedient devices designed to mask the disagreement between theory and experiment as long as we have not informed ourselves concerning the processes of cerebral physiology from some other source.

A theory which, without experimental support, posits forces in contrary directions evidently escapes being contradicted by experience since it can always bring into play at the right moment one of the two principles in default of the other. For the same reason it is not susceptible to any experimental justification. Far from being patterned on the facts, Pavlov's categories are imposed upon them. The terms *excitation, inhibition* and *disinhibition* properly designate certain descriptive aspects of behavior which are made known to us by our internal and external experiences. On the other hand, inhibition as Pavlov defines it—that is, as a positive nerve process released by certain stimuli—is a physico-mechanical symbol which should not profit from the same evidential privilege.[22] Because he carried descriptive notions found in the observation of behavior directly over into the central nervous system, Pavlov was able to believe that he employed a physiological method. In reality it amounts to an imaginary physiology, and it could not be otherwise. For a physiological method which appears to be recommended by the best scientific spirit is in reality the one which asks the most of conjectures and is the least direct of all.

There is an equivocation on the meaning of the term "physiological fact." [23] Sometimes it is used to designate phenomena directly observed in the brain, sometimes and more generally those which the analysis of behavior leads us to posit behind the actions of animals and men. And a privilege of objectivity is transferred to "physiological fact" in the second sense of the word which it has only in the first sense; moreover, a realistic prejudice is operative here. If we had a precise knowledge of the physiological phenomena of which the nervous system is the seat, to be guided by them in the analysis of behavior would be indicated. But in fact what we know about nerve functioning directly comes down to very little. One can wonder in all justice whether, in physiological knowledge, objectivity is not confused with the methods of physical and chemical measurement.[24] The application of physical and chemical excitants and the measurement of chronaxies allow us to note certain effects of nerve activity under determined conditions, which conditions, moreover, are rather different from those of its normal exercise. It is not certain that nerve functioning can be adequately characterized in this way. In the present state of our knowledge in any case, whether we examine the organism by means of the observation of behavior or by means of the measurement of reactions evoked in it by certain physical and chemical agents, only the manifestations of nerve functioning are grasped and the two procedures are equally indirect. Inferences are equally necessary in both cases. In this situation the more one is aware of the indirect character of physiological knowledge the less there is risk of error; consequently one can presume that such risk is at a maximum in those who, like Pavlov, pretend to start from physiology.

Since nobody can in fact start with physiology, Pavlov begins with a study of behavior, with a description of the reactions of the organism in the presence of certain situations—in spite of his own principles. And since he is not sufficiently aware of the constructive character of his physiology, he founds it on the least defensible principles of the older psychology. A deliberately descriptive and psychological method would offer more guarantees.

It remains for us to justify these criticisms of principle and to disengage a positive conception by analyzing some results of modern investigations concerning central nerve functioning and concerning the development of behavior.

The "Central Sector" of Behavior and the Problem of Localizations

The atomistic postulates which oblige Pavlov to consider a complex excitant as the sum of simple excitants excludes the notion of receptive coordination from nerve physiology. The model of nerve action is sought in the "elementary" process which associates a simple reaction to an isolated process. Since there is a one-to-one correspondence between them, the physiological substrate of the reaction is imagined in the form of connections (or disjunctions), and the points of arrival of the excitation are marked on the map of the brain; the positive and negative reactions which are observed are actualized in points of positive and negative innervation. If we move to more complex reactions, different stimuli will be found in competition at the level of these points. But their acquired powers will be combined only by an algebraic summation; their union can only permit or prohibit, reinforce or attenuate, but not *modify qualitatively* the reaction governed by the point of innervation.[25]

Pavlov's physiology excludes the idea of motor coordination in the same way. The excitation or inhibition of the innervation points of which we just spoke indeed depends on what happens in the rest of the cortex; the reciprocal induction and proprioceptive conditioning of a reaction by the one which precedes it are indeed "transverse functions." But although reciprocal induction gives a local phenomenon the power of inhibiting another, it does not permit the one to modify the other qualitatively. Thus it does not provide the instrument of a flexible regulation. Although the conditioning of a reaction by the preceding one makes it understandable that real fragments of behavior can be joined to each other or disassociated, it cannot render possible the adaptation of the parts to each other, such as in the rhythmic organization which is so remarkable in verbal behavior. "In virtue of the fact that, in the waking state, these two processes (excitation and inhibition) are mutually limiting, an immense mosaic is produced in the cerebral hemispheres in which stimulated points on the one hand and points which are inhibited and in a temporary state of sleep on the other are found next to each other. The presence of these intermingled points, now stimulated, now sleeping, determines the entire behavior of the animal."[26] As in the older conception of localizations, nerve phenomena constitute a mosaic and nerve activity is never an autonomous process of distribution. To the theory of conditioned reflexes as to the classical theory of reflexes, Buytendijk's question must be posed: in nerve phenomena "are we dealing in reality with functions of the structure or with functional structures?"[27] In particular, the nervous system will direct behavior by an action comparable to that of the rudder of a boat or the steering wheel of an automobile:[28] the directing organ would exercise a quasi-mechanical action; thus only one position of this organ would be possible for a given direction of walking. This conception of nerve functioning is in any case applicable only to the cerebral cortex, where the afferent and efferent nerve fibers are punctually projected. The existence of conditioned motor reactions in fish which do not have a cerebral cortex or even in invertebrates and down to the protozoa[29] suggests that these reactions are not linked to any particular anatomical device and that they must express a general property of nerve phenomena or even of biological phenomena.[30] But with regard to the functioning of the cortex itself, does modern physiology move in the direction of Pavlov?

Although the discussion remains open both concerning the limits of this or that center and concerning the definition of mental functions to be localized in each particular case, agreement seems to have been established [31] concerning the meaning of localizations in general and concerning the significance of place in nerve substance. We would like to formulate some of the established results since they will allow us to become acquainted with the "central sector" of behavior and to understand its insertion in the body.

1. *A lesion, even localized, can determine structural disorders which concern the whole of behavior, and analogous structural disorders can be provoked by lesions situated in different regions of the cortex.*

The older theory of localizations underestimated two difficulties of fact—that of localizing the lesion and that of localizing the function—which Monakow has insisted upon,[32] but also a third difficulty: that of defining the illness studied and the corresponding normal function, which difficulty could not be surmounted without a methodological reflection and a theory of biological knowledge. It has long been known that the constitution of "nosological personalities," the discovery of the fundamental disorder from which the multiplicity of observable symptoms is derived, is a problem for pathology. But in general pathology the symptoms are sometimes given unequivocally: massive deficiencies are involved; often the organism ceases responding to certain physico-chemical excitations in all circumstances; the disorder affects certain real fragments of behavior. Or, to be more exact, since it is the fundamental adaptations with regard to the vital milieu which are compromised, the solicitations of this milieu are ordinarily sufficient to reveal and characterize the illness. Thus it will be possible rather often to define pathological behavior by means of a realistic analysis in which the characteristics conserved and those abolished are enumerated. In order to interrelate the symptoms and delimit a nosological entity, one will often be able to discover a real chain of effects and causes, observable in principle, which lead from the superficial manifestations to the essential disorder. This latter can then be designated as the causal origin of the illness; thus, even if it alters the functioning of the entire organism, it has a defined site and can be localized on the map of the body. Carried over into mental pathology, this method of realistic analysis and causal explanation has led to defining aphasia, or more generally the agnosias, by certain circumscribed disorders, by the absence of certain *contents* of behavior. It was believed that the symptomatology of mental illness could also be content with noting deficiencies. It was not realized that the symptom is an organism's response to a question from the milieu and that the tableau of symptoms varies then with the questions which are posed to the organism.[33] The symptom always corresponds to an expectation of the mind, which expectation must be precise in order that the symptoms be significative. Taking over the confused classifications which are given in the language, the physician wondered only *if* the sick person could speak, understand, write or read. The psychologists, on the other hand, although they had abandoned the "faculty of speaking" or the "faculty of remembering," had limited themselves to giving the empiricist equivalents of these; the concrete act of speech or of reference to the past was reduced to the possession of certain specific contents of consciousness, to "representations" or "images." Thus, aphasia and amnesia necessarily had to be defined from the beginning as the loss, or the loss of control, of certain collections of mental states. Physicians unknowingly singled out in the behavior of the aphasic that which could be interpreted as a disorder of the verbal images. If other symptoms presented themselves they were either attributed to supplementary lesions—they were put aside as altering the "purity" of the case—or, since the observation of the patient almost always went beyond the theoretical framework of the illness, one sought to derive the disturbing symptoms from the "primary" disorders: paraphasia from psychic deafness, disorders of writing from the destruction or inefficacy of the "verbal images." [34]

The force of the facts and the contradictions of theory have obliged psychology and physiology to become aware of the postulates which had guided them in the classical conception of localizations. Like the philosophy of faculties, the theory of verbal images was at the same time realistic, since it analyzed acts into real fragments, and abstract, since it isolated them from their context. The anatomical spirit sought to actualize nerve functioning in visible connections and circumscribed areas. Modern investigations, on the contrary, proceed by concrete description and ideal analysis. Cortical lesions rarely give rise to elective disorders involving certain fragments of normal behavior in isolation.[35] Ordinarily the organism does not become purely and simply indifferent to certain sectors of the physico-chemical milieu and does not lose the aptitude for *executing a certain number of movements*. It is known that the aphasic or apraxic subject is capable or incapable of certain verbal or real actions depending on whether the latter are situated in a concrete and affective context or whether, on the contrary, they are "gratuitous." In certain amnesic aphasias observation shows that the subject has not, properly speaking, lost the *words,* which he remains capable of employing in automatic language; he has lost the power of *naming* because, in the act of denomination, the object and the word are taken as representatives of a category and are thus considered from a certain "point of view" chosen by the one who names; this "categorial attitude" is no longer possible in a subject reduced to concrete and immediate experience.[36] What is inaccessible is not then a certain stock of movements but a certain type of acts, a certain level of action. As a consequence, we can understand why the disorder is not limited to a particular faculty but is discovered in varying degrees in all those which demand the same attitude of gratuitousness.[37] "Each problem which forces [the patient] beyond the sphere of immediate reality to that of the 'possible' or to the sphere of representation, insures his failure";[38] this happens whether it is a question of action, perception, will, feeling or language.

Thus, a specific disorder should always be put back into the context of the total behavior; from this point of view a comparison becomes possible between the picture presented by aphasia and that by other illnesses. It is always a question in some measure of the deficiency of a fundamental function which Gelb and Goldstein call "categorial attitude"; Head, power of "symbolic expression"; and Woerkom, "mediation function" (*darstellende Funktion*).[39] Since the behavior of the patient adheres much more closely to the concrete and immediate relations of the milieu than the behavior of the normal person, the fundamental disorder could also be defined as "the impairment of the capacity to comprehend the essential features of an event"[40] or, finally, as the incapacity of clearly disengaging a perceived, conceived or exercised grouping, as a *figure,* from a *ground* treated as indifferent.[41] Pathological transformation takes place in the direction of a less differentiated, less organized, more global and more amorphous behavior.[42] It may happen in alexia that the patient can read his name as a word, but not the letters which compose it taken separately; in motor aphasia, that he can pronounce a word inserted in a verbal ensemble, but not if it is isolated. In hemiplegia the global movements, the "legato," sometimes remain possible while the detailed movements, the "staccato," are compromised.[43] It is evident that here the sickness does not directly concern the content of behavior but rather its structure and consequently that it is not something which is *observed* but rather something which is *understood.* The conduct of the patient is not deduced from the conduct of the normal person by simple subtraction of parts; it represents a *qualitative* alteration; and it is to the extent that certain actions demand an attitude of which the subject is no longer capable that they are electively disordered.

There appears here a new kind of analysis which no longer consists in isolating elements but in understanding the character of a whole and its immanent law. Sickness is no longer, according to the common representation, like a thing or a power from which certain effects follow; nor is pathological functioning, according to a too wide-spread idea, homogeneous with normal functioning. It is a new *signification* of behavior, common to the multitude of symptoms; and the relation of the essential disorder to the symptoms is no longer that of cause to effect but rather the logical relation of principle to consequence or of signification to sign.

The works of Gelb and Goldstein bring to light very clearly the structural character of disorders following cortical lesions and justify the idea of a comparison between different cerebral maladies. They find, in a war-wounded man (Schneider, designated by his initial in their works), disorders which at the same time involve perception, visual recognition and memory,[44] the spatiality of tactile givens and tactile recognition, motor reactions (the patient is incapable of initiating or accomplishing a movement with his eyes closed) [45] and finally, memory, intelligence and language.[46] For this patient, classical conceptions would authorize a diagnosis of psychic blindness, astereognosis, and disorders of intelligence with diffuse lesions of different parts of the brain all at the same time. But it is a question of a man wounded in the war who seems to present a unique lesion caused by a piece of shell. Moreover, the integrity of feeling and of elementary motor reactions and the normal appearance of bodily and mental behavior in practical living makes the hypothesis of multiple lesions most unlikely. The disorders have a systematic character; but it appears impossible to derive these different deficiencies from one of them—for example, from the disorder of visual perception which had been observed first and to which an unwarranted weight had been given as a consequence.[47] All the deficiencies seem to express a fundamental alteration of behavior: "The patient failed whenever it was necessary, in order to react correctly, to possess a given all at once as an articulated whole, while he acted quickly and happily each time a successive process was sufficient for the accomplishment of his task." [48] Thus we find ourselves in the presence of a disorder of structure determined by a circumscribed lesion. This correlation had already been observed by Head,[49] who considered it a general law of nerve functioning.

Goldstein himself compares the observation which we have just summarized to those which other authors have presented and which this time are concerned with aphasics. The patient studied by Boumann and Grunbaum[50] presents disorders which at first glance are rather different from those of S. . . . Gelb and Goldstein's patient sometimes recognized an object from certain characteristic details in spite of his visual disorders —for example, a die from certain black dots marked on it. On the contrary, Boumann and Grunbaum's subject did not perceive details and these authors concluded from this that no rapprochement could be made between the two cases. But in reality, even though it may happen that S . . . is troubled by details which are too precise (he is, for example, incapable of recognizing a "bad circle" in a badly drawn circle), this is always because his perception is not directed toward the essential; the incapacity of surmounting details and the incapacity of perceiving any at all are in reality disorders of the same form.[51] In the two cases we are equally removed from the organized perception of the normal person, who is capable both of seizing wholes without their being confused and of bringing to light details when they have a signification. The two patients present the same fundamental deficiency of the "figure and ground structure." With S . . . the details are not chosen as essential and integrated into a whole; they are not properly perceived. Even though he recognizes an object by its height and its width, these properties are not apprehended directly but reconstructed and deduced from certain confused signs.[52] Thus, in reality there are only superficial differences between the perceptive disorders in Gelb and Goldstein's subject and in Boumann and Grunbaum's. Moreover, the latter presents disorders of attention, thought, spontaneous language, reading, denomination and articulation, the form of which is common and similar to that of the disorders of S . . . : in all of these domains "the mental or psycho-motor process is fixated at a primitive phase of development which goes from an impression of an amorphous whole to a more differentiated structuration (*Ausgestaltung*) . . ." [53]

The comparison between Gelb and Goldstein's observations and those concerning Woerkom's aphasic is even more demonstrative.[54] The differences of the two cases are evident: in the visual domain Woerkom's patient possesses much better organized givens than those of S . . . , which amount to colored spots with neither contours nor precise dimensions. Inversely S . . . speaks much better than Woerkom's patient; he has the use of a great many more expressions and he is constantly correcting grammar. These differences—to which we will return in a subsequent paragraph—should not mask the traits which absolutely coincide in the two observations. The two subjects are equally incapable of executing an action based on simple verbal indication; in order to succeed they must put themselves back into the corresponding mental situation (which S . . . achieves by repeating the order which was given him). Neither of them can designate the direction from which a sound is coming without orienting their body in this direction. Both can localize a pain in their body by means of touch, but they are equally incapable of indicating on a diagram the point where their hand stops. Woerkom has insisted on the superiority of S . . . in the use of language and the manipulation of concepts and on the deficiencies of his patient in this domain. But in order to appreciate exactly the situation of S . . . in this regard, account must be taken of the substitutions which mask the gravity of these deficiencies in him. In reality an attentive observation shows, for example, that for him addition is reducible to a manual operation without any intuition of numbers.[55] With respect to language, it is not at all normal in S . . . in spite of appearances. The subject cannot follow a sermon or a discourse. He speaks fluently only in response to the solicitations of a concrete situation; in every other case he must prepare his sentences ahead of time. In order to recite the words of a song, he is forced to take up the attitude of the singer. He cannot subdivide a sentence which he has just spoken into words and, inversely, words which are coherent but separated by a pause never constitute a phrase for him. He can neither spell the letters of a word which he pronounces well as a whole nor write them separately, although he possesses the word as an automatic motor ensemble. This shows to what extent language is deficient in him, although these insufficiencies are especially marked in the intuition of simultaneous wholes.[56]

Lashley's experiments,[57] which were resumed by Buytendijk, confirm this description of morbid behavior in central cortical lesions. Neither the elementary movements which "compose" the behavior of a rat—the acts of walking, jumping, standing up on its hind legs—nor the sensory discriminations which govern them seem to be compromised after cauterization of the central and frontal cortical regions. But the animal is maladroit; all his movements are slow and rigid, although in the normal state he is lively and agile. If the rat has to walk on a wooden lath a few centimeters wide, his foot often slips sideways; the animal falls when he tries to turn around or get down. Everything takes place as if the impressions "which in the normal state govern movements by their space-time relations, by their configuration, [could] no longer sufficiently determine the operated animal."[58] Its movements are no longer linked together: it takes a morsel of biscuit but bites a stick placed near it, grasps the food with its teeth but does not at the same time execute the movements of the feet which would be necessary. While normal rats learn rather quickly to go down a stair head first in order to go to their nest and, after a little hesitation, accustom themselves to finding their nest at the bottom of a stair oriented in the opposite direction, in the operated rats, on the contrary, learning takes much longer and, once acquired, is not easily transferred to a different situation. Everything happens as if the behavior of the operated animal were no longer governed by the spatial relation of the stair to the nest but by the concrete grouping in which this spatial structure is, as it were, submerged. Intact animals in a T labyrinth accustom themselves without difficulty to choosing the path on the right which will lead them to their nest and also quickly accustom themselves to choosing the path on the left if they no longer find the goal at the end of the first. On the contrary, the operated rats persevere in the acquired habits even after six days and twenty-five unfavorable trials. Thus, in them adaptation to the right side is not of the same nature as in normal rats. One could say that in the case of the operated animal the path on the right determines the orientation of the walking by its particular concrete properties and that in the normal animal, on the contrary, adaptation is acquired in relation to a certain typical structure; this would explain why it can easily be transferred to another situation materially different from the first. Finally, rats accustomed to traversing a long L-shaped pathway in order to arrive at their food will prefer another shorter one if the goal is visible at the end. Operated animals, however, continue to utilize the longer pathway as if the spatial relations of objects had ceased to be reflexogenic for them.[59] One could summarize these observations by saying that the operated rat, like the man with a brain injury, ceases to regulate his behavior by that which is essential in a situation and which can be found in other analogous situations.[60] "The general functional disorder consists in a reduced perception [61] of wholes (*Gestalten*) and in a reduced differentiation of actions." [62]

How can we represent nerve functioning for ourselves in keeping with this description of pathological phenomena? The existence of disorders of structure suggests the disorder of a general organizational function of behavior. This function must characterize the central cortical region, that region which has long been called the "association zone." We should not expect to find a multitude of anatomical devices in it, each one predisposed to a certain movement, but rather a regulatory system capable of giving certain general characteristics to behavior which depends on it, whole processes which imitate, as it were, the structural character of the disorders which we have described. Here structure must take precedence over content, physiology over anatomy. Here a circumscribed lesion would act by interrupting processes and not by curtailing organs. The place of the lesions could vary within this central zone without the clinical picture of the illness being noticeably modified. The nerve substance located there would not be a container in which the instruments of such and such reactions were deposited, but the theater where a qualitatively variable process unfolds.

Moreover, this hypothesis is confirmed by the facts. Lashley[63] had already pointed out that the effect of a central lesion—which is, as we have seen, to disassociate the behavior and to compromise its articulation—depends much less on the place of the lesion than on its extent. The deficiencies in the case of a central lesion are too different from those which are observed in the case of a peripheral lesion for us to be able to suppose a functioning of the same type in the two places: after enucleation an animal is capable of relearning a labyrinth with six errors; the destruction of the visual zone of the cortex permits the habit to be restored again only after three hundred and fifty-three errors.[64] If the central regions of the nervous system were, like its receptive terminations, only a bundle of autonomous conductors, the disorders evoked by central lesion ought to have the same character as disorders of peripheral origin: they ought to be at the same time more elective and less durable than those which are in fact observed; a disorder of the learning attitude in general would be inconceivable. But the general function of organization of which we spoke should not be located in the most central region of the cortex; it would suppose the integrity of the whole and eccentric lesions could compromise it. Asymmetrical lesions in certain octopi, in addition to their particular effects,[65] determine general disorders analogous to those brought on by the ablation of the cerebral ganglia and a part of the central ganglia: incompleteness of action comparable to apraxic disorders of man,[66] insufficient cooperation between the two halves of the body, incoordination of the movements of the arms, general excitability increased or lowered and lability of behavior.[67] The analogous disorders of structure which we encountered in Goldstein's subject and in that of Boumann and Grunbaum correspond to lesions localized very differently in the two cases: in the first case it most probably involves a unique lesion in the extra-calcarine optic region caused by a piece of shell; in the second case, a left frontal lesion is probably involved.

2. *Nevertheless, nerve functioning cannot be treated as a global process where the intervention of any of the parts would be of equal importance. The function is never indifferent to the substrate by which it is achieved.*

The same authors are as a matter of fact in agreement in recognizing that the location of lesions determines as it were the point of principal application of disorders of structure and their preferential distribution.[68] As in the case of Schneider, marked deficiencies predominantly in the perceptual domain will correspond to the lesions of the posterior regions of the brain next to the optic sector. On the contrary, disorders affect language particularly (psychic deafness, aphasia) when the lesions are situated in the anterior region of the brain, as in the case of Woerkom's patient, or in the auditive region. Thus, there can be no question of relating all behavior to an undifferentiated activity.[69] In spite of the hasty observations of wartime pathology, substitutions can be observed after the destruction of a specialized region of the cortex,[70] but never the restoration of the function.[71] The reorganizations and the substitutions which Goldstein describes mask the deficiency without making in disappear.[72] S . . . always remains incapable of grasping visual wholes, and the imitative movements by means of which he succeeds in identifying such wholes by retracing their principal lines do not improve the visual givens as such. Inversely, in tactile agnosia the visual forms assume the function of tactile wholes without restoring them.[73] The blind demiretina remains blind in the hemianopic.[74] Most frequently, if the effect useful for the organism remains the same, the substitution represents a detour and the replacing activity is different in its nature and origin from the original activity.[75] Concerning the alleged assumption of the functions of one hemisphere by the other, it would be established only if it were a case of the total destruction of the first and if it could be established that the second had not collaborated to some extent in the actions involved before the lesion. But this last condition could never be fulfilled if it is true, as many facts suggest,[76] that the two hemispheres work together in an infant; thus, the privilege of one of them in the adult does not exclude the hypothesis of a collaboration of the other.

But how do these specialized regions of the cortex function themselves? "There is no doubt that differently situated sources do not lead to the same tableau of symptoms, that the place [of the lesions] has an essential significance in the constitution of a particular tableau of symptoms. The whole question is to discover the nature of this significance and the manner in which the lesion of a particular place causes a particular set of symptoms to appear." [77] The facts which force us to admit a specialization of the cerebral regions do not eliminate the relation of these regions to the whole *with regard to functioning.* Authors are also in agreement in accepting that the regions are not specialized in the reception of certain contents, but rather in the structuration of these latter. Everything happens as if they in turn were not the seat of certain anatomical devices but the terrain for the exercise of an activity of organization, applied, it is true, to a certain type of materials.

We were saying that the occipital situation of the lesion involves, in Gelb and Goldstein's subject, a predominance of perceptual disorders which asserted themselves first in the analysis.[78] Subsequent investigations have shown that, more generally, it is the simultaneous intuition of wholes that is deficient in S . . .[79] Should this gnosic disorder be derived from the perceptual disorder observed initially? Is it *because* the visual forms are dislocated that the simultaneous intuition of wholes has become difficult? Is it made of visual forms as a house is made of stones? Correlatively, is the total functioning of the cortex the sum of the local functioning?

Psychological empiricism and physiological atomism are allied in this matter. The facts give no indication which would be favorable to them. Since there are substitutions and since the intuition of simultaneous multiplicities, when it is impossible by means of visual givens, is achieved in one way or another by means of the successive givens of touch, it is not as such absolutely conditioned by the existence of visual forms and, correlatively, cannot be localized in the injured occipital region. The inverse hypothesis becomes more probable: the constitution of visual forms in the normal person would depend on a general organizational function which would also condition the possession of simultaneous wholes; the natural functioning of the occipital region would demand the collaboration of the central cortical region. But we have seen on the other hand that substitutions are never restorations; the apprehension of simultaneous wholes becomes rudimentary when the visual contents are not available, not because it depends upon them as an effect depends upon its cause, but because they alone furnish it with an adequate symbolism and are in this sense irreplaceable auxiliaries. Thus, the constitution of visual forms can neither be attributed properly to the occipital region as if it did not need the collaboration of the center, nor can the apprehension of simultaneous wholes be localized in central activity as if it owed nothing to the special materials of the optic zone. An occipital lesion compromises the apprehension of simultaneous wholes by withdrawing from central activity its most appropriate instruments. The relations of local functioning to central functioning are understood in the same manner by Piéron: occipital lesions evoke disorders of visual thought and left temporo-parietal lesions evoke disorders of verbal thought,[80] not because these regions are the seat of corresponding modes of thought, but because they find there the privileged means of their realization. "Modes of thought and the associative processes can be carried out around a predominant sensory nucleus with differences according to individuals and, in a given individual, according to the circumstances."[81]

3. *Consequently, place in nerve substance has an equivocal signification. Only a mixed conception of localizations and a functional conception of parallelism can be accepted.*

Certain forms of behavior depend on the central cortex, not that they are made up of the same elementary movements whose memos or orders would be located there, but inasmuch as they are of the same structure, permit classification under the same idea and are situated on the same human level. Normal sexual initiatives and the lucid handling of numbers, equally compromised in the case of S . . . , have no elementary movement, no real part, in common; they permit comparison and even definition only by means of certain "anthropomorphic" predicates: it could be said, for example, that these two behaviors are "adaptations to the virtual." Consequently, the functioning in this central region cannot be understood as the activation of specialized mechanisms each one of which would correspond to a movement in space, but as a global activity capable of conferring the same typical form, the same value predicate or the same significance on movements which are materially different. From one action to another this central functioning would not vary by the number of devices put into play; the same substrate would function in two actions in a qualitatively different manner. If a mass of cells and conductors is called "brain," the higher forms of behavior would not be *contained* in the brain taken in this sense; they would be related to the brain only as a functional entity. If one understands by space a multiplicity of parts external to each other, they would not be in space. We can always consider the brain in a space defined by the mutual exteriority of homogeneous parts. But it must be understood that the physiological reality of the brain cannot be represented in this space.

A lesion in the central region of the cortex produces the observed effects not inasmuch as it compromises this type of functioning or that level of conduct. Thus, whatever the location and development of the lesions, a systematic disintegration of function will be observed. These are the localizations which have been designated by the name of "vertical localizations." On the other hand it is clear that, on the level of the conductors which carry messages received by the senses to the brain or distribute the appropriate excitations to the different muscles, each part of the nerve tissue has the role of guaranteeing "the relationship between the organism and a certain part of the outer world." [82] To each point of nerve substance and to the phenomena which are produced in it there corresponds a point of the sensitive surfaces or of the muscles and an external stimulus or a movement in space, at the least a component of bodily movement. At this level lesions will have the effect of withdrawing the organism from the influence of certain stimuli or of eliminating a certain stock of movements, without their being anything systematic in the sensory or motor deficiency. The activation of different regions of the substrate ("horizontal" localizations) corresponds at this level to different perceived contents or to different executed movements.[83] Nevertheless, in normal functioning and excepting the case of peripheral lesions, do nerve conductors bring a contribution to total behavior which would be assignable in isolation? No, since we have seen that they are in functional relation with the center. The situation of elementary stimuli on the receptors does not determine in a univocal manner the spatial or qualitative characteristics of the corresponding perceptions, which also depend on the constellation of simultaneous stimuli. And we will encounter in disorders of elementary vision (colors and light), not a deficit which depends on the place of the lesion, but a systematic destruction of visual function which proceeds from the seeing of colors—which is more "integrated" and fragile—to the seeing of light, which is less integrated and more solid.

Thus, subordinated vertical localizations must be accepted within the visual area which, given that it is connected with the center in functioning, is defined as "horizontal" localization. It is in this regard that the classical distinction of zones of projection and association is not satisfactory. Local excitations distributed at the surface of the receptors undergo, from the moment of their entrance into the specialized sectors of the cortex, a series of structurations which disassociate them from the context of spatio-temporal events in which they were really engaged and which orders them according to the original dimensions of organic and human activity.

H. Piéron clearly seems to agree with the other authors concerning this mixed conception of localization. Without employing this language, he describes a series of horizontal and vertical localizations which intersect in nerve functioning. He accepts the fact that touch properly so called and depth touch, sensitivity to heat and cold, "painful" sensitivity, bone sensitivity, and finally arthro-muscular sensitivity, which psycho-physiological analysis disassociates and whose conductors remain distinct at the level of the medullar fasciculi and way stations,[84] do not possess a distinct representation in the cortex. The cortical receptors correspond to different regions of the body and not to the different types of sensitivity. In case of lesion these latter are affected according to the degree of their "susceptibility," which amounts to saying, it would seem, that they do not correspond to locally distinct nerve apparatuses but rather to so many different modes of functioning of the same substrate. Likewise, while pathology permits us to disassociate sensitivity to colors (hemiachromatopsia), sensitivity to volume (hemiastereopsia) and sensitivity to light (hemiaphotopsia), it confirms the fact that the occipital-visual area corresponds point for point to the retina. Thus, it seems definitively impossible to assign a special center within the visual area for the seeing of color, another for the seeing of form, and a third for the seeing of lights.[85] And if, following a lesion, one of the three sensitivities is electively affected, it is not because a particular region of the visual area has been put out of use; rather it is because the lesion, depending on its severity, systematically destroys visual functioning beginning with its most fragile forms.[86] With regard to language, H. Piéron accepts a series of horizontal localizations more precise than those of P. Marie, at least for the agnosias (coordinating centers for speech, writing and "verbal thought" movements and, within this latter, coordinating centers for words read and for those heard). But in each of these centers functioning is conceived according to a double principle: on the one hand, as a mosaic functioning; on the other, as a global functioning; and from this latter point of view the unity of cerebral physiology is reestablished across the frontiers of "coordinating centers." For example, since there are pure verbal blindnesses, it is accepted that the evocation of the "visual images" of words utilizes certain specialized devices and that there is a coordinating center for this function distinct from the one which generally assures the visual evocation of absent objects.[87] But this coordinating center is not a place in the brain where the "cerebral traces" of different words would be juxtaposed, while those of other visual images would be deposited in another place in the brain and while, finally, "perception centers" should be sought outside of these "image centers."

Everything demands conceiving of the physiological processes which accompany perception and mnemonic evocation as the execution, on a unique ensemble of receptors, of analogous melodies whose initiative is peripheral in the first case and central in the second.[88] Nor can there be any question of distinguishing a center *of* visual verbal images, and a center *of* general visual images: the coordinating centers which were enumerated above could only be the points of origin and the regulating organs of processes which extend through the cortex to the same receptors situated in the visual area.[89] It would be all the more impossible to suppose individually distinct traces for each word. When a word is evoked, the localized coordinating center is limited to *distributing* the nerve influx according to a characteristic rhythm in such a way as to play the melody which corresponds to this word on the visual receptors.[90] Thus, the function of the cerebral regions which are called coordinating centers is of a completely other type than that of the peripheral conductors; their activity concerns the structure, the organization, the configuration of behavior.[91] Here the different words evoked no longer correspond to locally distinct nerve activities but to different modes of functioning of the same substrate: function appears to prevail over anatomical devices, organization over juxtaposition. The author even appears to think that anatomical specifications, if they exist, are subsequent and result from the functioning itself, since he indicates (with respect to motor coordination centers, it is true) that the coordinating centers are not innate and result from a progressive development which involves individual variations.

Thus, the older physiology was not mistaken in drawing a parallel between nerve activity and the operations of consciousness. But the method of elementary analysis—which decomposes the whole into a sum of real parts—disassociated the nerve functioning into a mosaic of juxtaposed processes, distributed them among autonomous centers and reduced acts of consciousness to the association of real contents or to the combined interplay of abstract faculties. The parallelism obtained was illusory. Local excitations can still be made to correspond to isolated sensations. But it is on the condition of working in the artificial milieu of the laboratory experiment; and the excitations as well as the sensations obtained in this way are not the integrating elements of normal nerve functioning or of living consciousness. The discrediting of realistic analysis in psychology as well as in physiology brings about the substitution of a functional or structural parallelism for this parallelism of elements or contents.[92] "Mental facts" and "physiological facts" are no longer brought together in pairs. It is recognized that the life of consciousness and the life of the organism are not made up of a collection of events external to each other like the grains of sand in a pile, but rather that psychology and physiology are both investigating the modes of organization of behavior and the degrees of its integration—the one in order to describe them, the other in order to determine their bodily foundation.[93]

Until now we have limited ourselves to summarizing the ideas concerning which the authors are in agreement, that is in short, to criticizing psychological and physiological atomism. It remains to be seen under what categories the phenomena brought to light by this critique can be conceptualized positively. In the theory of central functioning as in that of the reflex, most authors act as if it were sufficient to *correct* the atomism by the notions of *integration* and *coordination*. To our way of thinking these notions are equivocal. They may represent a genuine reform of psychological and physiological understanding, but they may also represent the simple antithesis or counterpart of atomism. This is what we shall attempt to establish by the analysis of three examples taken from spatial perception, chromatic perception, and the physiology of language.

The very facts which call most imperatively for the hypothesis of a global functioning are interpreted in such a way as to take as little as possible away from the atomistic interpretations. It is known that the localization of a perceived point does not depend solely on the location occupied by the excitation on the retina or by the corresponding process in the calcarine area. The simple existence of normal vision in a strabismic subject shows that the spatial values of the retinal points and the points of the calcarine area which are in one-to-one correspondence with them can be redistributed. Still more simply, stereoscopic perception of depth shows that two processes initiated by "disparate" points can give rise to the perception of a single point whose localization is determined by no "local sign" inherent in the points stimulated, since it depends only upon their separation. The permutation of local signs in cases of this kind is interpreted by Piéron in a purely anatomical language.[94] It is supposed that a spatial value is conferred on the calcarine neurons by their integration in a determined associative and reflex circuit. Thus the modification of their spatial values could be understood only as the establishment of new connections. We are told nothing concerning the causes which could evoke this reworking of synchronizations and regulate it in such a way that the points on the two retinas on which the same object is projected are connected in pairs. The very influence of the stimuli itself would probably be invoked here: the projection of the image of an identical object on two noncorresponding points of the retinas—that is, in classical vocabulary, the disparity of the images—would in some way invoke the integration of these two points in the same associative circuit. But Koffka has rightly pointed out the anthropomorphic element in this notion of retinal disparity. An external observer who *knows* that the same real point is projected on two noncorresponding points of the retinas can speak of disparity; but the eye does not know that these two images come from the same object, and the question is precisely to understand how perception makes them fuse.

Will it be claimed that the two stimuli are immediately indicated as identical·by their resemblance, which latter is an objective characteristic? But one of Helmholtz's experiments shows that it is not the similitude of two retinal images which provokes the integration of the corresponding processes into a single circuit.

If a white piece of paper marked with two black dots B and A is presented on one side of a stereoscope and, on the other side, a black piece of paper with two white dots B^1 and A^1, which are closer together, then when the left eye fixates B and the right B^1, dots A and A^1 are seen as a single dot on a plane situated behind the plane, B–B^1. In this case, however, the dot on the right retina corresponding to the one where A is projected is black like dot A itself. The dot on the left retina corresponding to the one where A^1 is projected is white like A^1 itself. The two dots A and A^1 do not present any common qualitative characteristic.[95] They have nothing in common except being *dots on a homogeneous ground*. Thus it is the function, completed by a stimulus in the constellation in which it is integrated, which is determining.

This is the equivalent of saying that the permutation of local signs in the calcarine area is not a phenomenon which can be accounted for point by point: the permutation takes place in each point according to what is demanded by the whole. It is indeed, if you wish, the disparity of images which is the cause. But this disparity is a physiological reality only if it is represented in the visual sector by forces which tend to relate similar excitations; and this similarity exists only with regard to the function completed respectively by each of these excitations in the whole of which it is a part. The projection of two identical images on two noncorresponding points of the retinas is never sufficient, as a local phenomenon, to produce an effect.

One of Jaensch's experiments, interpreted by Koffka, shows that two luminous filaments on a black ground, even when they are unequally distant from the subject, are seen as situated on the same plane. But once they are presented in full light they are arranged in depth. It is reasonable to attribute the difference of the effects to the difference of the circumstances: the localization in depth to the presence in the second case of a ground of objects which are projected on the retina at the same time as the two threads. This ground reinforces the disparity of the two images of the thread which remained inefficacious until then. Thus, the localization in depth assigned to the thread and the spatial value of the excitation which it projects depend in the final analysis on those of the whole field. Since the same reasoning could apply to each of the points which, it is believed, "compose" it, it follows that the disparity of retinal images and the attribution of a spatial value are not punctual phenomena but phenomena of structure, that they do not depend on the properties of the excitation in each place or in all places, but result from the properties of the whole as such.[96]

Thus, if we postulate the intervention of a "disequilibrium" between the excitations coming from the two eyes in the correct perception of a strabismic subject or in the stereoscopic vision of depth —as one can postulate a disequilibrium between visual excitations and those furnished by the other receptors in order to explain the functional reorganization in hemianopsia[97]—we will only be developing the classical notion of the disparity of images by stripping it of its anthropomorphic character. To the extent that the calcarine area represents a punctual projection of the retina and to the extent that the retina is treated as a bundle of autonomous nerve terminations, "the retina, like the calcarine area, seems only to have the role of mediating the stimuli . . . the construction of the total visual field is evidently not the expression of the activity of the calcarine area: it is only an intermediary which furnishes the materials with the help of which the entire visual field is constructed by the fundamental function of the brain." [98] Is integration in the associative circuits sufficient to make possible this construction of the spatial field? Psycho-physiology had imagined attributing a determined "local sign" to each point of the two retinas; experience having shown that local signs are not immutable, Piéron no longer relates their distribution to pre-established anatomical devices in the retinas but to coordinating circuits; in this way it is conceived that two noncorresponding points of the two retinas, integrated into the same associative circuit, can enter into functional relationship and receive the same local sign. But *which one?* Where does the associative circuit in turn obtain the local specificity which it communicates to the partial excitations? If one thinks that it belongs to it by construction, one is only referring the anatomical theory of local signs to a higher system and we come up against the difficulties which it has encountered: the spatial localization of a determined excitant is modified by the introduction of additional points into the field. The local specificity of an associative circuit does not *belong to* and is not inherent in it; it depends on its relations with other associative circuits which at the same time are distributing concordant local signs to other points of the retina.

We are referred back, then, to a higher coordinating system. In the same manner every anatomical conception of coordination will leave the explanation incomplete by always deferring it. There can be no question of anything but a functional conception. This is to say that local specificities are distributed to the associative circuits themselves at each moment according to what is demanded by the equilibrium of the total constellation. One could wonder by what chance the retinal images of two objectively similar points, or ones which exercise the same function in two colored wholes, happened precisely to be linked to the same local sign. The problem disappears as soon as the local specificity of associative circuits is assigned to them in each case by the structure of the whole. For then the construction of the spatial field is no longer a centripetal but a centrifugal phenomenon. It is not *because* two retinal excitations are integrated into the same associative circuit that their mental correspondents receive the same function in perceived space; rather it is this common function which designates them to be linked by an associative circuit.[99] Coordination itself appears as a result: the effect of a phenomenon of structure or "form."

The analysis of the physiological conditions of chromatic perception will lead to the same conclusions. Here again we choose the expositions which H. Piéron gives of them as typical and we will raise the question as to whether the idea of integration or coordination is sufficient to resolve the difficulties of physiological atomism. Although Piéron rejects the hypothesis of a special center for color vision, he accepts that the receptor cones of the retina are related to a keyboard of chromatic neurons, each one of which is susceptible to the perception of a nuance. The wave length of the luminous excitant would itself assure the shifting of the nerve influx toward one of the chromatic keyboard notes which corresponds to the nuance of the light.[100] With regard to the degrees of intensity of the colors, their physiological substrate would again be found in different circuitings: when a differential threshold is crossed, it is because the nerve influx which until then was channeled toward a certain anatomical device is suddenly shifted toward another circuit.[101] Are we not brought back to anatomical representations which localize the function of chromatopsia and even the different degrees of this function in a certain nerve territory—although the author nevertheless wanted chromatopsia, stereopsis and photopsia to be affected in the order of their decreasing fragility in case of lesion? [102] We are dealing with a horizontal localization which attributes certain areas to certain contents. Just as above with regard to the "local signs," we can wonder if the chromatic values assigned to each of the objective points which are projected on the retina really depend solely on the properties of the afferent local influx.

The phenomenon of contrast, if we could adhere to the classical interpretation, would not be an obstacle to the punctual analysis of chromatic values related to each part of the field. For Hering's theory, for example, supposes in the most complex cases only a reciprocal action between the area which plays the role of "figure" and that which plays the role of "ground" in which the proper effects of each of the areas are added together. If the contrast of brightnesses is taken as an example, one will reason in the following fashion: white induces black around it; gray on a black ground will appear very clearly because this induction effect reinforces the proper color of the ground: gray on a gray ground will appear darker and emerge less distinctly because the two gray areas mutually darken each other. A large gray disc on a black ground will appear less clear than little gray pieces of the same nuance on the same ground since, by the same mechanism, the "internal contrast" causes the different parts of the large disc to darken each other. In this conception contrast depends only on the size and the geometric distribution of the stimuli; the total effect is the sum of local effects.[103] Thus the phenomenon would demand, in cerebral physiology, only the hypothesis of a reciprocal action of the local influxes which seems compatible with Piéron's schema.

But, in the case of color contrast, it has been possible to bring to light phenomena which it seems impossible to interpret in the same sense. It is known that a ring of gray paper on a yellow ground appears blue and, on the other hand, that a window illuminated by neutral daylight appears bluish in a room lighted by the yellow light of electricity. Initially, these two phenomena appear comparable. In reality they are not. While the yellow ground in the first case retains a very strong saturation after the gray ring has been introduced, walls lighted by electricity appear, on the contrary, faded and whitish. They take on a distinctly yellow tint only if they are observed through an opening in a screen. Thus, in the first case the contrast affects only the figure; in the second it simultaneously affects figure and ground and consequently accentuates in the first case the difference that one would find between the gray and the yellow in examining them separately, while in the second case, between the apparent blue of the daylight and the whitish yellow of the electric light, the difference is no greater than between the daylight when it is seen as neutral and the electric light when it appears to be a saturated yellow. This is because the second phenomenon obeys a very different law than the first. Everything happens as if the colored light (yellow) of the ground tended to appear neutral while the objectively neutral light of the "figure" tended to take on a color complementary to the objective color of the ground—in other words, with the electric light assuming the function of ground or of neutral light, as if the objectively neutral light took on an appearance such that the difference of the objective colors were transposed but maintained in our perception.[104] It is a question of a sort of "shift of level" by which the color which plays the role of ground becomes neutral while the color of the figure is modified in such a way that the difference between ground and figure remains invariable. "If two parts of the retina are differently stimulated, no constant relationship will exist between each part of the phenomenal field and its local stimulation, but under certain conditions there will be a constant relationship between the gradient in the phenomenal field and the stimulus difference."[105] Perhaps it would be better to find a new name for this new phenomenon which would distinguish it from the first, or to borrow the term "transformation" from Jaensch. In any case it is no longer a question here of increase, as in the classical phenomenon of contrast, but of transposition of a difference in colors. In the experiments on which Hering's theory was based, a color acted on a neighboring color; Hering supposed that the yellow of the ground acted as such on the gray of the figure to modify the appearance. In Koffka's phenomenon, on the contrary, the transformation cannot be related to either of the two terms present or to actions of one superimposed on the other.

This point, which is essential for our purpose, can be made evident by a crucial experiment. If the blue color of the figure really results from the yellow color of the ground, the effect should be accentuated by accentuating the coloration of the ground. Therefore let us place an opaque object on a sheet of white paper in a room lighted by diffuse daylight and by an electric light bulb so that the electric light is screened by the object. Only the daylight penetrates and this shadow appears to be a saturated blue. If all the surface surrounding the zone of shadow is covered with yellow paper, the coloration of the milieu is reinforced and the phenomenon of contrast should be accentuated, if the classical theory were true. In fact the blue coloration of the shadow disappears under these conditions and all the more completely as the yellow paper employed is more saturated. The result of the experiment does not vary if one arranges to eliminate the difference of clarity between the shadow and the yellow paper as well as the internal contours of the yellow sheet—factors which are unfavorable to contrast. The result still remains the same no matter what the color of the light used. Inexplicable in the classical thesis, this phenomenon justifies, on the contrary, the notion of "color level." At the beginning of the experiment, the yellow light which constituted the ground tended to be manifested in perception as neutral light and correlatively, the objectively neutral light appeared blue. When its yellow color is given back to the ground, the condition of the total "transformation" phenomenon is made to disappear.[106] The apparent color "of the enclosed field does not depend, as contrast theories maintained, on its own [objective] radiation of the surrounding field, that is, on two factors which combine in a summative way, but on a gradient between enclosed and enclosing radiation and on the color in which the latter appears." [107]

Under these conditions can we maintain Piéron's schema? The chromatic value which will be assigned in perception to some particular point of the visual field is not solely an effect combining local excitation and excitations simultaneously distributed on the retina. It also depends on the chromatic value assigned to the ground and this latter tends toward neutrality, no matter what the excitation received, in virtue of a law of equilibrium proper to the nervous system; which is to say that no summative combination of afferent influxes[108] explains that those which represent the "ground" go looking for the neutral "note" on the color keyboard or consequently that the others go looking on the same keyboard for this change of "color level." That "transverse function" by which the structure of the visual field is maintained while the absolute chromatic values are modified is interposed between the afferent influxes and the "keyboard."

But there is more. The chromatic value of a given excitation depends not only on the chromatic structure of the whole; it also depends on its spatial structure.

A gray ring drawn on a ground which is half green and half red appears gray when it is perceived as a single figure and appears half reddish, half greenish, if a line cutting the circle at the juncture of the grounds causes it to be seen as a whole composed of two half circles placed against each other.[109] No phenomenon of contrast is produced as long as a disc is perceived as situated in front of the ground from which it is distinguished; the effect of contrast appears when the disc is seen as placed on the ground. The recent study of transparency phenomena shows that a colored excitation which remains locally invariable produces very different color effects in perception depending on whether the eye takes in the whole apparatus or, on the contrary, observes through the aperture of a screen. If a wheel made up of blank sectors and solid blue sectors is rotated on a black ground in the lower part of which a yellow rectangle has been placed, observation through two holes of a screen gives a dark saturated blue at the level of the black part; a gray is seen at the level of the yellow rectangle, which results from the mixing of the complementary colors, yellow and blue (Talbot). These apparent colors represent excitations objectively produced on the retina.[110] But as soon as one observes without the interposed screen, one sees a black surface and a yellow rectangle through a transparent blue surface. Thus, the arrangement in depth has the effect of disassociating the color objectively given on the retina. Although the yellow rectangle is seen as yellow it can be established that this is not because it is so effectively; according to the law of Talbot, it sends only a gray light to the retina. The blue color of the wheel, visible at the level of the black part, is communicated to the central part of this wheel. Thus one of the elements into which the neutral gray will be decomposed is given by this. The other is determined at the same time. For it seems to be a law of perception that "if a neutral stimulation gives rise to the perception of two surfaces one of which is colored, then the other must be complementarily colored."[111] Heider[112] has shown that if a red figure is placed in the lower part of the yellow rectangle and a wheel similar to the first but with green sectors is placed on this—or more simply, a solid wheel with alternately black and white sectors—the gray tint obtained by the mixture of the red and green or of the black and white is, according to the law of Talbot, decomposed into a yellow plane seen through a blue plane exactly as in the first case when one observes without a screen. Thus, the coloration of the two planes, far from being explicable by the properties of the local stimuli, depends entirely on the organization of the whole field, that is, on the distribution of the spatial values which we discussed above. Inversely, moreover,[113] the organization in depth is conditioned by certain objective properties of the chromatic stimuli: there must exist a difference of color or at least of brightness between the back-

ground and the transparent plane in order for the transparency phenomenon to be produced; the clearer the background the darker the wheel, the
larger the empty sectors, the more perfect the transparence.

Thus just as authors must give up assigning a local specificity for
each point of the calcarine area and make the specificity depend on
the variable integration of this point into the associated circuits, just
so here one must give up constructing color vision on the basis of the
local characteristics of the influx in each of the neurons which trans-
mit it. It is not the afferent influxes and the external stimuli which
play on the chromatic keyboard; the melody of colors depends on a
transverse function which assigns its momentary chromatic value to
each part of the excitation. But should we adhere to this conclusion?
We saw above that the physiological problem of spatial perception
was not resolved if one limited oneself to carrying over to the associative circuits the absolute local signs which atomism attributed to each
point of the retina. Just so here, should a chromatic neuron be supposed for each nuance of light? This would be to admit a one-to-one
correspondence between different colors of the milieu and different
points of the cerebral cortex. But at the same time we are obliged to
superimpose on this realistic projection of the external world in the
cerebral cortex processes of distribution by which the proper activity
of nerve function is manifested. Is it not necessary to choose between
these two representations of the nervous system? And does not the
second make the first one useless?

Since perception of space and perception of color, each one taken
separately, are not only phenomena of structure but also, as we have
shown by the study of contrast and transparency, two abstract aspects
of a global function, if one wants these phenomena of form to be
translated on a color keyboard (and in a series of circuits gifted with
a fixed local specificity), one is obliged to posit functional connections the complexity of which it is difficult to imagine. Above all we
need to raise the question as to what validates this exigency. The
hypothesis of a color keyboard or that of a local specificity of associative circuits had a *raison d'être* only when topographically defined
devices to which they were related could alone confer a determined
chromatic and spatial significance on the afferent excitations. But
since in any case it is no longer the physical excitant and its proper
action on the nervous system which determines the perceived color
or spatial position, there is no longer any reason for positing in the
cortex a color keyboard or spatial positions uniquely destined for

receiving the qualified external excitations. Since chromatic and spatial determinations are moments of a global dynamic structure which assigns a certain coefficient to each part of the total excitation, there is no reason for relating these coefficients to a graduated scale of colors and places. The only punctual projection which experience reveals is that of the *receptive surfaces* on the cortex. The hypothesis of a keyboard of colors is bound up with the old conception of a parallelism of contents; it accords badly with the modern conception of a parallelism of nerve functioning and mental functioning.

Finally, in the physiology of language the notion of integration and coordination will appear once more as a compromise with atomism rather than as a solution to the problems which atomism poses. The coordinating centers are not storehouses of ready-made traces. They are command posts capable of executing the most different ensembles on a single keyboard of phonemes, just as an infinity of melodies can be played on a single piano. Thus, one would believe that what belongs to them in their own right, as it does to the pianist, is the distribution of intensities and intervals, the choice of notes and the determination of the order of their succession: in a word, the elaboration[114] of the structural properties of perception and movement. Elsewhere Piéron speaks of "notes" of the keyboard which would be susceptible to certain words[115] or of ready-made "memos" which would order their release;[116] he invokes the proximity of the "keys" which correspond to the confused words in order to explain paraphasia;[117] and he founds, it seems, the logical order of disintegration on considerations of topography even in cases where the lesion compromises the function in its entirety, from the least automatic to the most automatic, instead of attacking selectively one word or one determined type of language.[118] Is this not to forget that the improvisation, at each moment, of the necessary coordinations for playing the word in question on the keyboard of phonemes has been attributed to the centers as their principal function? Is this not to establish the structure of the word ahead of time and, in brief, to return to the notion of "cerebral traces" which the author had nevertheless wanted to surpass? [119]

"Leaves in a book" have an individuality demanding their own coordinating correspondent, and the leaves of a tree have another.[120] If the coordinating center, instead of achieving the coordinations of phonemes, possesses in itself as many regulatory devices as there are words, it is difficult to see what distinguishes them from "cerebral traces." If it is thought that similar words have neighboring keys in the brain which govern their evocation it is because, following the habits of the old parallelism, the idea of relating logical relations or relations of the similitude of words to the map of the brain has not been given up. Finally, if it is thought that the least automatized processes are tied to nerve substance *in the same manner* as processes which have created organs for themselves, it is because a functional point of view has not really been adopted.

The notions of integration and coordination can serve to designate certain rigid constructions by which partial activities become solidary with each other. Such is the mechanism which assures the release of a "Go" signal when all the doors of a train are closed. This is the kind of coordination which one seems to have in mind when one accepts the idea of a distinct note in the receptive coordination center corresponding to each word or even to homonyms. The telephone plug can only put one or more pre-established circuits into communication with one or more pre-established circuits. How does it happen, then, that the elementary influxes released by sounds which are registered one after the other on the auditory receptors act precisely on the right key, find immediately the pathways which are posited as prepared for them, while the initial phoneme can belong to so many different words and the resemblance of these words can extend to all the constitutive phonemes in case of homonymy?

Even the hypothesis of a coordinating device which is all ready to function does not dispense us from looking for what it is in the actual word or sentence ensemble which directs and guides the elementary influxes corresponding to the phonemes or words toward these already prepared paths. The circuits, it will be said, are constituted only by momentary synchronizations. As a word is being pronounced before a subject, what is it then which guarantees that the influxes will find synchronizations ahead of them capable of conducting them to the appropriate keys of the phonemic center? They must create them themselves. Everything happens as if we are dealing with an automatic central in which a prior message itself opens up the appropriate pathways for the oscillations which will follow. But it would be a question of a central capable of responding to an indefinite number of indicators, to unplanned combinations of indicators already received, and one which does not limit itself to totaling them by taking them for what they are but which interprets them by taking them for what they represent.

A machine is capable only of operations for which it has been constructed; the idea of a machine which would be capable of responding to an indefinite variety of stimuli is a contradictory one, since automation is obtained only by submitting the initiation of work to certain chosen conditions. Thus we are led to a type of coordination very different from that which was defined above. Here the coordinated elements are not only coupled with each other, they constitute together, by their very union, a whole which has its proper law and which manifests it as soon as the first elements of excitation are given, just as the first notes of a melody assign a certain mode of resolution to the whole. While the notes taken separately have an equivocal signification, being capable of entering into an infinity of possible ensembles, in the melody each one is demanded by the context and contributes its part in expressing something which is not contained in any one of them and which binds them together internally. The same notes in two different melodies are not recognized as such. Inversely, the same melody can be played two times without the two versions having a single common element if it has been transposed. Coordination is now the creation of a unity of meaning which is expressed in the juxtaposed parts, the creation of certain relations which owe nothing to the materiality of the terms which they unite.

The physiology of language has need of a coordination of this kind. Homonyms must give rise to an elaboration which eliminates the equivocal; a few syllables of a word must designate it without ambiguity, as happens most of the time in current language. And this will be possible if the influxes which they provoke in the nervous system do not, like the final notes of a melody, simply confirm the details of a structure already traced in its ensemble. In the same manner, the sentence of a speaker must be organized all by itself, as it were, as happens in fact in the normal use of language in which an awareness of the means of expression for themselves, the contemplation of "verbal images," is already a pathological phenomenon. The first words must already have the kind of rhythm and accent which is appropriate to the end of the sentence, which is nevertheless not yet determined, except as the last notes of a melody are performed in its global structure. If one wants to establish the parallel between the "dynamism" of psychology and that of modern physiology which H. Piéron believes he must accept, it will be necessary to conceive of coordination, whether it be receptive or incito-motor, as Gestalt theory does, that is, as the constitution of "forms" or of functional structures.

In summary, whether it be a question of the comprehension of a word or of the perception of colors or of spatial positions, the putting into action of pre-established apparatuses which the stimuli, in virtue of their objective properties, would release from the outside cannot be seen in nerve functioning. The physiological process which corresponds to the perceived color or position or to the signification of a word must be improvised, actively constituted at the very moment of perception. Thus, function has a positive and proper reality; it is not a simple consequence of the existence of organs or substrate. The process of excitation forms an indecomposable unity and is not made up of the sum of the local processes. The color or the position which will be effectively perceived following such and such retinal excitations depends not only on the properties of these latter but on the laws proper to nerve functioning. It is not the stimuli which constitute the reactions nor which determine the contents of perception. It is not the real world which constitutes the perceived world. And physiological analysis, if it wants to grasp the true functioning of the nervous system, cannot recompose it from the effects which psychophysiology obtains by applying isolated stimuli to receptors. Seen through the opening of a screen, the same experimental set-up which gives rise to the transparency phenomenon in free observation appears as a uniform gray surface.[121] The living physiology of the nervous system can only be understood by starting from phenomenal givens.

Negatively, the conclusion is easy. Pavlov's conceptions are irreconcilable with modern pathology and physiology. If their inadequacy appeared already at the level where we have most often placed ourselves, it would be even more apparent in a complete analysis of perception. I do not perceive simply "things," but also use-objects: an article of clothing, for example. Between the actual appearance of the article of clothing placed in front of me, the position which it can occupy in space (for example, were I to take it and put it behind me in order to put it on) and the right and left regions of my own body, a series of regulated correspondences is established which permits the normal person to handle the article of clothing without hesitation and which is lacking in a person suffering from agnosia. Nerve functioning distributes not only spatial and chromatic values but also symbolic values. The conditioned reflex theory obliges us to treat these systematic transformations as a sum of local transformations, explicable in each point of the cortex by the conditioned efficacy of the stimuli. Suppose I am looking at a coat placed in front of me: for me to take it and put it on, the left sleeve, which is first situated at my right, passes to my left and it is my left arm which I must introduce into it. The correlation which is manifest in my behavior between "what was on the right" and "what will be on the left" would find its explanation, according to the conditioned reflex theory, in the reflexogenic power acquired by each partial stimulus in the course of experience. But now, when I am actually perceiving the sleeve of the coat, the index "on the right" with which it is marked cannot come from conditionings acquired by the points of the retina then stimulated: these conditionings are indeed multiple since a single retinal impression, depending on the position of the eyes, has been able to correspond to stimuli which are situated in an extremely variable way in objective space. Only the proprioceptive excitations which represent the current position of my eyes to the central system can choose, among the conditionings acquired by retinal impression, the one which will be evoked in each case. This comes down to saying that the situation perceived according to right and left, far from depending on the retinal stimulus as such, depends on a constellation of both proprioceptive and exteroceptive stimuli.

Once again the excitation, instead of being a longitudinal and punctual phenomenon, becomes a transverse and global phenomenon. But an adapted behavior demands something more: each point of the concrete expanse currently seen must possess not only a present localization but also a series of virtual localizations which will situate it with respect to my body when my body moves, in such a way, for example, that I thrust my left arm without hesitation into the sleeve which was on my right when the coat was placed in front of me. In other words, it is not sufficient that fragments of concrete expanse, circumscribed by the limits of my visual field and each one of which would have a spatial structure of its own, appear one after the other in the course of my movements. It is necessary that each point of one of these perspectives be put into correspondence and identified with those which represent it in the others. It is even less possible than in the first case for these new spatial indices to result only from retinal excitations and from the conditioned reactions which they would have released.

The reasoning processes which we have just gone through with respect to each of the spatial perspectives is *a fortiori* valid with respect to their integration in a space. Thus, the apparent position and its virtual variations must be a function of two variables: the afferent ocular excitations and, on the other hand, the ensemble of excitations which represent the current position of my body in the cerebral cortex. A reorganization of the spatial field will correspond to each change of this position: if, for example, I execute a half turn, what was "on the right" will be immediately marked with the index "on the left" and identified in this new position. It follows from this that neither for physiology nor for psychology can the spatial field of behavior be constructed point for point. Each "local sign" depends on a global process of excitation in which participate, in addition to the retinal excitations, those which come from the oculo-motor muscles, the devices of equilibrium and the ensemble of the muscles of the body. Each perceived position has a meaning only as integrated into a framework of space which includes not only a sensible sector, actually perceived, but also a "virtual space" [122] of which the sensible sector is only a momentary aspect. It is in this way that the perceiving subject can move himself in a stable space, in spite of the movements of the eyes and body which jostle the punctual excitations at the surface of the receptors at each instant. The conditioned reflex theory (in addition to the fact that it would suppose a long and difficult learning period and accords badly with the precocity of our adaptations to space) explains nothing since, in any case, the acquired conditioning would have to be put into play by a process of structured excitation which renders the hypothesis superfluous.

If pathology and physiology exclude physiological empiricism— the thesis according to which the functional structures realized by nerve activity would be reducible to the association by contiguity created in the course of experience—they are by the same token unfavorable to a dualism of perception and sensation, of form and matter. The cerebral regions assigned to elementary vision represent only way stations; we have no right to set up a correspondence between them and a first level of behavior or a first layer of "mental facts." [123] Disorders such as musical deafness or amusia[124] manifest the existence in normal persons of functions of auditive organization analogous to the distribution of chromatic and spatial values in the visual order. But if it is impossible to constitute the spatial field of behavior or that of perception from "localizing reflexes" or from punctual local signs, neither is it permissible to refer the organization to a higher system. There are agnosias which destroy the virtual space of which we spoke without compromising the spatial structures within the visual field. They may modify them but nevertheless they do not make them impossible. Concrete space, as it is grasped within our visual field, and virtual space in which concrete space is integrated in normal perception, are two distinct constitutive layers, even though the second integrates the first. We can be disoriented in virtual space without being so in concrete space. We can be incapable of conceptualizing space as a universal milieu without the horizon of virtual space which surrounds the properly visible expanse being abolished at the same time. The notion of form has value precisely because it goes beyond the atomistic conception of nerve functioning without reducing it to a diffuse and undifferentiated activity, because it rejects psychological empiricism without going to the intellectualist antithesis. The analysis of perception will lead to re-establishing a demarcation—no longer between sensation and perception, or between sensibility and intelligence, or, more generally, between a chaos of elements and a higher system which would organize them —but between different types or levels of organization.

Concerning the relations of behavior and the brain, the preceding analyses can have two meanings. Perhaps they require only changing categories and introducing the notion of form in physiology. Form, in the sense in which we have defined it, possesses original properties with regard to those of the parts which can be detached from it. Each moment in it is determined by the grouping of the other moments, and their respective value depends on a state of total equilibrium the formula of which is an intrinsic character of "form." In this sense it seems to fulfill all the conditions necessary for giving an account of nerve functioning. Thus it would be possible to define it as a process of the "figure and ground" type.[125] With regard to the dependence of forms in relation to certain topographical conditions, all degrees exist[126]—from the case of a membrane stretched over a metallic frame and submitted to pressures in relation to which it realizes a certain position of equilibrium, to the case of a drop of oil in water which realizes a stable structure without any topographical support. Again in this sense, form appears capable of explaining the ambiguity of place in nerve substance, from the horizontal localizations of the periphery to the vertical localizations of the center. These uncontested localizations represent points of the cortex where the essential processes unfold—the "figure" of the total process—without our ever being able to separate them completely from a ground, which is constituted by the activity of the rest of the cortex. Thus, on the condition that "form" is introduced in nerve functioning, a parallelism or a rigorous "isomorphism" [127] could be maintained.

But the very fact that we had to borrow the terms "figure" and "ground" from the phenomenal or perceived world in order to describe these "physiological forms"—just as above with the metaphor of melody[128]—leads us to wonder if these are still *physiological* phenomena, if we can in principle conceive of processes which are still physiological and which would adequately symbolize the relations inherent in what is ordinarily called "consciousness." We have seen, for example, that two disparate excitations are fused in vision if they fulfill the same function in the two colored surfaces, be it only that of "dot on a homogeneous ground." But how can it be understood that this community of function can be the *cause* which makes them fuse?

The function, "dot on a homogeneous ground," or more generally, the function, "figure and ground," has a meaning only in the perceived world: it is there that we learn what it is to be a figure and what it is to be a ground. The perceived would be explicable only by the perceived itself, and not by physiological processes. A physiological analysis of perception would be purely and simply impossible. On the basis of a word as a physical phenomenon, as an ensemble of vibrations of the air, no physiological phenomenon capable of serving as a substrate for the signification of the word could be described in the brain; for we have seen that, in audition and also in speaking, a word as an ensemble of motor or afferent excitations presupposes a word as a melodic structure and this latter presupposes a sentence as a unity of signification. As one moves toward the center of the cortex the conditions of behavior, instead of being found in the nerve substance as such, as may happen on the periphery, are more and more to be found in the qualitatively variable modes of its global functioning. A logical hierarchy of functional levels is substituted for the spatial juxtaposition of the peripheral conductors and, in case of lesion, disorders of structure are substituted for deficiencies of contents. Since this structure of behavior and the cerebral functioning which supports it can only be conceived in terms borrowed from the perceived world, this latter no longer appears as an order of phenomena parallel to the order of physiological phenomena but as one which is richer than it. Physiology cannot be completely conceptualized without borrowing from psychology.

And, in the final analysis, what does the failure of a physiology of space perception signify? It signifies that a model of space as perception reveals it cannot be constructed either in real space or in real "mental facts" by an assemblage of parts; or it signifies, as Kant had said, that real extension, *partes extra partes,* presupposes known extension. Thus it is to the ideality of space to which these simple remarks would lead. It will be possible to establish the conclusions only after a stricter analysis of the notion of form.

The Structures of Behavior

The preceding paragraphs show that, for reasons of principle—the impossibility of reducing the whole of behavior to a sum of real parts—physiology could not achieve the reduction of behavior on the basis of cerebral functioning as it is known by chronaxic measures or more generally by physical methods; inversely, it shows that it is the psychological analysis of morbid behavior, confronted with the presumed extent and location of lesions, which allows us to construct hypotheses concerning its central sector. Thus, what we have just said concerning their physiological substrate only anticipates the direct examination of higher forms of behavior. And our reason for not beginning with such an examination was to show that the method which is called physiological refers us back to behavior. The image which Pavlov gives of behavior and the results of recent investigations must now be compared—without any hypothesis concerning cerebral physiology being implied in this discussion.

Since the theory of the conditioned reflex has attempted above all to explain the expansion of the reflexogenic field of the animal, the decisive point for it should be to explain the acquisition of a new and adapted mode of behavior. As a theory of learning, it joined forces with the principle of "trial and error." Presented with a new situation, the animal would react by a series of attempts to which no intentional character, that is, no internal relation to the situation, should be attributed. Enclosed in a cage outside of which its food is placed, the animal would execute, under the pressure of need, a multitude of gestures (grasping and shaking the bars, etc.), among which could be found the decisive gesture (biting or pulling the lever which regulates the opening of the door). Those of the trials which are not followed by success would be eliminated from future behavior, the others set and acquired.

But how can the same situation evoke new trials in the case of the failure of the first? And by what mechanism are the favorable responses, and only those, established? Concerning the first point, the existence of multiple connections established in advance between an afferent path and several efferent paths was invoked (Thorndike), which we have seen is hardly compatible with the data of modern physiology. With regard to the second point, the pleasure of the success was appealed to anthropomorphically in order to explain the fixation of useful reactions.

The conditioned reflex theory provides strict behaviorism with a more satisfactory explanation. After a failure the organism undertakes a new trial because, according to the laws of reciprocal and internal induction, the points of the cortex which were inhibited until then pass to a state of excitation. If a rat in a labyrinth can be trained always to choose the path marked by a white curtain at the end of which it finds its food, and never the path marked by a black curtain which is obstructed and where it receives an electric shock, it is because the white curtain becomes the conditioned stimulus of the "positive reactions" to the goal.[129] Inversely, the bars of the cage in our first example and the black curtain in the second give rise to a conditioned inhibition. The privilege of the acquired response will be confirmed by repetition since, coming at the end of each series of experiments and sometimes at the very beginning, it is more frequent than any one of the others. Learning and the development of behavior do not, properly speaking, achieve anything new. They only transfer to certain stimuli the power of releasing certain movements, the motor conditions of which are considered as given in advance. The development of behavior consists only in the different association of pre-existent elements.

But is the frequency of favorable responses sufficient to explain why they become rooted in behavior? Is it not, on the contrary, because they are preferred that they become durable acquisitions? It is not true to say that they are produced more often than the others in virtue of the very conditions of the "trial" which, in the laboratory as in life, comes to an end only at the moment when favorable responses do occur and as soon as they do. It is forgotten that fruitless trials, in experiments like those of Thorndike, are repeated many times before the animal turns to other means.[130] Moreover, frequency cannot intervene in inhibition which is acquired once and for all with regard to dangerous stimuli. Conditioned inhibitions should become weakened by the very fact that they anticipate the return of painful experiences,[131] and one should see "stupid" reactions reappear as the training progresses. Finally, favorable responses seem to be able to be established after a single test, as is adequately shown by the sharp rise of the curves in motor learning.[132] These facts suggest the idea that the value of positive or negative behavior would intervene in some manner in its fixation. But how can this intervention of values be represented? What is it in the organism which can, as it were, appreciate them? Let us return to the acquisition of behavior in order to determine whether it can be understood as an accidental connection.

Behaviorism made its task easy by supposing, in our example, that the lever which regulates the door can become the conditioned stimulus, not only of reflexes of prehension and mastication which take place in the presence of the goal, but also of the manipulations which have *preceded* the opening of the door. In the same way behaviorism is content to say that the white curtain becomes the conditioned stimulus of the "positive" reactions, thereby confusing—under the same name—reactions to the goal, which could indeed be evoked by it after training, and reactions preparatory to the solution which it could not establish.[133] In reality the difficulty is one of principle. The conditioned reflex theory presents stimulations and responses which succeed each other in an organism like a series of events external to each other and between which no relations can be established other than those of immediate temporal contiguity. The manipulations which the animal executes on the lever are in themselves only the effects of cerebral mechanisms; they will in fact bring about liberation and success, but they have no relation whatsoever to the "perception" of the food, except perhaps insofar as it awakens the need and thus provokes a state of agitation favorable to the activation of pre-established conditionings. But on this point the useful manipulations are in no way privileged: they owe as much or as little to the goal pursued as the useless attempts which have preceded them. And it would be necessary that the goal, because it had been attained, be capable subsequently of stimulating them again. Any prospective relation between the preparatory attitudes and the goal is eliminated; one would like the goal, by a retroactive effect, to be able to bring back the conditions which have permitted its attainment.

But if learning is really only a particular case of physical causality, it is difficult to see how the order of temporal passage would reverse itself, how the effect could become the cause of its cause. For the "perception" of the lever or the goal to bring back the useful manipulations, it is not sufficient for them to have preceded it in objective time. The attitudes which will lead to the goal, or their physiological substrate, must possess, either before the animal has "tried" them or after they have succeeded, some distinctive property which designates them for success and integrates them into the "perception" of the goal. It remains to understand the relation which is established between the goal and the preparatory actions, giving a meaning to the multiplicity of elementary movements which the latter combine and making of them an act in the proper sense of the word, a new creation after which the behavioral history is qualitatively modified.

Rigorously described, moreover, learning does not appear to be the addition to old forms of behavior of certain determined connections between such and such stimuli and such and such movements, but rather to be a general alteration of behavior which is manifested in a multitude of actions, the content of which is variable and the significance constant. Conditioning could establish only useful responses which are like those produced the first time. This is not what we observe. A cat, trained to obtain its food by pulling on a string, will pull it with its paw on the first successful trial but with its teeth on the second.[134] If, as often happens, the first favorable attempt has been mixed with useless movements or partial errors, these accidents will disappear from subsequent responses.[135] Thus, to learn never consists in being made capable of repeating the same gesture, but of providing an adapted response to the situation by different means. Nor is the response acquired with regard to an individual situation. It is rather a question of a new aptitude for resolving a series of problems of the same form. It is known that, in children, the acquisition of differential behavior with respect to colors is slow and difficult. When the child has succeeded in distinguishing red and green and naming them correctly, what is acquired is not properly speaking the discrimination of these two qualities as such; it is a general power of comparing and distinguishing *colors:* all pairs of colors benefit from the distinction of red and green and differential behavior progresses not from one to the other but by a finer and finer discrimination with regard to all of them.[136]

In Buytendijk's experiments, this systematic learning is discovered in fish. If one accustoms sunfish to seeing first black and then white bread and, once the habit is acquired, one mixes pieces of chalk with the white bread, a differential behavior with regard to the chalk and the bread as visual stimuli is acquired little by little. If one then mixes pieces of black rubber with the black bread, a differential behavior is again acquired after a period of "disorientation," but much more rapidly than in the first case. If one comes back to white bread, the readaptation is made after a much shorter delay. Thus the inhibitions acquired with regard to the pieces of chalk made it possible for the animal to acquire inhibitions more rapidly with regard to the pieces of rubber, and inversely. It is not to a certain material therefore that the animal has adapted but, to speak a human language, to a certain kind of deception. The effectively acquired learning could not be understood as an association between such and such a visual stimulus (the proper color of the chalk and the rubber) and the negative result. It is an aptitude for choosing, a "method of selection," which is established in the animal.[137]

The facts of habit transfer would confirm this interpretation and the general character of all learning. It is true that the conditioned reflex theory does not necessarily suppose that learning is directed to the individual characteristics of the stimuli and is translated by the exact repetition of the movements to which the first favorable experience has given rise. The acquired conditioning can be condensed and the act abridged because each of its phases becomes, by repetition, the conditioned stimulus of the following one. It is precisely the behaviorist school which has brought to light the "abstract" character of certain animal reactions: the adequate stimulus of the reactions of the spider is neither the visual aspect of the fly nor the noise by which its presence is announced, but only the vibrations which it communicates to the web by struggling in it. This accounts for the fact that, if a fly is put in its nest, the spider does not treat it as bait. Its instinctive behavior is not a reaction to the fly but a reaction to a vibrating object in general; it would be initiated just as readily by placing a tuning fork in the middle of the web. Moreover, in almost all species the very structure of the receptors determines an automatic "abstraction" in the same manner. Far from manifesting an activity directed toward the essential, these general reactions would rather be comparable to the stereotyped behavior of the demented person who does not take into account the details of the situation because he no longer perceives them. But this is precisely the question: is it possible to explain in the same manner stereotyped behavior or the "absurd" errors of the animal which attempts the same solution in essentially different situations when they have a single common trait and, inversely, no longer has the use of its instinctive powers if the situation is the least bit unexpected, on the one hand, and on the other, the flexibility of habits which are equally efficacious in the face of materially different situations provided that they have the same *meaning*?

This would be to confuse the universal and the abstract. "Absurd" errors are encountered, in Koehler's observations for example, especially when the animal is cold, tired, or too excited.[138] Such errors bring more clearly to light the originality of "true solutions."

When the problem is for a chimpanzee, working through a grill with a stick, to maneuver a piece of fruit placed in a box toward itself, and if it is arranged so that only the upper part and the side of the box opposite to that of the animal is open, the animal will most frequently begin by pulling the fruit directly toward itself as it did in other more simple experiments. But this time the side of the box placed between the animal and the goal does not allow it to succeed. This first movement, which represents a blind perseverence, is to be contrasted with the "good solution" which can be obtained if the opening through which the goal is accessible had been placed laterally. Here the least "intelligent" monkeys succeed immediately even though the experiments to which they had been previously submitted had only taught them to execute these detours by themselves or to make use of a stick without an obstacle.[139] In the first case we are dealing with a reaction which retains from the situation only its vague resemblance to prior situations and neglects the precise data of the present problem. It is to actions of this kind that the conditioned reflex theory applies, the presence of certain "stimuli" (the goal, the bars of the cage and the stick) evoking the movements for which they have become the conditioned excitants. In the second case, on the contrary, even though the problem is different from those which the animal has encountered until then, the monkey's behavior is related to that in the situation which makes it a new form of already "known" problems.

If, instead of considering positive habits, we were now to analyze the inhibitions created by experience, the demonstration would be still easier. It is not the violent reactions which follow a painful experience which are established in the behavior of a child but reactions of protection which, although they have the same *meaning,* do not have the same appearance. In the presence of a flame, a child who has burned himself will not repeat the sudden withdrawal of the hand which the burning evoked.[140] This indicates that learning is not a *real* operation, not a correlation established between two individual realities—a certain stimulus and a certain movement—which would not be modified by their association. The conditioned stimulus acts only as the representative of a whole category of stimuli which have become reflexogenic along with it; the original response movement is established only as a particular instance of a general aptitude which can vary around the same fundamental theme.

The true stimulus is not the one defined by physics and chemistry; the reaction is not this or that particular series of movements; and the connection between the two is not the simple coincidence of two successive events. There must be a principle in the organism which ensures that the learning experience will have a general relevance.

If these observations did not impose themselves on psychologists earlier, it is doubtless because the problems presented to the animal in the older experiments were not favorable to true learning, as Koehler and Koffka have indicated. If the opening of a cage is made to depend on the manipulation of a lock or even of a lever, the relation of the preparatory movement to the result can only be one of simple succession, since the mechanism of the lever or of the lock is not visible from the cage; in addition, it involves multiple connections that even man is not always capable of mastering. In the same manner the choice of a white or black curtain for marking the entrances of a labyrinth is completely arbitrary. Thus these are not the proper experimental conditions for bringing to light an internal relation between the goal and the acquired responses, and one should not be surprised if the animal proceeds by trial and error in situations of this kind. But even in this case the empiricist theory of learning is not verified. As soon as there is learning it is necessary that a relation be established between the signal, the preparatory reactions and the access to the goal which makes the ensemble something other than an objective succession of physical events. Chimpanzees which do not know how to build can nevertheless place cases on top of each other in order to attain a goal. But the grouping always remains very unstable and is utilizable only by an animal like a monkey which is adroit in compensating for the oscillations of the structure by its own movements.[141] The monkey proceeds by blind trials, setting a case on its edge for example and starting over again each time the edifice falls down without giving up. Thus the trial and error schema applies here. *But there is also no learning;*[142] the clumsiness of the animal is definitive. Thus the development of behavior would *never* find its explanation in the contiguity realized by experience between such and such a situation and such and such a favorable response.

The decisive factor lies in the manner in which fortuitous contiguities are utilized by the organism, in the elaboration which the organism makes them undergo. If it were otherwise it is difficult to see why all species of animals, as soon as their bodily structure included the receptors and permitted the required gestures, would not be apt at every kind of learning. The difference between absurd errors and good solutions does not lie solely in the specific nature of the sensory receptors and the affector apparatuses, since success and failure are found with respect to the same problem within the same species,[143] and in the behavior of the same animal depending on the moment and the degree of freshness and fatigue. In reality it is never the trials by themselves (by this we mean the visible movement) which can contribute in any way to the acquisition of a habit. These trials must occur in a certain organic framework which gives them meaning and efficacy; they presuppose a "sensory-motor *a priori*,"[144] practical "categories"[145] which differ from one species to another. Even when the nature of the problem posed demands a series of prior explorations and excludes an immediately correct solution, these "trials" always have a systematic character. A rat introduced into a labyrinth will follow the general direction of the initial elements. Everything happens as if the animal adopted a "hypothesis" which "is not explained by the success since it is manifested and persists before the success can confirm it."[146] Clearly it must be accepted that what is tested here is not just any series of independent choices but a definite "path," each part of which is determined only by its relation to the direction of the ensemble, by its participation in the law of the whole. After the complete exploration of the labyrinth, inhibitions are also manifested in a systematic order: impasses which are parallel and in the direction contrary to the general direction of the goal are the first to be eliminated, then those which are perpendicular to the direction of the goal, and finally those which are parallel and in the same direction. "The first explorations followed by a sanction at the end have the effect of classifying the alleys according to their relation to this general direction, of affecting them as it were with a particular vector." [147]

Even in these cases least favorable to our interpretation, either the "trials" involve no internal law, but then they never result in learning; or there is learning, in which case the organism must be capable, on the one hand, of creating relations among the different possible "solutions" and, on the other hand, among all of them and the "problem," by which their *value* is measured. Even when the relation of signal to goal is a relation of pure succession, as happens in Tolman's experiment,[148] we can presume that learning does not consist in recording *de facto* contiguities. It is necessary that the succession in-itself (*en soi*) become a "succession for the organism." This is possible in Tolman's experiment because the curtain, the alley which it signals, and the goal together enter into a spatial structure which has a meaning. But if one accustoms a cat to obtaining its freedom by scratching or licking itself, the animal reduces this movement little by little until it becomes imperceptible and does not renew it in case of failure.[149] If it is a question of obtaining a piece of food by a gesture which is without objective connection with success, the animal, in executing this gesture, does not look at the goal; if, on the contrary, there is a relation which we will call logical between the conditioned stimulus and a natural stimulus, the animal does not take its eyes off the goal. One is clearly obliged to note that in the second case the goal has acquired the power of evoking, in addition to the motor reactions, reactions of the visual apparatus which in fact converge with them. Finally, the rhythm of the movements, their distribution, and their coordination in time are different depending on whether the response in question has a meaning and is related to the very essence of the problem, or whether, on the contrary, it is a stereotyped reaction evoked by an aspect of the situation which is abstract and external to it.[150]

How did the conditioned reflex theory account for these variations of behavior which correspond to a like number of internal connections between the goal and a preparatory reaction, since for this theory all relations are equally external? Behaviorism opposes an objection of principle to these descriptions: in saying that the acquired reaction is related to the essence of the situation and that it admits of a series of variations around a fundamental theme, and in distinguishing true solutions from the results of training by the continuity of the movements which they integrate and by their melodic development, we would be attributing characteristics to observed behavior as if they were essential to it when they are only the result of our human manner of perceiving and interpreting such behavior. It is for the human observer, who compares reactions distributed in different moments of time, that the acquired aptitude is general. It is also for him that a continuous curve is distinguished from a broken line.

If we consider behavior objectively, that is, instant by instant and in the framework of the real stimuli which initiate it, we are never dealing with anything except particular movements responding to particular excitations; all other language would be "anthropomorphic." But it would still have to be explained why this so-called anthropomorphic interpretation is possible with respect to certain ways of behaving and impossible with respect to others. Even if we have been at fault in employing words like "essence" or "problem," which were convenient for purposes of description, there remains the statistical difference between an organism which, after training, has acquired the power of responding to a definite stimulus and an organism which, after learning, succeeds in varied adaptations to situations which are themselves varied. If one refuses to take into consideration, as the object of science, every property of phenomena which is not manifested in the intuition of a particular case and which appears only to reflective consciousness—by an analysis of the varied concordances or by a reading of the statistics—it is not anthropomorphism which is excluded, it is science; it is not objectivity which is defended, it is realism and nominalism.

Scientific laws, which are not *given in* the facts but which one finds *expressed* in them, would be subject to the same grievance. When one speaks of the structure of the situation and its meaning, these words evidently designate certain givens of human experience and are consequently suspect of anthropomorphism. But "colors," "lights," and "pressures" or their expression in physical language are no less so. It is clear that all the terms of which we can make use refer to phenomena of human experience, naive or scientific. The whole question is to know whether they are truly constitutive of the objects intended (*visés*) in an inter-subjective experience and necessary for their definition.

Precisely the preceding observations show that we cannot treat reactions to the structure of the situation as derived or give a privilege of objectivity to those which depend on elementary excitations. For instance, the excitations received on the sensory terminations and the movements executed by the effector muscles are integrated into structures which play a regulating role in their regard. These structural processes account for the laws of learning which we formulated above: since they establish a relation of meaning between situation and response, they explain the fixation of adapted responses and the generality of the acquired aptitude. In the stimulus-response schema, they bring into play not the material properties of the stimuli, but the formal properties of the situation: the spatial, temporal, numerical and functional relations which are its armature. It is to the extent that relations of this kind emerge and become efficacious by themselves that the progress of behavior is explicable.

An early experiment of Ruger[151] presents us with these original properties of wholes in behavior. A subject trained to execute on each piece in turn, but in a systematic order, all of the operations necessary for taking apart a metallic puzzle, behaves as if he had no practice with it when presented with the entire puzzle. Learning acquired with respect to a "part" of a situation is not acquired with respect to this "same" part assimilated into a new whole. In other words, the real parts of the stimulus are not necessarily the real parts of the situation. The efficacy of a partial stimulus is not tied solely to its objective presence. It must make itself recognized as it were by the organism in the new constellation in which it appears. There is reason for distinguishing the presence of the stimulus in-itself (*en soi*) and its presence "for the organism" which reacts. But what we have just said of the entire puzzle could be said of each of the pieces which compose it. It is not with respect to the luminous rays reflected by it that a habit had been acquired, but with respect to the metallic piece considered according to its form (in the ordinary sense of the word) and its mechanical properties. Since the decomposition into real parts can never be completed, it is never as an individual physical reality that the stimulus becomes reflexogenic; it is always as a structure.

If these remarks are founded, it should be possible—and it is necessary—to classify behavior, no longer into elementary and complex behavior as has often been done, but according to whether the structure in behavior is submerged in the content or, on the contrary, emerges from it to become, at the limit, the proper theme of activity. From this point of view, one could distinguish "syncretic forms," "amovable forms" and "symbolic forms." These three categories do not correspond to three groups of animals: there is no species of animal whose behavior *never* goes beyond the syncretic level nor any whose behavior *never* descends below the symbolic forms. Nevertheless, animals can be distributed along this scale according to the type of behavior which is most typical of them. So we will speak of reactions to space and time above all with regard to the "amovable forms." It is nevertheless clear that an instinctive movement, tied to a syncretic situation, is adapted to the spatial characteristics of the instinctual object and involves a temporal rhythm. The fundamental dimensions of space and time are found, if you like, at the three levels which we have just distinguished. But they do not have the same meaning at each level. In order to become the unlimited milieus that human experience finds in them, space and time demand symbolic activity.

THE SYNCRETIC FORMS

At this level behavior is tied either to certain abstract aspects of the situations[152] or to certain complexes of very special stimuli. In any case, it is imprisoned in the framework of its natural conditions and treats unexpected situations only as allusions to the vital situations which are prescribed for it.

The simplest forms of behavior, those for example that are found in invertebrates, are never addressed to isolated objects and always depend upon a large number of external conditions. An ant placed on a stick allows itself to fall on a white paper marked with a black circle only if the sheet of paper is of definite dimensions, if the distance from the ground and the inclination of the stick have a definite value, and finally if there is a definite intensity and direction of the lighting. This complex of conditions corresponds to natural situations which release the "instinctive" acts of the animal. The training which can be achieved with the starfish scarcely goes beyond the framework of the situations in which the animal finds itself in its natural life. Even when learning is possible, it does not take into account the details of the experimental apparatus; it is a global response addressed to vital situations which are somewhat analogous. If one attempts to establish conditioned reflexes in a toad, one realizes that the responses of the animal depend on the resemblance which can exist between the experimental situations and those for which it possesses instinctual equipment much more than on the associations and disassociations achieved by the experimenter. If an earthworm is placed in front of a toad but separated from it by a glass, the animal perseveres in its attempts at prehension in spite of the failures which ought to be inhibiting because, in natural life, the instinctual equipment prescribes repeated attempts when confronted with a mobile objective. On the other hand, if an ant which tastes bad is presented to the animal, this unique experience is sufficient to provoke an inhibition with regard to all other ants because, in the natural condition, the instinctual equipment assures a general halting of positive reactions with regard to all the ants of an anthill when a sample has given rise to reactions of disgust. Finally, if the animal is presented with a little piece of black paper which is dangled at the end of a thin wire and which it succeeds in nabbing, this "deceptive" experience does give rise to an inhibition but one which ceases at the end of a few minutes; thus we can presume that it depends less on the gustative properties of the paper than on the instinctual rhythm which, in natural life, orders the animal to undertake new attempts at prehension only if it has not succeeded in nabbing the bait. Thus it is never to the experimental stimulus that the frog reacts; the stimulus is reflexogenic only to the extent that it resembles one of the dimensionally limited objects of a natural activity; and the reactions which the stimulus evokes are determined, not by the physical particularities of the present situation, but by the biological laws of behavior.[153] If one wishes to give a precise meaning to words, behavior of this kind, which responds literally to a complex of stimuli rather than to certain essential traits of the situation, should be called instinctive. The kinds of behavior which are ordinarily called instinctive imply structures which are much less "adherent" than those we just described. Thus, it is often difficult to distinguish them from "intelligent" behavior.

THE AMOVABLE FORMS

Behavior of the preceding category certainly does include a reference to relations. But they remain involved in the matter of certain concrete situations and this is why they are not available for true learning. As soon as we observe, in the history of behavior, the appearance of *signals* which are not determined by the instinctual equipment of the species, we can presume that they are founded on structures which are relatively independent of the materials in which they are realized.

In signal behavior, the "situation" to which the organism adapts is the simple temporal or spatial contiguity of a conditioned and an unconditioned stimulus. But, as we indicated above and must now show, signal learning is not a simple transfer of this *de facto* contiguity into behavior. It must become a contiguity "for the organism." If spatial contiguity is involved, the unconditioned stimulus is not linked to the conditioned stimulus which is the object of the training, but to a structure of the ensemble of which it is only a moment and from which it derives its meaning: this is what is shown by Koehler's well-known experiments.[154] If one accustoms a domestic chicken to choose, between two equal piles of grain, the one which is signaled by a light gray (G 1) and to leave aside the one which is signaled by a medium gray (G 2) and if, in the critical experiment (that is, after from four to six hundred training experiences), one eliminates G 2 and introduces a new gray (G °) which is lighter than G 1, the subject, faced with a reflexogenic color and a neutral color should, it would seem, choose the first. In fact, four subjects submitted to this training chose the new neutral color 59 times while the positive color was chosen only 26 times. A counter-proof is obtained by conserving in the critical experiment, not the positive color, but the color to which an inhibition should have been acquired (G 2) and by presenting it with a new gray darker than it. The negative color is chosen. Thus the reflexogenic power is not bound up with a certain nuance of gray but "to the lighter" of the two. Correlatively, the acquired motor reaction is not a sum of individual movements. During the course of the experiment care is taken to exchange the relative positions of the lightest and darkest gray in order to avoid any interference of an adaptation to the right and left with the differential reaction to the colors. Thus the motor responses involve widely variable bundles of muscles and nerves. It is an afferent structure which releases and regulates a motor structure. Thus, the relation of the conditioned stimulus to the conditioned response is a relation between relations. The training does not transpose a *de facto* contiguity into behavior. The signal is a configuration (Sign-Gestalt).

Tolman[155] comes to the same conclusion concerning temporal contiguity. The white curtain which indicates the "good path" at the end of which the animal will find its food would not derive its reflexogenic power from the simple fact that it was always presented to the animal before each favorable experience; it would owe it to the fact that, along with the favorable result, it constitutes a configuration. Tolman seeks to prove this by establishing that the reflexogenic power of the curtain disappears if the animal receives an electric shock when placed directly at the end of the path. The inhibiting value acquired by the end of the path would rebound on the entrance, which would presuppose some internal relation between them. All the same, this counter-result has not been observed by Tolman himself, who worked with tired animals, it is true. And the strict behaviorists[156] add that, even if it is produced, it can be explained in terms of conditioned reflexes. The electric shock does as a matter of fact cause the white curtain to lose its value as a positive stimulus only when the rat, at the moment that it received the shock, was beginning the prehension and mastication reactions themselves which take place in the presence of the goal. If it is shocked at the moment it is executing reactions to the goal (reactions in water) different from those which ordinarily take place in the experimental apparatus (reaction to the food), the influence of the shock on the reflexogenic power of the white curtain is weak (the rat still enters the path marked by a white curtain but he goes through it more slowly). This influence is the more sensitive as the two goals are more similar.[157] The counter-result of the electric shock could then be explained without having recourse to a configuration-signal. It is a general law of the conditioned reflex that the acquired reaction tends to be anticipated by the stimuli which precede the conditioned stimulus itself. Animals, trained to enter a food box in which they should turn toward the right, take and follow the right side of the alley from the moment of their entry into the labyrinth. Likewise, the rat anticipates reactions to the goal at the entrance of Tolman's apparatus. Since these latter have become inhibiting as an effect of the electric shock, the animal will not enter the path which it followed before. Thus it is the reactions to the goal and not the structure of the situation which would serve as a vehicle for the acquired inhibition and would cause it to intervene from the moment of entry into the experimental box. To which one could reply, as has already been said, that the attitudes of the rat when it refuses to enter the path marked by the white curtain are not identical with the behavior which was initiated by the electric shock and that likewise the movements necessary for following the right side of the path are materially different from those which the rat will execute in the presence of the turn. The reflex is not *anticipated;* it is *prepared* and *pre-formed.* Thus the phenomenon cannot be accounted for by saying that the same movements have been transferred from one stimulus to another prior stimulus. Rather it should be said that the latter initiates movements which have a meaningful relation to the change of sign of the final stimulus. This retroactive action, which is not a simple displacement in time, would in the final analysis be favorable to the notion of "Sign-Gestalt." The activity of the organism would be literally comparable to a kinetic melody since any change in the end of the melody qualitatively modifies its beginning and the physiognomy of the whole. It is in the same manner that the closing of an alley in a labyrinth immediately confers a negative value, not only on the entrance to this alley, but on that of a second alley which, after a detour, falls on this side of the barrier; and this is so even if the animal has not just gone through it. The failure has the effect of changing the sign of all the stimuli which have a determined structural relation to the place where it took place.[158]

Although, taken in itself, the relation of the signal and that which it "announces" is simple (it is encountered in otherwise slightly differentiated behavior), all degrees of complexity are observed in the structure of signals; and the nature of the signals to which a species responds can serve

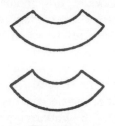

Figure 1

as a measure of its "intelligence." Domestic chickens, accustomed to choosing the smaller of two figures, treat as smaller that one of Jastrow's equal figures which appears smaller in human perception because of its position (Figure 1).[159] Even if it could be said that the contrast between two grays is contained in the colors as physical stimuli, here at least the differential behavior could not be elicited by the physical stimuli since objectively the two figures are equal. On the other hand, it is difficult to see what equipment, what empirical connections would explain it. Nothing would be gained by saying that the convex part of the lower segment is rendered different from the corresponding part of the upper segment by the nearness of a concavity: this would be precisely to recognize that the adequate stimulus is not found in the objects nor in the objective relations of the physical world, but in another universe where local properties depend on ensembles. A counter-test is possible: an animal trained to choose a black object will respond positively even when the object is presented under conditions of extreme illumination in which it reflects a thousand times more light than the objects employed during training. If we restrict ourselves to the physical phenomenon, to the light effectively received by the eye of the animal, the constancy of its behavior is even less intelligible since, under other conditions, a difference of two percent in the stimulation will be sufficient to suspend the acquired reactions.[160] But the power of adapting to the structure of signals rather than to their material properties is not without limit in animals. If eight similar boxes are placed in front of a child at increasing distances from him and if, without his seeing it, a piece of chocolate is placed in turn in the first, then in the second, then in the third, etc., from the second trial on the child will systematically look for the goal, not in the box where he just found it, but in the next one. The lower monkeys fail.[161] Perhaps they could be[162] trained to visit each of the boxes in turn. But this is not the proper object of our experiment, since a training of this kind could consist in creating inhibitions with respect to each box just visited. It would not exclude the hypothesis of an individual action of each of these stimuli, the sign of which would be reversed only as the experiment unfolds; or again the possibility that each of the boxes visited would act—for example, as a positive stimulus, then as inhibiting—in terms of the relations of position which exist between them and all the others and its place in the sequence of executed operations. There would not be progress throughout a series, but the *same* monotonous operation begun again with respect to each one —a concrete reaction which depends only on an isolated and individual stimulus, or an abstract reaction which treats them all in the same manner because of the real parts which they have in common: in either case the training would not be a reaction to *order*. On the contrary, in the child, who has learned the appropriate movement from the second trial on, the generality of the reaction can result neither from an addition of particular reflexes nor from organic equipment which would abstract from each stimulus that which makes it identical to the preceding ones. The first interpretation would be possible only if the entire series of boxes had been run through at least once; the second, only if a sufficient number of experiences had, by an interplay of appropriate inhibitions, permitted disengaging the positive reaction from the ties which it can have with the particular characteristics of each box in order to make it depend on their common characteristics. And still it would not permit us to understand how the boxes are visited in the order of their increasing distances. Indeed, it is this order which must be explained above all. The adequate stimulus of this reaction consists in a constant relation which unites the next stimulus and the preceding one, the box to be visited and the box visited, which relation we express by saying that it is necessary "to always take the next one." This relation is invariable in itself; but its point of application is different in each new trial and it would be useless without it. This is to say that the adequate stimulus is defined by a double reference to the spatial order on the one hand, and the order of executed operations on the other. A reaction to these two relations is not abstract since they take on a singular value in each case; nor is it a reaction to that which is individual in each box since it is the order of the ensemble which confers on each one its value as a positive stimulus. The success of the child and the failure of the monkey in this experiment manifests the aptitude in the first and the inability in the second of a disengagement from the elementary structure (which confers a positive reflexogenic value on the place where the goal was attained) in order to be open to more complex structures in which the reflexogenic value is distributed *in terms* of space and time.

Thus the objective description of behavior uncovers in it a more or less articulated structure, a more or less rich interior signification and reference to "situations" which are sometimes individual, sometimes abstract and sometimes essential.

The same variety would be noticed if we were to consider modes of behavior—in themselves more "difficult" and more "integrated" than elementary signal behavior—in which the conditioned stimulus and the unconditioned stimulus, instead of being simply contiguous, present a relation which we would call logical or objective. From then on, the conditioned stimulus gives rise to special reactions which are more and more clearly distinguished from reactions to the goal. In human language, one can say that it becomes the *means* to a certain *end*.

A first example of behavior of this kind is furnished by cases in which a stimulus becomes reflexogenic as a direct result of its *spatial or temporal relations* with the goal. If a dog is placed in front of a trellis with only two openings and if, behind the trellis and at the level of the first opening, one arranges a mobile goal which moves along the trellis toward the second opening, the dog always runs toward the spot where the goal was initially placed on the first trials. In the course of later experiments, it follows the goal in its movements along the trellis and grasps it at the moment when it reaches the level of the second opening. Finally the dog will go directly toward the second opening, where it will precede and wait for the goal.[163] If it were accepted that the second opening of the trellis has become the conditioned stimulus of the animal's reactions, this stimulus would not be able to overcome the action of the unconditioned stimulus which is in competition with it, since it borrows all its power from the latter, and one would not explain why the dog leaves its bait in order to go and wait for it at a point where it is not yet. Thus the goal must cease to be defined by the stimulations which it exercises here and now on the animal and be integrated into the spatial and temporal structures which mediate it, which bind together its present position, the opening of the trellis and the point where the dog is stationed. We can see a substitution of this kind in another of Buytendijk's experiments. Buytendijk asked himself what the behavior of a rat would be if it had to choose between a path which goes in the direction of a goal at the beginning (Tolman's experiments had shown that, with equal distance, this path is preferred), and a second path which deviates from it at first but is found to be the shorter.[164] The experiment shows that the simple structure—direction of the goal–direction of the path—can, in the rat, be displaced by a more complex structure in which the length of the path enters in (Figure 2). Six rats introduced into the apparatus first try to reach the goal directly and are stopped by the glass barrier G, then take path AEDZ of their own accord. When they have completed the course they are conducted by the shorter path ABCZ.

A first crucial experiment is then instituted. The animals are put at A and left free. Five of them take the longer path, the initial elements of which are in the direction of the goal; the sixth starts along this way, then retraces its steps and takes the path ABCZ. But if the animals are put back at point

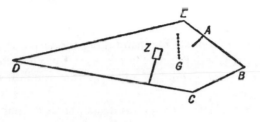

Figure 2

A several times, by the end of the first day (five trials) two of the four remaining rats choose the shorter path; the second day, on the sixth trial, the two others also choose it. In order to eliminate the influence of habit, the animal is conducted along the longer path after each correct choice; in order to establish that it is not a question of a conditioned reaction to the right and left, the animals are placed in a new apparatus which is a mirror-image of the preceding one. These precautions do not change the result which remains in favor of the shorter path. Will it be contended that the "path which goes in the direction of the goal" has become inhibiting as a consequence of the first trials? But it has never given rise to a failure. At the very most, it could be said that it leads to the goal less quickly. Is this circumstance sufficient for creating an inhibition? If one accepts this, one recognizes that the conditioned stimulus is not a real element of the physical world but a relation, a temporal structure.[165] And we shall see that in reality the intervention of spatial structures as such is much more probable.

For other experiments show that spatial structures are much more precise than temporal structures in the behavior of the rat. If one uses a labyrinth in which movable partitions permit varying the path which the animal must traverse in order to gain the exit, and if the open path sometimes involves two turns to the left, sometimes two turns to the right, the animal can be trained, in two series of experiments, to traverse each of these two paths without false movement. But the alternation of these two patterns of behavior, which we will indicate by the symbols *ll rr ll rr,* is not successfully obtained. If the animal is now placed in a longer labyrinth which requires the same alternation from the entrance to the exit, the training succeeds.[166] Since care was taken to eliminate every other factor, the difference in behavior can only be the result of the difference in structures which, in the first case, are ordered with relation to time, in the second case, with relation to space. The same sequences of movement are possible or impossible depending on whether they are developed along an open space or whether they only succeed one another in time. What is achievable in the unity of an action which is continuous through space is no longer achievable if it is a question of several cycles of movements connected in time. The living body does not organize time and space indifferently; the one is not available to it in the same way as the other. Nothing is more appropriate for manifesting the insufficiency of Pavlov's views. The spatial labyrinth and the temporal labyrinth are indiscernible from his point of view; and one could say that for him there are only temporal labyrinths.

But at the same time these experiments put us on our guard against another error which is symmetrical with and the inverse of Pavlov's. The terms "space" and "time" should not be taken here in their human meaning, according to which relations of time can be symbolized by relations of space. This spatio-temporal correspondence does not exist for animal behavior; and space is, as it were, a more solid and more manipulable structure than time. One would find something analogous in man at the properly perceptual level in which the dimensions of space and time interfere. The privilege of space in animals and the presence of a sort of space-time in perceptual behavior presents the same difficulty to the philosopher. In both cases it is a question of explicitating modes of behavior or experience which present themselves as original, without deforming them by an intellectualist interpretation. The temporal relations which play a role in animal behavior manifest "adhesions" and something like a viscosity of which it is difficult for us to conceive on the basis of pure and manipulable concepts of space and time.

The relations of means to end can still be *subtended* by *mechanical and static structures*. They represent a higher degree of integration, since they seem to play no role in the behavior of dogs which, as we have just seen, adapt themselves to relations of space. If a piece of meat is placed on a box with one end of a string tied around the meat and the other end hanging to the ground, dogs do not learn to pull the morsel of meat toward them as long as they limit themselves to "looking"; they must make it fall fortuitously by playing with the string.[167] A dog observed by Koehler, one which in other experiments had shown itself to be very "intelligent," multiplied reactions to the goal but tried nothing with the string which was placed in front of it.[168] Cats acquire an adapted behavior only if the string is rubbed with a piece of fish.[169] On the other hand, lower monkeys[170] and even more so chimpanzees, seem capable of adapted reactions to mechanical and static relations as such. There is no point in describing the well-known experiment in the course of which one of Koehler's chimpanzees adapted a bamboo stick of small diameter to one of larger diameter and used the instrument to reach a goal which was not directly accessible. We would only like to insist upon the role which could have been played by the fortuitous position of the bamboo sticks in the hands of the animal in the moment which preceded his discovery. It can be established that it was the favorable occasion, perhaps even the necessary occasion, but not the cause of the learning. If, as a matter of fact,[171] one makes use of four tubes of increasing diameters, with the difference from one to the other being constant, and presents the three possible pairs one after the other to the animal in such a way that the same tube is in one case the larger and in another the smaller of the two, one observes that the reaction of the animal is not acquired with respect to each tube considered individually. In fact, from the first manipulations of this kind on, it was observed that it is always the thinner of the two rods which is pushed toward the other and, consequently, that the animal always grasps it in the right hand, which is more adroit, the other rod being held passively in the left hand. But, during the course of the second series of experiments which we are describing—whether the thinner or the thicker tube was closer—in eight cases out of twelve the monkey grasped the thicker tube with the left hand and the thinner one with the right. In four other trials the animal re-established the normal distribution of the tubes as soon as it had them in hand, without any groping and even before trying to bring them together. Thus the assembling reaction is in no way tied to the absolute properties of each one of the tubes; it is regulated at each moment by the relation of their diameters. Since it is this relation which the animal has learned to take into consideration, one must therefore suppose that it played a decisive role as such in the course of the initial experiment.

But it is rather generally accepted that the behavior of chimpanzees goes beyond the level of the conditioned reflex adapted to individual stimuli. For us it is of more value to note the lacunae and the insufficiency of mechanical and static relations. There is something artificial in the descriptions of behavior which we have given up to now: by soliciting reactions to geometric and physical relations from the animal, one gives the impression that they are the natural framework of his behavior just as, for man, they are constitutive of the world. In reality, before they find access to animal behavior, other more natural structures have to be broken up; they emerge from ensembles which are difficult to disassociate. Let us recall Koehler's experiment in which a chimpanzee which has already utilized the rods is left alone in its cage in the presence of an inaccessible goal and a dried bush from which the branches can easily be cut. The results are very unequal with different subjects; and, in any case, a solution never comes about except after a long phase of inactivity. The tree branch as a stimulus is not then the equivalent of a rod, and the spatial and mechanical properties which permit it to assume this function are not immediately accessible to animal behavior. One of Koehler's subjects, which had nevertheless learned to manipulate cases in preceding experiments, does not use one which is offered it as long as another monkey is sitting on it. It leans against it; thus it cannot be said that it has not seen it; but it remains for him a means of support or rest; it cannot become an instrument.[172] Thus mechanical structures can become reflexogenic only if stronger structures which assign a useful value to objects are first reorganized. The constant error of empiricist and intellectualist psychologists is to reason as if a tree branch, since, as a physical reality, it has in itself the properties of length, breadth, and rigidity which will make it usable as a rod, also possesses these characteristics as a stimulus, and so much so that their intervention in behavior would follow automatically. What is not seen is that the field of animal activity is not *made up of* physico-geometric relations, as our world is.[173] These relations are not virtually present in the stimuli and it is not a simple abstraction which makes them appear in the regulation of behavior. They presuppose a positive and novel "structuration" of the situation. It should not be astonishing, then, if the physico-geometric relations which are scarcely disengaged from stronger biological connections are readily overlaid by the latter or even if they never appear in a pure state. In lower monkeys a rod or a rake is employed as an instrument only if it is arranged ahead of time in an appropriate way,[174] if, for example, the rake is already placed behind the fruit and its handle within reach of the hand. Something analogous is noted in less intelligent chimpanzees which, in the first experiments at least, employ the rod only if it is in "optical contact" with the goal, that is, if the goal and the rod can be encompassed in a single glance.[175] The instrumental value of an object decreases to the extent that it is more removed from the goal, which is to say that it is not made up of precise mechanical properties which would be independent of its position. Even when the chimpanzee succeeds in extending its field of action in time as well as space, as when it goes toward a final goal while passing by several intermediate ones, it often happens that the principal goal which is too close attracts to itself the operations which were addressed to the secondary goal. This "short circuit" phenomenon[176] shows that the chimpanzee does not succeed in developing, in an indifferent space and time, a mode of behavior regulated by the objective properties of the instrument, that it is always exposed to the solicitation of the near future or of the spatial proximity which contracts or dislocates the structure of the action. Even in the cases where the chimpanzee utilizes mechanical connections, it is probable that they do not influence its behavior by means of the properties which human perception ascribes to them. If chimpanzees are presented with several cords which all go toward a goal but only one of which is attached to the fruit, they grasp any one just as often as the others; their behavior is not governed by the mechanical relation of the cord to the goal; it depends much more on the length of the cords presented, the shorter being most frequently chosen.[177] This is probably why the chimpanzee fails as soon as the mechanical relations which *de facto* exist become complicated, since they can no longer be translated into the imperfect equivalents possessed by animal behavior; the chimpanzee can neither untie a knot nor separate a ring from a nail on which it is hung.[178] Thus a sort of animal physics immanent in behavior could be described, but its originality could only be understood by a psychology and a philosophy capable of making a place for the indeterminant as such, capable of comprehending that a mode of behavior or an experience can have a "vague" and "open" signification without being empty of signification. A young chimpanzee, in the presence of fruit hanging from the ceiling and a box placed in its cage, begins by jumping toward the goal in order to attain it directly; then its eye falls on the box; "it approached it, looked straight toward the objective, and gave the box a slight push, which did not, however, move it . . . it lifted the box, took a few paces away from it, but at once returned, and pushed it again and again with its eye on the objective, but quite gently, and not as though it really intended to alter its position." [179] A few moments later the solution will be "found." One could say that the box "had something to do" with the problem but that the function has not yet been made precise. Will it ever be completely? The verbal behavior of man furnishes an analogy. In Ruger's puzzle experiment, when a subject succeeds accidentally in separating two pieces, "the region in which the work is being done, or the particular kind of movement that is being made, is now emphasized, and becomes the focus of the whole procedure. In a large number of cases the solution, therefore, is almost entirely a matter of 'locus' or 'place-analysis'." [180] But the manner in which such a local intervention will produce the expected effect does not enter into the reaction. Again, one can think of the situations which set in motion the reaction of the player in a game of tennis: we would express this situation in a later analysis by saying that the direction of the ball, the angle which the trajectory makes with the court, the rotation with which the ball can be animated, the position of the adversaries and the dimensions of the court all contribute in regulating the strength and direction of the response, the manner in which the ball will be hit in return. But it is clear that the situation at the moment of the hit itself is not articulated so completely, even though with a good player all these determinations enter in. An analogous problem is posed by the description of the behavior of chimpanzees with regard to mechanical relations which must be poorly distinguished in them from "visual context" and must belong to an original category comparable to those of the physics of children[181] or to the "participation" of primitives. The same can be said concerning static relations which are very lacunar in chimpanzees. One of Koehler's subjects, in order to balance a ladder, places one of the sides against the wall.[182] The static characteristics of the situation enter in by way of interoceptivity rather than by the intermediary of the visual receptors. A chimpanzee treats a box as if it were in a state of equilibrium when it does not wobble at all, even if that equilibrium is very unstable, and on the other hand recommences his whole construction if the box, firmly set on its base, is nevertheless not absolutely immobile. Once the construction has been made "every movement or every suspicious inclination is admirably counteracted by a displacement of the center of gravity of the body, a raising of the arms or a bending of the trunk so that the boxes themselves under the animal obey, to a certain extent, the statics of its labyrinth and cerebellum." [183] "Structures grow under its hands, and often enough it can climb them, but they are structures which, according to the rules of statics, seem to us almost impossible. For all the structures which *we* know (and are familiar with optically) are achieved by monkeys by chance at best and, as it were, by a 'struggle for not wobbling'." [184]

If we say now that the chimpanzee is "intelligent," do we not risk forgetting the original characteristics of the physico-geometric relations in its behavior and confusing them with the "objective" geometry and physics of man? Doubtless, definitions are free and the one which Koehler gives of intelligence seems appropriate to the chimpanzee. Koehler takes as criterion: "the appearance of a complete solution without reference to the whole layout of the field" [185] and the appearance of behavior, the constituent parts of which "taken separately are meaningless in relation to the task, but which become significant again, when they are considered as part of the whole." [186] But the structure of the field can be more or less articulated, that of behavior more or less complex. And also is there only a difference of degree between the static and mechanical structures of the chimpanzee and those of human behavior? Is the insufficiency of the static relations in the chimpanzee only a "visual infirmity," following Koehler's expression, that is, in brief, a deficit comparable to blindness? Or is it not rather, inasmuch as these relations presuppose a superior mode of structuration, that they are inaccessible to the chimpanzee? And is it not to this mode of organization that the term "intelligence" ought to be reserved?

We have seen that the box-as-seat and the box-as-instrument are two distinct and alternative objects in the behavior of the chimpanzee and not two *aspects* of an identical *thing*. In other words, the animal cannot at each moment adopt a point of view with regard to objects which is chosen at its discretion; rather the object appears clothed with a "vector," invested with a "functional value" which depends on the effective composition of the field. For us, this is the principle of the insufficiencies that are noticed in the chimpanzee's behavior. We would like to establish this principle by means of two examples: that of the detour with objects, and that of static relations. The chimpanzees, who are presented with the task of obtaining a piece of fruit separated from them by the vertical sides of a box and who must push the food away from them toward the open edge of the box in order to succeed, can all make detours such as going outside to look for a piece of fruit that has been thrown through the window. Thus it is clear that executing a detour and arranging that one be made at the goal constitute two different and unequally difficult tasks for the animal organism. The spatial relations in the two cases must present some difference of nature. They are accessible to animal behavior only in one direction, that is when their pattern consists in a movement of the organism toward the goal; the goal is the fixed point, the organism the mobile point, and they cannot exchange their functions. The organism is not an object among objects, it possesses a privilege. What is it that prevents exteroceptive structures from acquiring the same plasticity which is found in proprioceptive structures? The analogy of human behavior in certain cases of agnosia and in fatigue furnishes an example. It is easier to go through a complicated itinerary than to explain it to someone, and often in the course of the explanation we make use of a motor mimic without which we would not be able to go through the route mentally, especially if we are tired. We have encountered this same recourse to motor attitudes in Gelb and Goldstein's patient.[187] It is not sufficient to say that we appeal to "kinesthetic data" in order to make up for the faltering "visual data." One would have to know precisely why they are faltering. Moreover, the motor attitudes are not *substituted* for the visual data. As a matter of fact, the gestures of orientation have a meaning in this case only in relation to some visual representation of the route which we form for ourselves. What the motor attitude contributes is not the content, but rather the power of organizing the visual spectacle, of tracing the relations which we need between the points of represented space. The alleged recourse to tactile data is in reality a recourse to lived space, in opposition to the virtual space in which our indications were situated at first. By the gestures which we sketch we make the principal directions of the virtual field in which our description is unfolding coincide momentarily with the strong structures—right and left, high and low—of our own body. The difficulty of a pure description of the itinerary is of the same order as that of reading a map or of orienting oneself on a plan; and it is known that a plan is practically unusable precisely in certain cases of agnosia. The purely visual sketch demands that we represent the itinerary for ourselves from a bird's-eye view, from a point of view which has never been ours when we traversed it; it demands that we be capable of transcribing a kinetic melody into a visual diagram, of establishing relations of reciprocal correspondence and mutual expression between them. In the same manner, arranging that a detour to an object *be made* is to trace by our very gesture the symbol of the movement which we would have to make if we were in its place; it is to establish a relation between relations; it is a structure or an intention of the second power. What is lacking in the chimpanzee is the capacity of creating relations between visual stimuli (and between the motor excitations which they elicit) which express and symbolize its most familiar kinetic melodies. The animal cannot put itself in the place of the movable thing and see itself as the goal. It cannot vary the points of view, just as it cannot recognize something in different perspectives as the same *thing*. But perhaps it will be said that we are presupposing a privilege of actuality in favor of the proprioceptive stimulations; it is only on this condition that the movements which ought to be imprinted on the object have need of a translation into proprioceptive language and that symbolic behavior is required. Why is the detour of the object not just as actual as the detour of the body proper? This is because, in animal behavior, the external object is not a thing in a sense that the body itself is—that is, a concrete unity capable of entering into a multiplicity of relations without losing itself. As a matter of fact, we do come up against the privilege of the body proper and it can only be a question of defining it correctly. What is really lacking in the animal is the symbolic behavior which it would have to possess in order to find an invariant in the external object, under the diversity of its aspects, comparable to the immediately given invariant of the body proper and in order to treat, reciprocally, its own body as an object among objects. In the same manner the monkey, which knows how to balance itself so well, that is, to re-establish the vertical position of its body by appropriate movements, does not succeed in balancing its construction. This is because the balancing of an object demands the establishment of a one-to-one correspondence between certain spatial relations of visual stimuli and certain interoceptive stimuli as representative of each other. But this solution, it will be said, presupposes what is to be explained: why do visual stimuli need to be related to interoceptive stimuli in order to be qualified according to the "high" and the "low," the "vertical" and the "oblique"? And how does it happen that their proper structures do not admit of these dimensions? Koehler indicates somewhere that chimpanzees never construct bridges and that, when a bridge is presented to them, one sees them get onto it, pull one of the arches, and give "signs of fright" when the whole thing collapses. "All other experiments," Koehler adds, "in which in principle the simultaneous intervention of *two* forces plays a role have failed as this one did." [188] Should not the failure of the animal when it is a matter of moving a piece of fruit away in order subsequently to bring it nearer, or its failure in relating two perpendicular components (as happens in the test with the ring and the nail,[189] and in that of the knot or of the cord wrapped around a beam)[190] be related to these experiments? And is not the same explanation still valid for the "maladdress" of the animal in the construction trials? For here again it is a question of establishing a correlation between two distinct forces, of simultaneously satisfying two conditions: the proper cohesion of the scaffolding and the orientation of the whole with respect to the vertical. The same difficulty is not found in the balancing of the body proper in which case the "scaffolding" is already constructed. Thus it is not properly an "optical weakness"[191] which is involved, or rather the visual infirmity is itself a result: the insufficiency of visual statics comes from the fact that, in the domain of external objects to which vision is related, equilibrium is obtained by the combining of two independent forces. Thus it is a question of treating two things as one, two forces as the analytic expression of a resultant which has no element in common with them. The visual infirmity only expresses the insufficiency of the relations of reciprocal expression, of symbolic behavior, or again of the "thing structure."[192] Vision is imperfect only because it is the sense modality of the virtual. And, indeed, in the detour experiments with objects, each time a chance movement of the goal anticipates the solution, the chimpanzee profits from this indication: this is because the chance movement has transposed the problem from virtual space, where it ought to be resolved by possible operations, into actual space, where it begins to be effectively resolved.[193] It is always the same behavioral incapacity to treat the whole field as a field of things, to multiply the relations in which a stimulus can be involved, and to treat all of them as different properties of the same thing which is in question.

Koehler indicates that the visual structures of the high and the low as well as the vertical and horizontal coordinates are coupled with the upright position. In fact, the child does not acquire them before standing up, and in chimpanzees, who do not possess them, the upright position never becomes a natural attitude.[194] The considerable development of the cerebellum and the labyrinth in the chimpanzee evidently corresponds to these two traits of its behavior. But what exactly is the relation between these three facts? It is indeed, if you wish, *because* of the visual infirmity and of the privilege of proprioceptivity that the upright position remains an exceptional attitude. However, it would be contrary to the spirit of Gestalt theory to *explain* the mode of locomotion of the monkey by the development of the labyrinth and cerebellum. If one recalls how Koehler conceived the relations of anatomy and physiology,[195] it will be necessary to say that this anatomical peculiarity itself is not separable in the genesis of a mode of total functioning of the organism to which it contributes. It is clear that the same reasoning is valid concerning the *visual infirmity* of the chimpanzee. The three concordant facts which we are recalling are not three events external to each other; all three have the same meaning; all three express a single structure of organic function, a single style of existence; they are three manifestations of a behavior adapted to the immediate and not to the virtual, to functional values and not to things. According to the very principles of Gestalt theory, this behavior must be *understood* in its immanent law, not *explained* by a plurality of separated causes; and the insufficiency of the static structures in monkeys should not be presented as a "visual infirmity." This is to give the impression that a deficiency is possible which does not have its reason in the global structure of behavior; it is to return to the old psychology of contents.[196] Beyond the "amovable" forms which are at the disposal of the chimpanzee, a level of original conduct must be accepted in which structures are still more disengaged—transposable from one meaning to another. This is symbolic behavior in which the thing-structure becomes possible.

THE SYMBOLIC FORMS

In animal behavior signs always remain signals and never become symbols. A dog which is trained to jump up on one chair on command, then to pass from it onto a second chair, will never use—lacking a chair—two stools or a stool and an armchair which are presented to him.[197] The vocal sign does not mediate any reaction to the general signification of the stimuli. This latter use of the sign demands that it cease to be an event or a presage (even more so a "conditioned excitant") and become the proper theme of an activity which tends to *express* it. An activity of this kind is already found in the acquisition of certain motor habits such as the aptitude to play an instrument or to type.[198] It is known that the connection between such and such a visual stimulus (a note, a letter) and such and such a partial movement (toward this or that note on the keyboard) is not essential to the habit; it may happen that trained subjects are incapable of designating separately on the keyboard the key which corresponds to such and such a note or to such and such a letter.[199] The keys are aimed at in behavior only as the transition points of certain motor ensembles corresponding to words or to musical phrases. The habit does not even consist in establishing determined kinetic melodies corresponding to known visual ensembles. A subject who "knows" how to type or to play the organ is capable of improvising, that is, of executing kinetic melodies corresponding to words which have never been seen or music which has never been played. One would be tempted to suppose that at least certain elements of the new musical phrase or of the new words correspond to rigid and already acquired sets. But expert subjects are capable of improvising on instruments unknown to them and the exploration of the instruments, which is evidently a preliminary necessity, is too brief to permit a substitution of individual sets.

The new correlation of visual stimuli and motor excitations must be mediated by a general principle so as to make immediately possible the execution, not of determined phrases or pieces, but of an improvised piece if necessary. And as a matter of fact the organist does not inspect the organ part by part;[200] in the space where his hands and feet will play he "recognizes" sectors, direction markings, and curves of movement which correspond, not to ensembles of definite notes, but to expressive values. The adjustment of motor excitations to visual excitations is accomplished by their common participation in certain musical essences. Doubtless the correspondence of such and such a musical sign, of such and such a gesture by the player, and of such and such a sound is conventional: several systems of musical notation are possible as are several dispositions of the keyboards. But these three ensembles—between which there exist, term for term, only chance correspondences—considered as wholes communicate internally. The character of the melody, the graphic configuration of the musical text and the unfolding of the gestures participate in a single structure, have in common a single nucleus of signification. The relation of the expression to the expressed, which is one of simple juxtaposition in the parts, is internal and necessary in the wholes. The expressive value of each of the three ensembles with respect to the two others is not an effect of their frequent association: it is a reason for it. Musical notation would not be a language and the organ would not be an instrument if the manner in which one writes and in which one plays a note did not comprise a systematic principle and did not as a consequence include the manner in which one writes and in which one plays the other notes. The true sign represents the signified, not according to an empirical association, but inasmuch as its relation to other signs is the same as the relation of the object signified by it to other objects. It is because of this that we can decipher unknown languages.

If all musical texts were lost with the exception of one page concerning which one did not even know that it represented music, it would be noticed that the signs on the page can be distinguished by their position on the staff, by adjoining secondary signs (those which distinguish a white from a black) and by their variable groupings within certain units of space (measures); the internal analysis of the text would determine the external contours and the principal dimensions of the universe which is expressed in it. If by chance another universe than the universe of sound possesses the same characteristics of structure, the text remains ambiguous. But this ambiguity does not prove that the relation of signs to the signified is contingent: on the contrary, it is due to the fact that two possible significations have the same structural properties in common. There must be a structural correspondence between the motor ensembles necessary for playing a piece on two different organs, just as the equations of a physical theory can be expressed in the language of another theory. This structure of structures which, abstracting from the rhythms (they obviously remain the same for the same piece on all instruments), establishes an intrinsic relation between movements which are not superimposable is the musical significance of the piece. Thus genuine *aptitudes* demand that the "stimulus" become efficacious by its internal properties of structure, by its immanent signification; and they demand that the response symbolize along with the stimulus. It is this possibility of varied expressions of a same theme, this "multiplicity of perspective," which is lacking in animal behavior. It is this which introduces a cognitive conduct and a free conduct. In making possible all substitutions of points of view, it liberates the "stimuli" from the here-and-now relations in which my own point of view involves them and from the functional values which the needs of the species, defined once and for all, assign to them. The sensory-motor *a prioris* of instinct bind behavior to individual stimulus-wholes and to monotonous kinetic melodies. In the behavior of the chimpanzee, the themes, if not the means, remained fixed by the *a priori* of the species.[201] With symbolic forms, a conduct appears, which expresses the stimulus for itself, which is open to truth and to the proper value of things, which tends to the adequation of the signifying and signified, of the intention and that which it intends. Here behavior no longer *has* only one signification, it *is* itself signification.

The preceding descriptions permit us to situate the conditioned reflex in its true place. Since vital behavior is attached to syncretic wholes, and since it is only at the level of symbolic behavior that we encounter an activity regulated by objective stimuli such as those which are defined by physics, the conditioned reflex is either a pathological phenomenon or a higher mode of behavior. We have had occasion to call attention, in dogs submitted to conditioning experiments, to the appearance of eczema and even of genuine experimental neuroses. Pavlov speaks of a dog which after some time refused any new experience: "The longer the session was prolonged the more excited it became; it wanted to get loose, scratched the floor, gnawed the bench, etc. Dyspnoea and a continuous salivation resulted from this uninterrupted muscular work; the animal became completely unsuitable for our work." [202] Pavlov interprets this conduct as a "freedom reflex." But the word "reflex" has no meaning if it does not designate a specific reaction to certain determined excitants: the reaction in question, however, is an indeterminate refusal to respond to stimuli. The general inhibition which is presented to us is not constructed according to the mechanical laws of conditioning; it expresses a law of a new kind: the orientation of the organism toward modes of behavior which have a biological meaning, toward natural situations, that is, an *a priori* of the organism. Thus there is a norm inscribed in the facts themselves.

Inasmuch as it is a phenomenon of disintegration we will not be surprised to find the conditioned reflex more often and more easily "in children than in adults, in younger children than in older ones, and, at an equal age, in the retarded rather than in the normal." [203] But if the practice of reflex conditioning involves a pathological alteration, it is also because reacting to absolute stimuli is a difficult operation which the animal cannot execute for very long. We have seen that in the reactions of domestic chickens to colors, absolute choices were produced. [204] But the adaptation to an absolute chromatic value is not stable. [205] On the other hand, an adult man submitted to analogous experiments would hesitate on the principle of choice; only in the instance in which the three nuances of gray were very close would he choose according to the relations of one to the other. [206] In fact, one observes that reactions to absolute stimuli become more frequent as older children are tested.

Finally, it is known that, in general, conditioned reflexes are all the more perfect as the cerebral development of the species considered is more advanced.[207] We have said that trained subjects cannot designate letters separately on the keyboard of a machine. They succeed indirectly by cross-checking with a few of the motor structures which they are capable of executing and of which the same letters form a part. This operation of the second power, this reaction to reactions, presupposes the structures which it analyzes. We see how the reference to absolute stimuli can have two meanings: it represents either a pathological disassociation or a new type of organization which, without destroying the existing structures, disposes them according to different perspectives. It is clear that it is not the explanatory principle of behavior in its first meaning.

But it is no more so in the second meaning. At the same time that one delineates the originality of the higher structures, one establishes that they do not account for the others. At the same time that he was maintaining a psychological empiricism Pavlov was borrowing his postulates from intellectualism. Empiricism and intellectualism carry over into primitive modes of behavior structures which belong to a very high level: structure of pure juxtaposition—the atom—or structure of pure interiority—the relation. It will be maintained perhaps that, in refusing to construct behavior on the basis of these notions which are constitutive of what we understand by nature, in rejecting them as anthropomorphic, we are implicitly referring to some reality in-itself (*en soi*), to some *Grund* from which intelligence emerges and with relation to which it can be called superficial. But this same reality, it will be added, can neither be named nor conceptualized except by the intellect. We will have to distinguish intellect and intellectualism and perhaps to acknowledge the existence of significations which are not of the logical order.[208] Here, it can be only a question of a preliminary description which does not resolve the transcendental problems of "confused thought" but which contributes to posing them.

Conclusion

The preceding chapters teach us not only not to explain the higher by the lower, as they say, but also not to explain the lower by the higher. Traditionally, lower or mechanical reactions which, like physical events, are functions of antecedent conditions and thus unfold in objective time and space are distinguished from "higher" reactions which do not depend on stimuli, taken materially, but rather on the meaning of the situation, and which appear therefore to presuppose a "view" of this situation, a prospection, and to belong no longer to the order of the in-itself (*en soi*) but to the order of the for-itself (*pour soi*). Both of these orders are transparent for the mind: the first is transparent for the mode of thinking in physics and is like the external order in which events govern each other from the outside; the second is transparent for reflective consciousness and is like the internal order in which that which takes place always depends upon an intention. *Behavior,* inasmuch as it has a structure, is not situated in either of these two orders. It does not unfold in objective time and space like a series of physical events; each moment does not occupy one and only one point of time; rather, at the decisive moment of learning, a "now" stands out from the series of "nows," acquires a particular value and summarizes the groupings which have preceded it as it engages and anticipates the future of the behavior; this "now" transforms the singular situation of the experience into a typical situation and the effective reaction into an aptitude. From this moment on behavior is detached from the order of the in-itself (*en soi*) and becomes the projection outside the organism of a *possibility* which is internal to it. The world, inasmuch as it harbors living beings, ceases to be a material plenum consisting of juxtaposed parts; it opens up at the place where behavior appears.

Nothing would be served by saying that it is we, the spectators, who mentally unite the elements of the situation to which behavior is addressed in order to make them meaningful, that it is we who project into the exterior the intentions of our thinking, since we would still have to discover what it is, what kind of phenomenon is involved upon which this *Einfühlung* rests, what is the sign which invites us to anthropomorphism. Nor would anything be served by saying that behavior "is conscious" and that it reveals to us, as its other side, a being for-itself (*pour soi*) hidden behind the visible body. The gestures of behavior, the intentions which it traces in the space around the animal, are not directed to the true world or pure being, but to being-for-the-animal, that is, to a certain milieu characteristic of the species; they do not allow the showing through of a consciousness, that is, a being whose whole essence is to know, but rather a certain manner of treating the world, of "being-in-the-world" or of "existing." A consciousness, according to Hegel's expression, is a "penetration in being," and here we have nothing yet but an opening up. The chimpanzee, which physically can stand upright but in all urgent cases reassumes the animal posture, which can assemble boxes but gives them only a tactile equilibrium, in this way manifests a sort of adherence to the here and now, a short and heavy manner of existing. Gelb and Goldstein's patient, who no longer has the "intuition" of numbers, no longer "understands" analogies and no longer "perceives" simultaneous wholes, betrays a weakness, a lack of density and vital amplitude, of which the cognitive disorders are only the secondary expression. It is only at the level of symbolic conduct, and more exactly at the level of exchanged speech, that foreign existences (at the same time as our own, moreover) appear to us as ordered to the true world; it is only at this level that, instead of seeking to insinuate his stubborn norms, the subject of behavior "de-realizes himself" and becomes a genuine *alter ego*. And yet the constitution of the other person as another I is never completed since his utterance, even having become a pure phenomenon of expression, always and indivisibly remains expressive as much of himself as of the truth.

There is, then, no behavior which certifies a pure consciousness behind it, and the other person is never given to me as the exact equivalent of myself thinking. In this sense it is not only to animals that consciousness must be denied. The supposition of a *foreign consciousness* immediately reduces the world which is given to me to the status of a private spectacle; the world is broken up into a multiplicity of "representations of the world" and can no longer be anything but the meaning which they have in common, or the invariant of a system of monads. But in fact I am aware of perceiving the world as well as behavior which, caught in it, intends numerically one and the same world, which is to say that, in the experience of behavior, I effectively surpass the alternative of the for-itself (*pour soi*) and the in-itself (*en soi*). Behaviorism, solipsism, and "projective" theories all accept that behavior is given to me like something spread out in front of me. But to reject consciousness in animals in the sense of pure consciousness, the *cogitatio,* is not to make them automatons without interiority. The animal, to an extent which varies according to the integration of its behavior, is certainly *another existence;* this existence is perceived by everybody; we have described it; and it is a phenomenon which is independent of any notional theory concerning the soul of brutes. Spinoza would not have spent so much time considering a drowning fly if this behavior had not offered to the eye something other than a fragment of extension, the theory of animal machines is a "resistance" to the phenomenon of behavior. Therefore this phenomenon must still be conceptualized. The structure of behavior as it presents itself to perceptual experience is neither thing nor consciousness; and it is this which renders it opaque to the mind.

The object of the preceding chapters was not only to establish that behavior is irreducible to its alleged parts. If we had had nothing other in view, instead of this long inductive research—which can never even be finished, since behaviorism can always invent other mechanical models with regard to which the discussion will have to be recommenced—a moment of reflection would have provided us with a certitude in principle. Does not the *cogito* teach us once and for all that we would have no knowledge of any *thing* if we did not first have a knowledge of our thinking and that even the escape into the world and the resolution to ignore interiority or to never leave things, which is the essential feature of behaviorism, cannot be formulated without being transformed into consciousness and without presupposing existence for-itself (*pour soi*) ? Thus behavior is constituted of relations; that is, it is conceptualized and not in-itself (*en soi*), as is every other object moreover; this is what reflection would have shown us. But by following this short route we would have missed the essential feature of the phenomenon, the paradox which is constitutive of it: behavior is not a thing, but neither is it an idea. It is not the envelope of a pure consciousness and, as the witness of behavior, I am not a pure consciousness. It is precisely this which we wanted to say in stating that behavior is a form.

Thus, with the notion of "form," we have found the means of avoiding the classical antitheses in the analysis of the "central sector" of behavior as well as in that of its visible manifestations. More generally, this notion saves us from the alternative of a philosophy which juxtaposes externally associated terms and of another philosophy which discovers relations which are intrinsic to thought in all phenomena. But precisely for this reason the notion of form is ambiguous. Up until now it has been introduced by physical examples and defined by characteristics which made it appropriate for resolving problems of psychology and physiology. Now this notion must be understood in itself, without which the philosophical significance of what precedes would remain equivocal.

III. THE PHYSICAL ORDER;
THE VITAL ORDER;
THE HUMAN ORDER

Introduction

Pavlov's reflexology treats behavior as if it were a thing, inserts and resorbs it into the tissue of events and relations of the universe. When we tried to define the variables on which behavior actually depends, we found them, not in the stimuli taken as events of the physical world, but in relations which are not contained in the latter—from the relation which is established between two nuances of gray to the functional relations of instrument to goal and the relations of mutual expression in symbolic conduct. Gray G 1 and gray G 2 are part of nature, but not the "pair" of colors constituted by the organism in their regard and which it "recognizes" in another ensemble in which the absolute colors are different. On analysis, the equivocal notion of stimulus separates into two: it includes and confuses the physical event as it is in itself, on the one hand, and the situation as it is "for the organism," on the other, with only the latter being decisive in the reactions of the animal. Against behaviorism, it has been established that the "geographical environment" and the "behavioral environment" cannot be identified.[1] In the hierarchy of species, the efficacious relations at each level define an *a priori* of this species, a manner of elaborating the stimuli which is proper to it; thus the organism has a distinct reality which is not substantial but structural.

Science is not therefore dealing with organisms as the completed modes of a unique world (*Welt*), as the abstract parts of a whole in which the parts would be most perfectly contained. It has to do with a series of "environments" and "milieu" (*Umwelt,*

Merkwelt, Gegenwelt)[2] in which the stimuli intervene according to what they signify and what they are worth for the typical activity of the species considered. In the same manner the reactions of an organism are not edifices constructed from elementary movements, but gestures gifted with an internal unity. Like that of stimulus, the notion of response separates into "geographical behavior"[3]— the sum of the movements actually executed by the animal in their objective relation with the physical world; and behavior properly so called—these same movements considered in their internal articulation and as a kinetic melody gifted with a meaning. The time necessary for a rat to get out of a labyrinth and the number of errors which it commits are determinations which belong to its geographical behavior and which may sometimes have more, sometimes less value than its behavior properly so called. It may happen that an act which is not being guided by the essential traits of the situation will encounter them by chance, as when a cat pulls a piece of meat toward itself while playing with a string; and inversely, it may happen that a movement which is in fact fruitless will be a "good" error, as when a chimpanzee, in order to reach a distant object, pushes a stick toward it with the aid of a second stick which it holds in its hand.[4]

One cannot discern in animal behavior something like a first layer of reactions which would correspond to the physical and chemical properties of the world and to which an acquired significance would subsequently be attached by the transference of reflexogenic powers. In an organism, experience is not the recording and fixation of certain actually accomplished movements: it builds up aptitudes, that is, the general power of responding to situations of a certain type by means of varied reactions which have nothing in common but the meaning. Reactions are not therefore a sequence of events; they carry within themselves an immanent intelligibility.[5]

Situation and reaction are linked internally by their common participation in a structure in which the mode of activity proper to the organism is expressed. Hence they cannot be placed one after the other as cause and effect: they are two moments of a circular process. Everything which impedes the activity of the animal also eliminates the reflexogenic power of certain stimuli, cuts them off from its "sensory universe."[6] "The relation of the internal world[7] to the external world of the animal cannot be understood as that of a key with its lock."[8] If behavior is a "form," one cannot even designate in it that which depends on each one of the internal and external conditions taken separately, since their variations will be expressed in the form by a global and indivisible effect. Behavior would not be an effect of the physical world, either in the crude sense of productive causality or even in the sense of the relation of function to variable. The original character of a physiological field beyond the physical field—a system of directed forces—in which it has its place, of a second "system of stresses and strains" which alone determines actual behavior in a decisive manner, will have to be acknowledged.[9] Even if we take symbolic behavior and its proper characteristics fully into account there would be reason for introducing a third field which, by nominal definition, we will call, mental field. Are we not brought back to the classical problems which behaviorism tried to eliminate by leveling behavior to the unique plane of physical causality?

It is here that the notion of form would permit a truly new solution. Equally applicable to the three fields which have just been defined, it would integrate them as three types of structures by surpassing the antimonies of materialism and mentalism, of materialism and vitalism. Quantity, order and value or signification, which pass respectively for the properties of matter, life and mind, would no longer be but the dominant characteristic in the order considered and would become universally applicable categories. Quantity is not a negation of quality, as if the equation for a circle negated circular form, of which on the contrary it attempts to be a rigorous expression. Often, the quantitative relations with which physics is concerned are only the formulae for certain distributive processes: in a soap bubble as in an organism, what happens at each point is determined by what happens at all the others. But this is the definition of order.

There is therefore no reason whatsoever for refusing objective value to this category in the study of the phenomena of life, since it has its place in the definition of physical systems. In the internal unity of these systems, it is acceptable to say that each local effect depends on the function which it fulfills in the whole, upon its value and its significance with respect to the structure which the system is tending to realize.[10] If we consider an ellipsoid conductor in which electrical charges are placed, the law according to which they are distributed does not enunciate simple coincidences; the relation which obtains between the size of the axes, the coordinates of the point in question and the charge which is stabilized there only expresses the internal unity of the process of distribution, its total character in which it finds its *raison d'être.* "To explain and understand are not different forms of dealing with knowledge but fundamentally identical. And that means: a causal connection is not a mere factual sequence to be memorized like the connection between a name and a telephone number, but is intelligible." [11] Thus the use of the categories of value and significance can *a fortiori* be accorded to the moral sciences. The world, in those of its sectors which realize a structure, is comparable[12] to a symphony, and knowledge of the world is thus accessible by two paths: one can note the correspondence of the notes played at a same moment by the different instruments and the succession of those played by each one of them. Thus one would obtain a multitude of laws which permit prediction. But this sum of coincidences is not the model of all knowledge. If someone knew a fragment of a symphony and the law of the construction of the whole, he could derive the same predictions and, in addition, he would find in the whole the *raison d'être* of each local event. But if knowledge in physics, to the extent that it deals with structures, accepts the very categories which are traditionally reserved for the knowledge of life and mind, biology and psychology should not in contrast withdraw in principle from mathematical analyses and causal explanation.

The theory of form is aware of the consequences which a purely structural conception entails and seeks to expand into a philosophy of form which would be substituted for the philosophy of substances. It has never pushed this work of philosophical analysis very far. This is because "form" can be fully understood and all the implications of this notion brought out only in a philosophy which would be liberated from the realistic postulates which are those of every psychology. One can only fall back into the materialism or the mentalism which one wanted to surpass as long as one seeks an integral philosophy without abandoning these postulates.

In fact, to the extent that a philosophy of structure maintains the original character of the three orders and accepts the fact that quantity, order and signification—present in the whole universe of forms—are nevertheless the "dominant" characteristics in matter, life and mind respectively, their distinction must once more be accounted for by means of a structural difference. In other words, matter, life and mind must participate unequally in the nature of form; they must represent different degrees of integration and, finally, must constitute a hierarchy in which individuality is progressively achieved. By definition, it would be impossible to conceive of a physical form which had the same properties as a physiological form and a physiological form which was the equivalent of a mental form. There would be no means of finding a continuous chain of physical actions between the stimuli and the reaction: behavior would have to be mediated by physiological and mental relations. But as long as one remains within the point of view of psychology, as long as one views behavior as a mundane event, interpolated between antecedent and subsequent events and really contained in a sector of space and a segment of time, this vital and mental mediation can be understood only as the passage from one plane of reality to another; life and consciousness will be introduced as the additional conditions which supplement the inadequate physical determinants. Relations and physical and biological structures will fall back into the status of real forces, of motor causes. The old mentalism with its problems is found again in a new language; the notion of structure has been introduced in vain, and the sought-for integration is not obtained. The psychology of form is far removed from these conclusions and, most of the time, follows a path leading instead toward a materialism—the antithesis of the mentalist solution which we have just indicated.

Behavior, it is said, has its roots and its ultimate effects in the geographical environment even though, as has been seen, it is related to it only by the intermediary of the environment proper to each species and to each individual. "How can a cause in one universe of discourse produce an effect in another? All our causal laws refer to events within the same universe of discourse and, therefore, since the geographical environment belongs to the universe of physics, we require its effects to belong to it also." [13] "I admit that in our *ultimate* explanations, we can have but *one* universe of discourse and that it must be the one about which physics has taught us so much." [14] In a philosophy which would genuinely renounce the notion of substance, there could be only one universe which would be the universe of form: between the different sorts of forms invested with equal rights, between physical relations and the relations implied in the description of behavior, there could be no question of supposing any relation of derivation or of causality, nor then of demanding physical models which serve to bring into being physiological or mental forms.

On the contrary, for the psychologists of whom we are speaking, the problem of the relations between the physical, the physiological, and the mental remains posed without any regard for the structural character of these distinctions and is posed in the very terms in which psychology has always posed it. The human body is placed in the middle of a physical world which would be the "cause" of its reactions—without any questioning concerning the meaning which is given to the word "cause" here, and in spite of what Gestalt theory has done precisely to show that no form has its sufficient cause outside of itself. From then on, behavior can appear only as a province of the physical universe, and this latter functions as the universal milieu instead of the forms which ought to fulfill this function. In introducing considerations of structure, the psychology of form does not believe it has gone beyond the notion of the physical world as *omnitudo realitatis* because structures are already found in it. Already, in the physical world, the passage from conditions to consequences is discontinuous. The quantity of electricity in a conductor does not correspond point for point to the quantities which have been put there; it is distributed according to an internal law of electrical equilibrium which does not connect each part of the effect to a part of the cause, but rather local effects among themselves. Local topographical conditions never act separately on their own: the charge at one point can be very weak if it is situated in the area of a second which is that much stronger. With regard to external influences physical systems already present that remarkable autonomy which we have found in the organism with regard to the physical conditions of the milieu and in symbolic behavior with regard to its physiological infrastructure. Value predicates and immanent signification—without which an objective definition of behavior cannot be made—would be only the expression in a human language (which is legitimate, moreover) of structural processes of the nervous system, and these latter in turn would represent only a variety of physical forms.

The theory of form believes it has solved the problem of the relations of the soul and the body and the problem of perceptual knowledge by discovering structural nerve processes which have the same form as the mental on the one hand and are homogeneous with physical structures on the other.[15] Thus no epistemological reform would be necessary and the realism of psychology as a natural science would be definitively conserved. If a solid body is in front of me and if I treat it as such in my behavior, it is because the physical "form" by which it is distinguished from neighboring objects gives rise, through the intermediary of the luminous actions which it exercises on my retina, to a physiological structure of the same type in my nervous system. Although the stimuli which reach the sensory receptors are independent of each other on arrival and carry with them nothing of the physical structure from which they have issued (although, for example, the luminous rays reflected by a body have no more intrinsic relation with each other than they have with the luminous rays reflected by a contiguous object), psychology would furnish an adequate explanation of perceptual knowledge by uncovering the laws according to which the stimuli are organized in the body and by showing that certain of their objective characteristics (their proximity, their resemblances, their aptitude for constituting together a stable form) prescribe that they participate together in a single configuration and that these characteristics are related to the physical form of the corresponding external objects. For such an explanation would permit us to understand how physical things are duplicated in behavior by a representation of themselves.[16]

Thus knowledge remains defined, according to the simplest of schemata, as an imitation of things; consciousness remains a part of being. The integration of matter, life and mind is obtained by their reduction to the common denominator of physical forms. It matters little that the ultimate explanation is always physical if the physical structures posited in nerve functioning imply relations just as complex as those which are grasped by consciousness in the actions of a living being or a man. A complex physical structure is less "material" than the atoms of consciousness of the old psychology. "If we go to the roots of our aversion to materialism and mechanism, is it the *material properties* of combined elements which we find? To speak frankly, there are psychological theories and a good many manuals of psychology which treat expressly of the elements of *consciousness* and are nevertheless more materialistic, inanimate and deprived of meaning and significance than a living tree, which perhaps does not have a trace of consciousness. It matters little what material the particles of the universe are made of; what counts is the type of totality, the significance of the totality." [17]

But can the originality of biological and mental structures be really conserved, as Gestalt theory tries to do, while at the same time founding them on physical structures? A physical explanation of behavior supposes that physical forms can possess all the properties of the biological and mental relations for which they serve as substrate. In a philosophy which denies itself material distinctions, this amounts to saying that there is no difference between the three orders and that life and mind are different words for designating certain physical forms. Precisely if one is thinking in terms of structure, to say that physical forms in the final analysis account for human behavior amounts to saying that the physical forms alone exist. If there is no longer any structural differences between the mental, the physiological and the physical, there is no longer any difference at all. Then consciousness *will be* what happens in the brain, and, as a matter of fact, we see Koffka defining consciousness, following the tradition of materialism, as that property "which certain events in nature have of revealing themselves," [18] as if consciousness always had as *objects* the physiological processes which accompany it. This "conscious side of processes," although it does not enter into the causal explanations, must nevertheless be recognized as a fact; it would be one of the most remarkable of the physiological processes in man[19] which would be sufficient to distinguish Gestalt theory from epiphenomenalism.[20] But if the structures of consciousness are useless in explanation, it is because they have have their physical or physiological equivalent; and this "isomorphism" in a philosophy of form is an identity. The fact of becoming conscious adds nothing to the physical structures; it is only the index of particularly complex physical structures. It must be said of these structures, and not of consciousness, that they are indispensable to the definition of man.

We do not think that the notion of Gestalt is pursued to its most important consequences either in these materialist conclusions or in the mentalist interpretation which we indicated at first. Instead of wondering what sort of being can belong to form and, since it has appeared in scientific research itself, what critique it can demand of the realist postulates of psychology, it is placed among the number of events of nature; it is used like a cause or a real thing; and to this very extent one is no longer thinking according to "form." As long as one sees the physical world as a being which embraces all things and as long as one tries to integrate behavior into it, one will be driven from mentalism, which maintains the originality of biological and mental structures only by opposing substance to substance, to a materialism, which maintains the coherence of the physical order only by reducing the two others to it. In reality, matter, life and mind must be understood as three orders of significations. But it is not with the help of an external criterion that we will judge the alleged philosophy of form. On the contrary, we would like to return to the notion of form, to seek out in what sense forms can be said to exist "in" the physical world and "in" the living body, and to ask of form itself the solution to the antinomy of which it is the occasion, the synthesis of matter and idea.

Structure in Physics

The notion of form which was imposed upon us by the facts was defined like that of a physical system, that is, as an ensemble of forces in a state of equilibrium or of constant change such that no law is formulable for each part taken separately and such that each vector is determined in size and direction by all the others. Thus, each local change in a form will be translated by a redistribution of forces which assures the constancy of their relation; it is this internal circulation which *is* the system as a physical reality. And it is no more composed of parts which can be distinguished in it than a melody (always transposable) is made of the particular notes which are its momentary expression. Possessing internal unity inscribed in a segment of space and resisting deformation from external influences by its circular causality, the physical form is an individual. It can happen that, submitted to external forces which increase and decrease in a continuous manner, the system, beyond a certain threshold, redistributes its own forces in a qualitatively different order which is nevertheless only another expression of its immanent law.[21] Thus, with form, a principle of discontinuity is introduced and the conditions for a development by leaps or crises, for an event or for a history, are given. Let us say in other words that each form constitutes a field of forces characterized by a law which has no meaning outside the limits of the dynamic structure considered, and which on the other hand assigns its properties to each internal point so much so that they will never be absolute properties, properties *of* this point.

Taken in this sense, the notion of form seems scarcely assimilable for classical physics. It denies individuality in the sense that classical physics affirmed it—that of elements or particles invested with absolute properties; and on the other hand it affirms it in the sense that classical physics denied it, since grouped particles always remained discernible in principle while form is a "molar" individual. Nevertheless, Koehler has found examples of form in classical physics without difficulty: the distribution of electrical charges in a conductor, the difference of potential, and the electrical current.[22] If one considers the state of equilibrated distribution and maximal entrophy toward which the energies at work in a system tend according to the second principle of thermodynamics as a form,[23] one can presume that the notion of form will be present in physics everywhere that a historical direction is assigned to natural events.

But, in reality, what Koehler shows with a few examples ought to be extended to all physical laws: they express a structure and have meaning only within this structure. The electrical density in each point of an ellipsoid conductor can be successfully determined by a single relation which is proper to them all, and to them alone, because together they constitute a functional individual. In the same manner, the law of falling bodies is true and will remain so only if the speed of the rotation of the earth does not increase with time; on the contrary hypothesis, the centrifugal force could compensate for and then go beyond that of gravity.[24] Thus the law of falling bodies expresses the constitution of a field of relatively stable forces in the neighborhood of the earth and will remain valid only as long as the cosmological structure on which it is founded endures. Cavendish's experiment gives us an independent (*en soi*) law only if it is supported by the Newtonian conception of gravitation. But if the notion of gravitational field is introduced and if, instead of being an individual and absolute property of heavy bodies, gravitation is tied to certain regions of qualitatively distinct space as the theory of generalized relativity holds, the law could not express an absolute property of the world; it represents a certain state of equilibrium of the forces which determine the history of the solar system.[25] Upon reflection, one finds in these laws, not the principal traits as it were of an anatomical constitution of the world, the archetypes according to which the physical world would be made and which would govern it, but only the properties of certain relatively stable wholes.

In our image of the physical world, we are obliged to introduce partial totalities without which there would be no laws and which partial totalities are precisely what we understood above by form. The combined interplay of laws could withdraw existence from structures which had become stable and bring about the appearance of other structures, the properties of which are not predictable.[26] Thus there is a flow of things which supports the laws and which cannot be definitively resolved into them. To treat the physical world as if it were an intersecting of linear causal series in which each keeps its individuality, as if it were a world in which there is no duration, is an illegitimate extrapolation; science must be linked to a history of the universe in which the development is discontinuous. We cannot even pretend to possess genuine "causal series," models of linear causality, in our established science. The notion of causal series can be considered a constitutive principle of the physical universe only if the law is separated from the process of verification which gives it objective value. The physical experiment is never the revelation of an isolated causal series: one verifies that the observed effect indeed obeys the presumed law by taking into account a series of conditions, such as temperature, atmospheric pressure, altitude, in brief, that is, a certain number of laws which are independent of those which constitute the proper object of the experiment.

Properly speaking, therefore, what one verifies is never a law but a system of complementary laws. There could be no question of supposing a point-for-point correspondence between the experiment and the physical laws; the truth of physics is not found in the laws taken one by one, but in their combinations.[27] Since the law cannot be detached from concrete events where it intersects with other laws and receives a truth value along with them, one cannot speak of a linear causal action which would distinguish an effect from its cause; for in nature it is impossible to circumscribe the author, the one responsible as it were, of a given effect. Since we nevertheless succeed in formulating laws, clearly all the parts of nature must not contribute equally in producing the observed effect. The only valid formulation of the principle of causality will be that which affirms, along with the solidarity of phenomena in the universe, a sort of lessening—proportional to the distance—of the influences exercised on a given phenomenon by prior and simultaneous phenomena.[28] Thus laws and the linear relation of consequence to conditions refer us back to events in interaction, to "forms" from which they should not be abstracted. ". . . one can wonder if . . . , in the different branches of pure physics—in the theory of weight in thermodynamics, in optics as in electromagnetics—a certain number of experimentally obtained coefficients are not introduced which are tied to the structure of our world as such, and without which the laws, or rather the fundamental relations, could neither be completely formulated nor exactly verified."[29] Without even leaving classical physics, corrected by the theory of relativity, one can bring to light the inadequacies in the positivist conception of causality, understood as an ideally isolable sequence even if *de facto* it interferes with others.[30] What is demanded by the actual content of science is certainly not the idea of a universe in which everything would literally depend on everything else and in which no cleavage would be possible, but no more so is it the idea of a *nature* in which processes would be knowable in isolation and which would produce them from its resources; what is demanded is neither fusion nor juxtaposition, rather it is structure.

But we must ask ourselves what exactly is proved by these rapprochements. When one says that there are physical forms, the proposition is equivocal. It is incontestable if one wants to express the fact that science is absolutely incapable of defining the physical universe as a homogeneous field from which reciprocal action, quality and history would be excluded. But, in speaking of physical forms, Gestalt theory means that structures can be found *in* a nature taken in-itself (*en soi*) and that mind can be constituted from them. However, the same reasons which discredit the positivist conception of laws also discredit the notion of forms in-themselves (*en soi*). The one is not corrected by the other; and these two dogmatisms misunderstand the vital meaning of the notions of structure and law in scientific consciousness. Much more than opposed, they are complementary and represent antinomies which must be surpassed.

If, against all right, the physical law is made a norm of nature, since the exercise of this law is possible only within a certain cosmological structure, this structure in turn will have to be posited as inherent in "nature," as Lachelier has shown clearly. The positivist universe of independent causal series ought therefore to be subtended by a universe of finality in which the synchronisms and ensembles which are presupposed by the causal laws provide the existential foundation of the latter, along with their *raison d'être*. But what makes the idea of a pure physical analysis chimerical is the fact that the cosmological given, the discontinuity of history, is not like a more profound layer of being, an infrastructure of the physical world upon which the law would rest. Law and structure are not distinguished in science as a real analysis and a real synthesis would distinguish them. The law of falling bodies is the expression of a property of the terrestrial field which in reality is supported and maintained at each instant by the ensemble of the relations of the universe. Thus the law is possible only within a *de facto* structure, but this latter, in turn, far from being a definitive given, the opaqueness of which would in principle defy analysis, can be integrated into a continuous tissue of relations. The relation of structure and law in science is a relation of reciprocal inclusion.

We were insisting above, against positivism, on the inclusion of law in a structure. Now it is appropriate to insist on the inclusion of structures in laws. It is not only from the outside and by linking structure to the ensemble of phenomena that laws penetrate structure. Science decomposes the reciprocal determinations internal to a physical system into separate actions and reactions, but is ready to consider them "each time with a determined number of empirical coefficients in such a way that it can obtain the synthetic combination which is destined to represent the total appearance which things present." [31] Koehler himself remarks that the structural character of a process does not find its expression in mathematical physics. The equation which gives the electrical density at each point of the surface of an ellipsoid conductor[32] could just as well represent the corresponding but purely mathematical values which one had arbitrarily assigned to different parts of a paper ellipsoid. "Consequently, the mathematical expression in and by itself does not reveal that moments of a form are involved; and it should not do so, since mathematical language—the general symbolism of any measurable object—must be able to express distributions just as well as structures." [33] The fact that each "moment" in the first case exists only as sustained by the remainder, which is characteristic of structure, does not appear in its law. Physical knowledge of a structure of this kind begins therefore at the moment when, in order to define them by a constant property, the different points are considered, points which in principle have no reality in the form. The form itself, the internal and dynamic unity which gives to the whole the character of an indecomposable individual, is presupposed by the law only as a condition of existence; the objects which science constructs, those which figure in developed physical knowledge, are always clusters of relations. And it is not because structure, by its essence, resists expression that physics only barely succeeds in formulating the laws of certain structures in mathematical language; it is because the existential solidarity of its moments renders the experimental approach difficult, prevents acting separately on one of them, and demands that a function which is appropriate to all of them be found initially.[34] One cannot even say that structure is the *ratio essendi* of the law which would be its *ratio cognoscendi,* since the existence of such a structure in the world is only the intersection of a multitude of relations—which, it is true, refer to other structural conditions.

Structure and law are therefore two dialectical moments and not two powers of being. What is demanded by physics is in no case the affirmation of a "physis"—either as the assemblage of isolable causal actions or as the place of structures—or the power of creating individuals in-themselves *(en soi)*. Form is not an element of the world but a limit toward which physical knowledge tends and which it itself defines.[35]

In this sense at least it must be conserved; and a theory of physical knowledge or, with even more reason, a theory of historical knowledge, which would not make room for form and which would define consciousness by the consciousness of laws, could not account for history and reality as objects of thought. After having rejected the dogmatism of laws, one cannot[36] act as if they were sufficient to provide the temporal field or spatial field with its meaning, as if the "non-relational ground"[37] on which the relations established by physics are based did not enter into the definition of knowledge. The effects of laws develop in time; and the appearance of a "synchronism" at the intersection of several laws, of an event which suddenly modifies the course of things and the distinction of a "before" and an "after" with respect to it, allows us to speak of a pulsation of universal duration. Doubtless it is by means of laws that we are able to reconstruct the architecture of a civilization which has disappeared: each step of progress in Egyptology modifies the history of Egypt.[38] But the reconstituted structures function to complete a "time" of the universe, the idea of which they presuppose. They are not themselves real forces which would direct the course of history or add a "causality of idea" to the causality which links together the partitive events. But Egypt, as an economic, political and social structure, remains an object of thought distinct from the multiple facts which have constituted it and brought it into existence. It is an idea, a signification common to an ensemble of molecular facts, which is expressed by all the facts and which is not contained completely in any one of them. In the same manner, the actions and reactions of which a physical form is the seat are conceived by the physicist as the components *of* a physical system, lacking which his science would be without object.

Against every attempt to treat primary qualities as autonomous objects of thought, it remains correct to argue with Berkeley that space presupposes color. The mathematical expressions by which physics characterizes its objects do not cease to belong to mathematics and express precisely a physical phenomenon only if one conceives them as laws of certain forms, of certain concrete wholes. Form, and with it the universe of history and perception, remains indispensable on the horizon of physical knowledge as that which is determined and intended by it. "Doubtless the sensible content of the perceptual given can no longer be considered as something true in itself (*en soi*), but the substrate, the carrier (the empty *x*) of the perceived determinations, must always be considered as that which is determined in terms of physical predicates by the exact methods." [39] Thus form is not a physical reality, but an object of perception; without it physical science would have no meaning, moreover, since it is constructed with respect to it and in order to coordinate it.

That in the final analysis form cannot be defined in terms of reality but in terms of knowledge, not as a thing of the physical world but as a perceived whole, is explicitly recognized by Koehler when he writes that the order in a form "rests . . . on the fact that each local event, one could almost say, 'dynamically knows' the others." [40] It is not an accident that, in order to express this presence of each moment to the other, Koehler comes up with the term "knowledge." A unity of this type can be found only in an object of knowledge. Taken as a being of nature, existing *in* space, the form would always be dispersed in several places and distributed in local events, even if these events mutually determine each other; to say that it does not suffer this division amounts to saying that it is not spread out in space, that it does not exist in the same manner as a thing, that it is the idea under which what happens in several places is brought together and resumed. This unity is the unity of perceived objects. A colored circle which I look at is completely modified in its physiognomy by an irregularity which removes something of its circular character and makes it an imperfect circle.

It is from the universe of perceived things that Gestalt theory borrows its notion of form; it is encountered in physics only to the extent that physics refers us back to perceived things, as to that which it is the function of science to express and determine. Thus, far from the "physical form" being able to be the real foundation of the structure of behavior and in particular of its perceptual structure, it is itself conceivable only as an object of perception. It sometimes happens that physics, in its increasing fidelity to the concrete spectacle of the world, is led to borrow its images, not from the poorly integrated wholes which furnished classical science with its models and in which one could attribute absolute properties to separable individuals, but from the dynamic unities, fields of force and strong structures which the world of perception also offers. It has been possible to say that, in abandoning homogeneous space, physics resuscitated the "natural place" of Aristotle.[41] But for the most part Aristotle's physics is only a description of the perceived world and Koehler precisely has shown very well that perceptual space is not a Euclidean space, that perceived objects change properties when they change place. In the same manner, system wave mechanics, which considers a group of particles in interaction, is obliged to "dismember" their individuality and to take into consideration not the waves associated with each particle, but a wave associated with the entire system which will propagate itself in an abstract space called "configurational space." The impossibility of attributing a localization in ordinary space to each particle and the appearance of properties in an ensemble which are irreducible to those of the assembled elements can very well be related to certain properties of perceptual space.

The ambivalence of time and space at the level of perceptual consciousness reminds one of the mixed notions by means of which modern physics goes beyond the abstract simplicity of classical time and space. It should not be concluded from this that forms *already* exist in a physical universe and serve as an ontological foundation for perceptual structures. The truth is that science, on the basis of certain privileged perceptual structures, has sought to construct the image of an absolute physical world, of a physical *reality,* of which these structures would no longer be anything but the manifestations. In accordance with the spirit of positivism, the perceptual given should be only the point of departure, a πρότερον πρὸς ἡμᾶς, a provisional intermediary between us and the ensemble of laws; and these laws—explaining by their combined interplay the appearance of such and such a state of the world, the presence in me of such and such sensations, the development of knowledge and even the formation of science—should thus close the circle and stand independently. On the contrary, as we have seen, the reference to a sensible or historical given is not a provisional imperfection; it is essential to physical knowledge. In fact and by right, a law is an instrument of knowledge and structure is an object of consciousness. Laws have meaning only as a means of conceptualizing the perceived world. The reintroduction of the most unexpected perceptual structures into modern science, far from revealing forms of life or even of mind as already in a physical world in-itself (*en soi*), only testifies to the fact that the universe of naturalism has not been able to become self-enclosed, and that perception is not an event of nature.

Vital Structures

The physical form is an equilibrium obtained with respect to certain given external conditions, whether it is a question of topographical conditions, as in the distribution of electrical charges on a conductor; or of conditions which are themselves dynamic, as in the case of a drop of oil placed in the middle of a mass of water. Doubtless certain physical systems modify the very conditions upon which they depend by their internal evolution, as is shown by the polarization of electrodes in the case of electrical current; and one can imagine some which are capable of displacing their mobile parts so as to re-establish a privileged state. But action which is exercised outside the system always has the effect of reducing a state of tension, of advancing the system toward rest. We speak of vital structures, on the contrary, when equilibrium is obtained, not with respect to real and present conditions, but with respect to conditions which are only virtual and which the system itself brings into existence; when the structure, instead of procuring a release from the forces with which it is penetrated through the pressure of external ones, executes a work beyond its proper limits and constitutes a proper milieu for itself. In a system of this kind the equilibrium that the internal reactions tend to produce is not an equilibrium gained at any cost nor the simple conservation of an established order, as in the distribution of electrical charges. The privileged state, the invariant, can no longer be determined as the result of reciprocal actions which actually unfold in the system.

It is known, for example, that an organism never realizes all the types of behavior which would appear possible if it were considered as a machine. If a subject points at an object placed in front of him, then on his right, and finally on the extreme right, one observes that trunk movements are executed at the same time so that the angle formed by the frontal plane and the arm remains fairly constant. This sort of constancy may be individual; two subjects asked to trace a circle with a piece of chalk on a plane parallel to the frontal plane generally do it according to different methods (the arm extended or the elbow bent) characteristic of each one of them. If one asks a subject to show his hand, he will not present it in just any position: the palm will ordinarily be turned down, the fingers slightly flexed, the thumb above the other fingers and the hand at the height of the middle of the body. It is rather well known that everyone has his own manner of carrying his head and his position of sleeping. Finally, perceptual behavior also has preferred determinations. An angle of 93° is designated as a "bad" right angle; a musician speaks of "false notes." [42]

Any behavior which is not preferred will be judged by the subject as difficult or imperfect behavior. But what is it that confers their preference on preferred modes of behavior? How does it happen that they are treated as "the simplest" and "the most natural," that they give a feeling of balance and facility? [43] Is the orientation toward these preferred modes of behavior comparable to the formation of a spherical soap bubble? In the latter case, the external forces exerted on the surface of the bubble tend to compress it into a point; the pressure of the enclosed air on the other hand demands as large a volume as possible. The spherical structure which is realized represents the only possible solution to this problem of minimum and maximum. Can it be said in the same way that the preferred modes of behavior of an organism are those which, in the *de facto* conditions in which it finds itself, objectively offer the greatest simplicity, the greatest unity? But most of the time they do not have any privilege of simplicity or of unity *in themselves*.

When I turn my head toward a source of sound in such a way that in fact the auditive excitations become synchronized at the level of the two ears, the process of excitation, considered part by part, is no simpler than before; it appears so only if one looks for an ensemble in it, for a whole, expressible by a unique law, and, finally, only by means of a resemblance with a model of simplicity which our mind suggests.

It is not because behavior is simple that it is preferred; on the contrary it is because it is preferred that we find it simpler.[44] And if one tried to hold with Koehler that preferred behavior is that involving the least expenditure of energy, besides the fact that its economic character is not objectively established, it is too clear that the organism is not a machine governed according to a principle of *absolute* economy. For the most part preferred behavior is the simplest and most economical *with respect to the task in which the organism finds itself engaged;* and its fundamental forms of activity and the character of its possible action are presupposed in the definition of the structures which will be the simplest *for it,* preferred *in* it. In certain patients, any passive movement of the head toward the right entails displacements of the members of the body in the same direction. But disassociation remains possible in the face of any concrete task which demands it. The reactions evoked by a stimulus depend upon the significance which it has for the organism considered, not as a group of forces which tend toward rest by the shortest paths, but as a *being* capable of certain types of action.[45] In the act of "pointing out," the preferred plane where the arm moves, far from being determined by the conditions of a physical equilibrium with the milieu, corresponds to the internal necessities of a vital equilibrium. It depends, not on local conditions, but on the total activity of the organism:

All the sensory stimuli—tactual, visual and auditive—as it were attract the preferred plane in their direction;[46] all movements of the body proper —whether of the head, the opposite arm, the eyes or the legs—modify it. And these motor conditions are no less efficacious when they are not perceived by the subject.[47] The same movement will displace the preferred plane in two opposed directions according to the significance which this movement has for the subject: for example, a displacement of the eyes toward the right pushes the preferred plane back toward the left if this displacement is gratuitous and without object; it draws it toward the right, however, if the subject turns his eyes in order to look at something. In reality it is only by abstraction that we can speak of preferred behavior, as if it were a question of local phenomena which ought to be explained one by one. Each preferred behavior is inseparable from the others and is united with them: it would seem that a lowering of tonus in one half of the organism should entail disorders of perception and of action; as a matter of fact it would entail them if the subject did not unknowingly incline his head or even his entire body toward the injured side. In this attitude, he does not fall, walks upright and perceives objectively vertical lines as vertical. The disorders reappear if the subject is obliged to hold his head up straight. Thus, through the slight slanting of the head, the course of the excitation in the whole organism has actually become ordered.[48] In brief, what is preferred in the healthy organism as well as in the sick one is not a certain position of the head on the one hand and a certain tonic gradient on the other, but a determinate relation of the one to the other.

Since the same remarks could be made with regard to the typical attitudes of each subject, one is led to the idea that there exists a general structure of behavior for each individual which is expressed by certain constants of conduct, of sensible and motor thresholds, of affectivity, of temperature, of blood pressure . . . in such a way that it is impossible to find causes and effects in this ensemble, each particular phenomenon expressing equally well what one could call the "essence" of the individual.[49] For the preferred behavior is the one which permits the easiest and most adapted action: for example, the most exact spatial designations, the finest sensory discriminations. Thus each organism, in the presence of a given milieu, has its optimal conditions of activity and its proper manner of realizing equilibrium; and the internal determinants of this equilibrium are not given by a plurality of vectors, but by a general attitude toward the world. This is the reason why inorganic structures can be expressed by a law while organic structures are understood only by a norm, by a certain type of transitive action which characterizes the individual. The thresholds of perception in an organism, as we were saying, are among the individual constants which express its essence. This signifies that the organism itself measures the action of things upon it and itself delimits its milieu by a circular process which is without analogy in the physical world.

The relations of the organic individual and its milieu are truly dialectical relations, therefore, and this dialectic brings about the appearance of new relations which cannot be compared to those of a physical system and its entourage or even understood when the organism is reduced to the image which anatomy and the physical

sciences give of it. Even its elementary reactions cannot be classified,
as we have said, according to the apparatuses in which they are
realized, but according to their vital significance.[50] Some obtain equilibrium at the least cost and in this sense come closer to a physical
process: these are local compensations which prevent the excitant
from being harmful. But others carry out a genuine work on the
outside in which the whole organism is engaged. Thus, it will be
necessary to distinguish an immediate behavior and an objective
behavior. The difference between abduction and extensor movements
(which in fact seem rather to be bound up with the activity of the
medulla) and adduction and flexor movements (which depend
rather on the cerebral cortex) is not expressible by these anatomical
designations nor by any physical notion. The science of life can be
constructed only with notions tailored to it and taken from our experience of the living being. It will be noticed for instance that movements of extension are particularly frequent with regard to objects
to which we do not pay attention. Yawning and the act of sneezing
are movements of pure extension. And inversely all precise movements (in opposition to movements of force) are flexor movements.
Thus, the true distinction between them is that of "different attitudes
of the organism to the world." [51] Flexion is an attitude in which the
organism takes possession of the world, as is seen by the example of
the movements of convergence and fixation and by the inclination of
the head in attention. On the contrary, extensor movements express
abandonment to things and the passive existence of an organism
which does not master its milieu.[52] Inspiration movements, more accentuated in a passive attitude, are bound up with extension behavior
in animals and even in man; on the contrary, expiration movements,
greater in man during meditation, are a particular case of flexion. An
analysis of this kind does not follow the articulations of anatomy: a
convulsive contraction of the flexors is not an act of flexion. The
biological value of an organism is not recognized purely and simply
by the organs which it uses; it cannot be understood in the language
of anatomy.[53] Thus one should anticipate finding a regulation in the
behavior of the simplest organisms which is different from that in
physical systems.

In fact, tropisms, which were long considered to be reactions to the
physical and chemical agents of the milieu, do not seem to exist in this
form in the normal life conditions of the animal. Positive phototropism
in young plaice does not take place in a large aquarium.[54] The sea-

anemone, placed on a trellis, sends its pedicle downward; and if the trellis is turned over several times, the pedicle enlaces the meshes of the trellis. But, after a certain number of trials, the animal disengages its pedicles and will settle itself in the sand. Which is to say that, here again, behavior cannot be defined as an adaptation to the given conditions and that the organism itself poses the conditions of its equilibrium.[55] Tropisms in Loeb's sense would represent laboratory reactions similar to those of a man whose conduct is disorganized by emotion and who runs toward the light or the dark.

Thus, the dialectic proper to the organism and the milieu can be interrupted by "catastrophic" behavior and the organism momentarily reduced to the conditions of the physical system. But it is a question here of pathological cases or of laboratory phenomena. These remarks hold not only against a mechanistic physiology; they also apply to Gestalt theory. Perceptual reactions can be explained by physical models only in the case in which they are artificially isolated from the context of action in which they are naturally integrated. Then the privilege of certain forms, instead of expressing the natural mode of action of the organism considered, depends only on the objective character of the stimuli presented. But these structures, not being centered in the total activity of the organism, are either labile formations—that is, pathological, precisely like Rubin's equivocal figures[56]—or else the process of physical equilibration from which one tries to make them emerge can itself unfold without interruption only with the guarantee and the guard of the total activity of the nervous system. Wertheimer's laws relate the formation of structures to the objective conditions in which the stimuli are presented—law of proximity, law of qualitative resemblance—or to the stability of "good forms," considered as a property which is inherent in them.[57] If it happens that our perception indeed obeys these laws, it is not because it is assimilable to a physical structure. It is because the functioning of the nervous system, in spite of the perpetual interactions of which it is the seat, is organized in such a way that Wertheimer's laws can work; in other words, it is because he had the good fortune of encountering constants in them which are admitted by the total activity of the organism.[58]

It is Gestalt theory's own principles which we are invoking against it here. In a form, the whole is not the sum of its parts. Even if one accepts the fact that the organism is accessible to a physical analysis which is unlimited in principle—since no one contests the fact that the physico-chemical analysis of the organism is the most complex there is—it is absolutely certain that these structures will not be able to find their equivalent in physical structures in the restricted sense of the word. To construct a physical model of the organism would be to construct an organism. The physical models of Gestalt theory have just as little relationship to the phenomena of life as crystallization has to karyokinesis.

We are upholding no species of vitalism whatsoever here. We do not mean that the analysis of the living body encounters a limit in irreducible vital forces. We mean only that the reactions of an organism are understandable and predictable only if we conceive of them, not as muscular contractions which unfold in the body, but as acts which are addressed to a certain milieu, present or virtual: the act of taking a bait, of walking toward a goal, of running away from danger. The object of biology is evidently not to study all the reactions which can be obtained with a living body in any conditions whatsoever, but only those which are *its* reactions or, as one says, "adequate" reactions. Everything which can occur to an organism in the laboratory is not a biological reality. One is not trying to do physics in the living being, but rather the physics of the living being; in other words one is attempting to trace the contour of a "natural" behavior which must be disengaged from *de facto* behavior. Which is to say that "organism" is an equivocal expression. There is the organism considered as a segment of matter, as an assemblage of real parts juxtaposed in space and which exist outside of each other, as a sum of physical and chemical actions. All the events which unfold in this organism possess the same degree of reality and there is not, for example, the distinction between the normal and the pathological. Is this the *true* organism, the sole objective representation of the organism? In reality the body thus understood is neither the object of biology nor even of physiology.

If we could describe the innumerable physical and chemical actions which make a living being pass from adolescence to adulthood, we would have a continuous sequence of phenomena in which it would be difficult to recognize the duration of an organism. The typical "functions" or "processes"—for example, anagenesis and catagenesis—the rhythm of which defines the phenomenon of growth or of aging for the physiologist, linked to chains of chemical reactions which condition them from all sides, would lose their proper contours, their individuality, to such an extent that the characteristic modifications which they undergo with age would cease to be perceptible. A total molecular analysis would dissolve the structure of the functions of the organism into the undivided mass of banal physical and chemical reactions. Life is not therefore the sum of these reactions. In order to make a living organism reappear, starting from these reactions, one must trace lines of cleavage in them, choose points of view from which certain ensembles receive a common signification and appear, for example, as phenomena of "assimilation" or as components of a "function of reproduction"; one must choose points of view from which certain sequences of events, until then submerged in a continuous becoming, are distinguished for the observer as "phases"—growth, adulthood—of organic development. One must mentally detach certain partitive phenomena from their real context and subsume them under an idea which is not contained, but expressed, in them. "The meaning of the organism is its being," [59] and the organism which biological analysis is concerned with is an ideal unity.

This method of organization of experience is not exclusive to biological knowledge. In history, to understand is also to break up the global ensemble of concrete events according to categories, then attempt to rejoin the real unity from which one has started by establishing concordances or derivations from one order to the other: from the political to the economic, from the economic to the cultural. It is also, in a becoming which is inarticulated at the molecular level, to mark breaks and phases, the end of one world and the beginning of another. The structures which one arrives at in this way are, as are those in the organism, neither supplementary causes which would direct the partitive phenomena, nor simple names for designating them, but ideas in which they participate without the ideas being contained in them. "Supply" and "demand" are neither real forces hidden behind the special causes which determine the production in each factory and the consumption of each individual, nor simple names for designating the arithmetical sum of these local phenomena, but objects of thought which science constructs and which give the immanent significance and truth of events. It is not otherwise that the history of the planets is written or that the ages of the earth are made to emerge through a continuous molecular evolution.

It is impossible for the intellect to compose images of the organism on the basis of partitive physical and chemical phenomena;

and nevertheless life is not a special cause. In biology as well as in physics the structures must be submitted to an analysis which finds in them the combined action of laws. What we are looking for in the idea of life "is not the terminal stone of a building, but the building itself in which the partial phenomena, at first insignificant, appear as belonging to a unitary, ordered and relatively constant formation of specific structure . . . ; we are not looking for a real foundation (*Seinsgrund*) which constitutes being, but for an idea, a reason in knowledge (*Erkentnissgrund*) in virtue of which all the particular facts become intelligible." [60] It is necessary only to accept the fact that the physico-chemical actions of which the organism is in a certain manner composed, instead of unfolding in parallel and independent sequences (as the anatomical spirit would want it), instead of intermingling in a totality in which everything would depend on everything and in which no cleavage would be possible, are constituted, following Hegel's expression, in "clusters" or in relatively stable "vortices"—the functions, the structures of behavior —in such a way that the mechanism is accompanied by a dialectic.

But are we not brought back to the classical alternative? If one grants that physical and chemical phenomena can only intelligibly depend on conditions which are themselves physical and chemical, and therefore that this physico-chemical analysis is in principle unlimited, do not the properly vital categories—the sexual object, the alimentary object, the nest—and the modes of conduct directed toward these objects cease to be intrinsic denominations of behavior and the organism; do they not belong rather to our human way of perceiving them; and, in the *final analysis* ought not constructions of stimuli and reflexes be substituted for them in an objective study?

Descriptive biology would be a preliminary inventory of the superstructures which are supported by the physics of living things; and explanation in biology as well as in physics would have to be reduced to the unique type of explanation by laws. The characteristics of the organic individual—the property which it has of itself setting the conditions of its equilibrium, then of creating its milieu—would be only the macroscopic result of a multitude of elementary actions identical to those of physical systems. Explanation could in principle be coextensive with description. One would have to grant only that, in biology as well as in physics, an exhaustive analysis of the *de facto* structures is inconceivable: the physical and chemical actions into which we decompose a function can themselves be produced only in a stable context; thus the laws explain a given structure only by presupposing another structure, and in this sense the physics of the organism is also obliged to start with a certain "historical given." But it does not differ from the other physics on this point, and the structures of the organism would be only a particular case of those of the physical world.

If, on the contrary, we want to maintain the properly biological categories as constitutive of the organism, we would be brought back to a sort of vitalism. We have accepted the fact that vital actions have an autochthonous meaning, as it were. The partial phenomena which physico-chemical analysis intercepts in the living organism are bound together by means of an original relationship. It is no longer a question of the reciprocal determination of the physicist, who ideally derives each of them from the others. They all participate in a single structure of behavior and express the organism's manner of modifying the physical world and of bringing about the appearance in the world of a milieu in its own image. The individual as a "specific capacity of reaction" [61] is an ultimate category or irreducible model (*Urbild*)[62] of biological knowledge. As soon as we try to predict the vital reactions of a given organism beyond statistical determinations, the individual coefficient which must be taken into account is "a specific structure which belongs to it with an internal necessity." [63] But quantum physics has doubtless taught us to introduce "acausal" givens into our image of the physical world,[64] behind which there is no reason in principle for affirming a causality of the classical type; and the physicists themselves[65] have made the comparison. But we have not restricted ourselves to saying that the organism was acausal. By accepting the fact that the organism itself modifies its milieu according to the internal norms of its activity, we have made it an individual in a sense which is not that of even modern physics. We have given a positive content to acausality, while the physicist limits himself to registering it as a fact and to circumventing the obstacle by means of indirect methods which permit a new cluster of mathematical relations to be thrown over the acausality. As we have described it, organic structure is not just one of these *de facto* structures which physics encounters; it is a structure in principle. In order to maintain definitively the originality of vital categories, it would be necessary to make every organism a whole which produces its parts, to find in it the simple act from which the partial phenomena derive their being, to return therefore to the notion of vital élan.

But the idea of *signification* permits conserving the category of life without the hypothesis of a vital force. The resistance of the concrete given to the approximate laws of physics is anonymous as it were: it is the opaqueness of the fact, the shock of the unexpected result, or the experience of an inexpressible quality. The incompleteness of lawful knowledge does not oblige physics to grant another mode of knowledge because the uncoordinated residue does not lend itself to any verifiable determination, except perhaps those which science will obtain later by the invention of new laws. The law remains therefore the model of all truth in physics.

But on the contrary, the "non-relational ground" which explanatory biology comes up against is represented to us by positive characteristics; it is the revelation of objective relations of an new kind. The local electrical charges in an ellipsoid conductor were determinable in terms of the coordinates of the point considered, of the size of the axes and that of the total charge. Local phenomena are not united in this manner in an organism, that is, by submission to a single law. Motor reactions, temperature and the proportion of calcium and calium are linked by their common appropriateness to the organism's mode of preferred activity. A law, in a physical system, gives at least the probable value of the present state in terms of the immediately preceding state, that of the local state in terms of the total state. When this double determination is impossible, the physicist introduces empirical coefficients, indivisible quanta of energy which express and do not explain the behavior of the atom. The organism is distinguished from the systems of classical physics because it does not admit of division in space and in time. Nerve functioning is not punctually localizable; a kinetic melody is completely present at its beginning and the movements in which it is progressively realized can be foreseen only in terms of the whole, as we have established above.

The organism is also distinguished from the systems of modern physics because, in physics, unities of indivisible behavior remain opaque givens, while in biology they become the means of a new type of intellection: the particularities of an individual organism are more and more closely connected with its capacity for action; the structure of the body in man is the expression of character. The unity of physical systems is a unity of *correlation,* that of organisms a unity of *signification*. Correlation by laws, as the mode of thinking in physics practices it, leaves a residue in the phenomena of life which is accessible to another kind of coordination: coordination by *meaning*. The same reasons which make a completely deductive physics chimerical also render a completely explanatory biology chimerical.

Nothing justifies postulating that the vital dialectic can be integrally translated in physico-chemical relations and reduced to the condition of an anthropomorphic appearance. To affirm this would be to reverse the logical order of scientific thought, which goes from that which is perceived to that which is correlated, without one's being able to follow the inverse path and make the πρός ήμας order rest upon the ηαθ'αύτο order. The significance and value of vital processes which science, as we have seen, is obliged to take into account are assuredly attributes of the *perceived* organism, but they are not extrinsic denominations with respect to the true organism; for the true organism, the one which science considers, is the concrete totality of the perceived organism, that which supports all the correlations which analysis discovers in it but which is not decomposable into them. It is true that the convergent efforts of intellectualism and mechanism withdraw any original determination from the perception of the organism. But, both in psychology and biology, the apprehension of structures should be recognized as a kind of knowing which is irreducible to the comprehension of laws.

Here let us say only that the perception of the living body—or, as we shall say from now on, of a "phenomenal body"—is not a mosaic of just any visual and tactual sensations which, associated with the internal experience of desires, emotions and feelings (or understood as the signs of those mental attitudes) would receive from them a vital signification. Every theory of "projection," be it empiricist or intellectualist, presupposes what it tries to explain, since we could not project our feelings into the visible behavior of an animal if something in this behavior itself did not suggest the inference to us. But it is not the resemblance of our own gestures to the gestures of other persons which can give to these latter their expressive value: a child understands the joyful meaning of a smile long before having seen his own smile, that of menacing or melancholy mimicry which he has never executed and to which his own experience therefore can furnish no content.

Finally, the living being is known long before the inorganic—which is ordinarily expressed rather poorly by speaking of infantile animism—and it is an anachronism to consider the perception of living beings as secondary. The gestures and the attitudes of the phenomenal body must have therefore a proper structure, an immanent signification; from the beginning the phenomenal body must be a center of actions which radiate over a "milieu"; it must be a certain silhouette in the physical and in the moral sense; it must be a certain type of behavior. In fact, modern psychology has brought to light this immediate apprehension of structure which is the condition of possibility of all judgments of recognition as well as of all associations of ideas. The physiognomy of the face and the writing, thoughts, brain and gestures of a man present intrinsic analogies which explain, along with the famous unreasonable antipathies, the success of reconstruction tests in which a subject must designate the profile which corresponds to a voice and the writing which corresponds to a physiognomy.[66] Likewise one finds, immanent to the phenomenal organism, certain nuclei of signification, certain animal essences—the act of walking toward a goal, of taking, of eating bait, of jumping over or going around an obstacle—unities which reflexology, as we have seen, does not succeed in engendering from elementary reactions, and which are therefore like an *a priori* of biological science. It goes without saying that this apprehension of structure is neither complete nor exact in common perception and, when one speaks of an "intuition" which grasps them, that one does not mean that this intuition is innate.[67]

The precocity of the perception of living things served us here only to exclude the constructive and projective explanations of classical psychology. It is precisely descriptive biology which, starting with the imperfect intuitions of common perception, reorganizes and corrects them. There is an exchange of service between the description of the phenomenal body[68] and causal explanation. Common knowledge contains, for example, a rich and confused notion of "male" and "female" which connotes certain behavioral constants, a general attitude recognizable well beyond sexual behavior properly so called. It is very unlikely that this notion is constituted in the experience of each one of us by the inductive rapprochement of a large number of isolated facts; on the contrary, it is likely that it was read in a single glance and revealed in a facial expression, in a gesture. The discovery of causal correlations—for example, endocrine influences which subtend the ensemble of sexual characteristics —has not only the effect of "completing" the common notion; it can also lead us to modify our view of the male and female being and integrate with it certain partial attitudes which had eluded common knowledge. But in any case, to understand these biological entities is not to note a series of empirical coincidences; it is not even to establish a list of mechanical correlations; it is to unite the ensemble of known facts by means of their significations, to discover in all of them a characteristic rhythm, a general attitude toward certain categories of objects, perhaps even toward all things.[69] Thus it is necessary in this sense to go beyond mechanism.

These remarks cannot serve to justify a vitalism, however—even the refined vitalism of Bergson. The relation of the vital élan to that which it produces is not conceivable, it is magical. Since the physico-chemical actions of which the organism is the seat cannot be abstracted from those of the milieu, how can the act which creates an organic individual be circumscribed in this continuous whole and where should the zone of influence of the vital élan be limited? It will indeed be necessary to introduce an unintelligible break here. If one prefers to say that matter consists of disintegrating life, the relation of life which is becoming to life which is disintegrating is no more comprehensible. But the critique of mechanism leads back to vitalism only if it is conducted, as often happens, on the plane of being. To reject the dogmatic thesis according to which the unity of the organism is a superstructure supported by a really continuous chain of physico-chemical actions would then be to affirm the antithesis, also dogmatic, which interrupts this chain in order to make place for a vital force—just as, before Kant, the negation of infinite divisibility was equivalent to the affirmation of an indivisible real. This is indeed the case as long as one remains on the plane of being.

It is inconceivable—this is the mechanist argument—that an existing physical or chemical action not have its real conditions in other physical or chemical actions. But—this is the vitalist argument —since each constant chemical reaction in the organism (for example, the fixation of oxygen on the hemoglobin of the blood) presupposes a stable context, which itself presupposes another one, the physico-chemical explanation always seems to be deferred; since no law is unconditional, it is difficult to see how they could be so together; and since there do exist organisms in fact, it seems necessary to relate the multiplicity of phenomena to the simple act of a vital élan which unifies them.

In reality, the two arguments consider the organism as a real product of an external nature, when in fact it is a unity of signification, a phenomenon in the Kantian sense. It is given in perception with the original characteristics which we have described. Scientific knowledge finds physico-chemical relations in it and little by little invests it with them. A counter-force which would intervene to break these correlations is inconceivable. But nothing forces us to think that the cycle of physico-chemical actions can completely enclose the phenomenon of the organism, that explanation can rejoin the givens of the description or that the phenomenal body can be converted into a physical system and integrated into the physical order. The totality is not an *appearance;* it is a *phenomenon.* If it is impossible to affirm in principle a discontinuity of physical correlations throughout this phenomenon, the affirmation of a real continuity is not any more permissible. Vital acts *have* a meaning; they are not defined, even in science, as a sum of processes external to each other, but as the spatial and temporal unfolding of certain ideal unities. "Every organism," said Uexkull, "is a melody which sings itself." [70] This is not to say that it knows this melody and attempts to realize it; it is only to say that it is a whole which is significant for a consciousness which knows it, not a thing which rests in-itself (*en soi*).

We cannot maintain that certain "centers of indetermination" appear in the universe of physical causality. Let us say rather that our external experience is that of a multiplicity of structures, of significant wholes. Some, which will constitute the physical world, find the adequate expression of their internal unity in a mathematical law. Others, which are called living beings, present the particularity of having behavior, which is to say that their actions are not comprehensible as functions of the physical milieu and that, on the contrary, the parts of the world to which they react are delimited for them by an internal norm. By "norm" here one does not mean a "should be" which *would make* it be; it is the simple observation of a preferred attitude, statistically more frequent, which gives a new kind of unity to behavior. One needs to introduce an active principle of order, an entelechy, only when one tries to compose the organism by means of the summation of separated processes. For it is then that the whole, with its remarkable constants, seems to demand an ordering factor which maintains them. From the moment that causality loses its mythical meaning of productive causality to be reduced to the functional dependence of variables, laws can no longer be conceived as that which engenders the existence of the facts. One can no longer say, as M. Lapicque writes, that order is an effect of the mechanisms by which it is realized. This would be to offer a support to the vitalist argumentation and to return to the antinomies.

Nor is order that which calls the mechanisms into existence. The whole in the organism is an idea, as Spinoza thought. However, while Spinoza believed he was able to rediscover the unity of the body beyond the fragmented extension of the imagination in a law homogeneous with the law of physical systems, it does not seem possible to understand life by a regressive analysis which goes back to its conditions. It will be a question of a prospective analysis which will look for the immanent signification of life, the latter again being no more a force of attraction than cause is a force of propulsion. "Signification" is to the final cause what the relation of function to variable is to the "producing cause." Following M. Brunschvicg's expression, the laws of physics presuppose the observation of a *de facto* state of our universe; an event can be deduced with necessity only from another given event (without the contingence of that which exists—each time pushed further back— ever being eliminated from the whole). Similarly, the ideal structure of behavior allows us to link the present state of the organism with a prior state taken as given, to see in the former the progressive realization of an essence already legible in this latter (without our ever being able to go beyond the limit or make of the idea a cause of existence).

The Human Order

In describing the physical or organic individual and its milieu, we have been led to accept the fact that their relations were not mechanical, but dialectical. A mechanical action, whether the word is taken in a restricted or looser sense, is one in which the cause and the effect are decomposable into real elements which have a one-to-one correspondence. In elementary actions, the dependence is uni-directional; the cause is the necessary and sufficient condition of the effect considered in its existence and its nature; and, even when one speaks of reciprocal action between two terms, it can be reduced to a series of uni-directional determinations. On the contrary, as we have seen, physical stimuli act upon the organism only by eliciting a global response which will vary qualitatively when the stimuli vary quantitatively; with respect to the organism they play the role of occasions rather than of cause; the reaction depends on their vital significance rather than on the material properties of the stimuli. Hence, between the variables upon which conduct actually depends and this conduct itself there appears a relation of meaning, an intrinsic relation. One cannot assign a moment in which the world acts on the organism, since the very effect of this "action" expresses the internal law of the organism. The mutual exteriority of the organism and the milieu is surmounted along with the mutual exteriority of the stimuli. Thus, two correlatives must be substituted for these two terms defined in isolation: the "milieu" and the "aptitude," which are like two poles of behavior and participate in the same structure.

It is this intrinsic connection which Bergson expresses when he finds in instinct a relation of "sympathy" with its object, or Koehler when he writes that each part of a form "dynamically knows" the other parts. In speaking here of knowledge and consequently of consciousness, we are not constructing a metaphysics of nature; we are limiting ourselves to denominating the relations of the milieu and the organism as science itself defines them as they should be denominated. In recognizing that behavior has a meaning and depends upon the vital significance of situations, biological science is prohibited from conceiving of it as a thing in-itself (*en soi*) which would exist, *partes extra partes, in* the nervous system or *in* the body; rather it sees in behavior an embodied dialectic which radiates over a milieu immanent to it.

There is no question—as we have said often enough—of returning to any form whatsoever of vitalism or animism, but simply of recognizing that the object of biology cannot be grasped without the unities of signification which a consciousness finds and sees unfolding in it. "The mind of nature is a hidden mind. It is not produced in the form of mind itself; it is only mind for the mind which knows it: it is mind in itself, but not for itself." [71] In reality then we have already introduced consciousness and what we have designated under the name of life was already the consciousness of life. "The concept is only the interior of nature," says Hegel;[72] and already it has seemed to us that the notion of the living body could not be grasped without this internal unity of signification which distinguishes a gesture from a sum of movements. The phenomenon of life appeared therefore at the moment when a piece of extension, by the disposition of its movements and by the allusion that each movement makes to all the others, turned back upon itself and began to express something, to manifest an interior being externally.

If now we continue our description—always from the point of view of the "outside spectator"—and if we consider the human order, we will at first see in it only the production of new structures. If life is the manifestation of an "interior" in the "exterior," consciousness is nothing at first but the projection onto the world of a new "milieu"—irreducible to the preceding ones, it is true—and humanity nothing but a new species of animal. In particular, perception should be integrated in its turn into the dialectic of actions and reactions. While a physical system equilibrates itself in respect to the given forces of the milieu and the animal organism constructs a stable milieu for itself corresponding to the monotonous *a prioris* of need and instinct, human work inaugurates a third dialectic. For, between man and the physico-chemical stimuli, it projects "use-objects" (*Gebrauchobjekts*)[73]—clothing, tables, gardens—and "cultural objects" [74]—books, musical instruments, language—which constitute the proper milieu of man and bring about the emergence of new cycles of behavior. Just as it seemed to us to be impossible to reduce the pair: vital situation-instinctive reaction, to the pair: stimulus-reflex, just so it will doubtless be necessary to recognize the originality of the pair: perceived situation-work.

It is by design that, instead of speaking of action as do most contemporary psychologists, we choose the Hegelian term "work," which designates the ensemble of activities by which man transforms physical and living nature. For, although nothing is more common than to link consciousness and action, it is rare that human action is taken with its original meaning and its concrete content. The pure image of *Matter and Memory* is accompanied by consciousness of itself at the moment when the physical forces, instead of passing through the body and releasing automatic responses in it, are dissipated in a "center of indetermination," that is, in a being capable of action proper; and thus the zone of our possible action will be marked out in detail by our perception. But the action of which Bergson is thinking is always vital action, that by which the organism maintains itself in existence. In the act of human work, in the intelligent construction of instruments, he sees only another manner of attaining the ends which instinct pursues in its way. In both cases there are "two equally elegant solutions to the same problem." [75] Beyond biological action, there remains only a mystical action which is directed to no determinate object.

Properly human acts—the act of speech, of work, the act of clothing oneself, for example—have no significance in their own right. They are understood in reference to the aims of life: clothing is an artificial skin, an instrument replaces an organ, language is a means of adaptation to the "unorganized mass." There is more. Although one finds in the conception of "kinetic melodies" a concrete description of consciousness in action, of the internal unity and the meaning of gestures, Bergson sometimes returns to a purely motor notion of action. Habit is finally only the "fossilized residue of a mental activity," the active gesture only a "motor accompaniment" of thoughts, and the practical aims of consciousness are reduced to the consciousness of "incipient movements." In the same manner Janet's "reality function" in the final analysis is the consciousness of certain displacements of our members[76] since the system of tendencies which governs them is, according to the author, only a representational hypothesis.[77] Moreover, if it were realized in consciousness, the relation of these natural forces and the thinking subject would scarcely be conceivable. But the purely motor notion of action which psychologists make use of is accepted by philosophy just as it is. "Following reflexive analysis, the psychologically simple, the specifically irreducible element of perception, is the affirmation which confers existence in the proper sense; it is the judgment: this is. Considered in itself, such a judgment doubtless implies no determination of any content whatsoever; the critical elimination of the successive contributions of memory and intelligence reduces the initial consciousness of the fact of experience to that sort of instantaneous shock, of fugitive sting, which we experience when, in the night, we believe without being completely sure of it that we have glimpsed a flash or heard a sound. This judgment, which in no way carries with it the determination of its object, which is not accompanied by any immediate intuition, is nevertheless that which marks the point of contact with reality, that which is irreducible in experience and without which our thought would no longer be rooted in being; it is that the capital importance of which contemporary psychologists have shown when they have tied the equilibrium of psychological life to the 'feeling which we have of present reality,' to the 'reality function'." [78]

One could say that psychology and philosophy tend toward a notion of *here-and-now consciousness* which they need in order to account for that which is specific in perception, for the individual existences which it reveals within and outside of us. But philosophy does not possess an idea of consciousness and an idea of action which would make an internal communication between them possible. Whether consciousness be continuous duration or a center of judgments, in either case this pure activity is without structure, without nature. Correlatively, perception and action taken in that which is specific to them, that is, as the knowledge and the modification of a reality, are rejected from consciousness. It is granted that their proper function is to "root" consciousness in being. But at the same time the determination of its content is denied to the judgment of existence. It follows that the relation between *what exists* and *the fact* of existence, between the consciousness of contents and the consciousness of action which roots them in being, remains necessarily external.

In the final analysis, consciousness is defined by the possession of an object of thought or by transparence to itself; action is defined by a series of events external to each other. They are juxtaposed; they are not tied together. Bergson himself pointed out what is abstract in psychologies which describe the empirical origin of perception as if its function were immediately contemplative, as if the original and primary attitude of man were that of a spectator. But he did not follow this idea all the way. To do it justice completely it would have been necessary first of all to stop defining consciousness by knowledge of self [79] and to introduce the notion of a life of consciousness which goes beyond its explicit knowledge of itself. But something further would also have been necessary: to describe the structures of action and knowledge in which consciousness is engaged, instead of leaving this life of consciousness indeterminate and being content with the "concrete in general" [80]—as if consciousness could not go beyond the melodies of instinct without being liberated from all determinate form. Consequently it can be seen that the psychology of perception in Bergson is not profoundly

modified by the fact that he brought it closer to action. Since action
is still understood in the narrow sense of a vital action and since
vital action tends to adapt us to the "unorganized mass," the problem is still to understand how the objects of nature are constituted
for us; and the question of whether or not it is indeed to objects
of this kind that human action and perception are first addressed
is not asked.

It has been clearly shown that animal perception is sensitive
only to certain concrete stimulus wholes, the form of which is prescribed by instinct itself; and, rightly, a lived abstraction by means
of which what does not correspond to the structure of the animal's
instinct is left purely and simply outside its sensory field has been
discussed.[81] But the thought of relating the content of human perception to the structure of human action in the same way does not
occur. Of course it is said that our "needs," our "tendencies," and
our attention oriented by them make the objects of our actual perception emerge from the possible sensory field. But what is ordinarily
implicitly understood by this is an ensemble of qualities—color,
weight, flavor—among which attention chooses; and it is from a
mosaic of preconscious sensations that one tries to rejoin the actual
content of infantile or original perception. The analysis is made
following the same postulates which we encountered in the theory
of the reflex: one tries to make a determinate content of consciousness correspond to each partial stimulus—a luminous vibration, for
example—exactly as reflex theory tried to decompose the instinctive
act into a sum of elementary reactions each one of which would
correspond to an elementary stimulus. And just as instinctual activity unfolds, as we have seen, according to the structures prescribed
by the organism itself, one could show likewise that sensations cannot be supposed, even ideally, behind the concrete unities of original
perception. But then the needs, tendencies and acts of spontaneous
attention—the forces, in a word, which are also preconscious—
which must be introduced in order to reconstruct the original syncretism on the basis of pure qualities appear in turn as hypothetical
constructions, as "faculties," which are rendered indispensable only
by the myth of sensations. They are abstract ideas which are formed
in order to explain the discrepancy between our *de facto* perception
and a perception which is in principle wholly conventional. Two
abstractions together do not make a concrete description. There are
not these impersonal forces on the one hand and, on the other, a

mosaic of sensations which they would transform; there are melodic unities, significant wholes experienced in an indivisible manner as poles of action and nuclei of knowledge. Primitive knowledge is not comparable to the result of an energic process in which the tendencies and needs would be released over a mosaic of pure qualities and would give directions to an impartial thinking subject which it will docilely execute. Perception is a moment of the living dialectic of a concrete subject; it participates in its total structure and, correlatively, it has as its original object, not the "unorganized mass," but the actions of other human subjects.

Lacking an adequate notion of real consciousness, thinkers have been led to construct perception arbitrarily and without being able to take into account its descriptive characteristics. Let us try, on the contrary, to start from these characteristics and indicate how they compel us to conceive of the structure of consciousness.[82] Nascent perception has the double character of being directed toward human intentions rather than toward objects of nature or the pure qualities (hot, cold, white, black) of which they are the supports, and of grasping them as experienced realities rather than as true objects. The representation of the objects of nature and of their qualities, the consciousness of truth, belong to a higher dialectic; and we will have to make them appear in the primitive life of consciousness which we are trying for the moment to describe. It is a known fact[83] that infantile perception attaches itself first of all to faces and gestures, in particular to those of the mother. As long as one conserves the hypothesis of sensations, the fact may appear insignificant: the tendencies and the affections of the infant would make the face emerge from the mosaic of sensations, and the expression from the face, so that finally the sensations would become the barely conscious signs of an expression. But we have seen that the hypothesis of sensations is not justifiable.

It follows from this that it is possible to perceive a smile, or even a sentiment in this smile, without the colors and the lines which "compose" the face, as one says, being present to consciousness or given in an unconscious. Thus, the frequently noted fact that we can know a physiognomy perfectly without knowing the color of the eyes or of the hair, the form of the mouth or of the face should be taken quite literally. These alleged elements are present only in virtue of the contributions which they bring to the physiognomy and it is from the latter that they are reconstituted in memory with great difficulty. It is the painters—certain painters—who have taught us, following Cézanne's expression, to regard faces as stones. The human signification is given before the alleged sensible signs. A face is a center of human expression, the transparent envelope of the attitudes and desires of others, the place of manifestation, the barely material support for a multitude of intentions. This is why it seems impossible for us to treat a face or a body, even a dead body, like a thing. They are sacred entities, not the "givens of sight."

One might be tempted to say that, after the human body, it is the use-objects created by man which compose the field of nascent perception. And, indeed, their preponderance is striking in adults. In adults, ordinary reality is a human reality and when use-objects—a glove, a shoe—with their human mark are placed among natural objects and are contemplated as things for the first time, or when events on the street—a crowd gathering, an accident—are seen through the panes of a window, which shuts out their sound, and are brought to the condition of a pure spectacle and invested with a sort of eternity, we have the impression of acceding to another world, to a surreality,[84] because the involvement which binds us to the human world is broken for the first time, because a nature "in itself" (*en soi*) is allowed to show through. Here again, a mode of esthetic perception which appears absurd to so many adults should not for this reason be made a part of primitive perception. Nevertheless, it should be noted that infants are unaware of the use of many objects even when they have seen them handled; we ourselves can remember the marvelous appearance which things had when we did not know what they were for; the child must see many use-objects without linking them to the human actions of which they are actually the support. But even then it is out of the question to suppose in children the perception of *objects* defined by an ensemble of "visual," "tactile" and "sonorous" properties. This would be to forget the role which language plays in the constitution of the perceived world.

Everything which we know of infantile perception and its lacunae permits us to think that the meaning of a word is not determined in the mind of the child by the comparison of objects which he designates in turn but by the cross-checking of the logical contexts of which it is successively a part. It is not because two objects resemble each other that they are designated by the same word; on the contrary, it is because they are designated by the same word and thus participate in the same verbal and affective category that they are perceived as similar. Thus, even when it is addressed to natural objects, nascent perception is still related to them through certain artifacts, the words; and nature is perhaps grasped initially only as that minimum of stage setting which is necessary for the performance of a human drama—a remark which is not new, if it is not taken in a strict sense. People have long spoken of infantile "animism"; but the expression seems improper to the extent that it evokes an interpretation in which the child would confer a signification on the qualitative givens which is distinct from them, would construct souls to explain things. The truth is that there are no things, only physiognomies—just as in adults a mescalin intoxication can give animal appearances to objects and *make* an owl out of a clock without any hallucinatory image whatsoever.[85] "In nature," says Goya, "there are as few colors as lines." [86] But even if there is no line which does not have a physiognomy for the child, still the physiognomy must be delineated in a minimum of matter. What can be the appearance of this sensible support?

It is here that the notion of "form" will permit us to continue the analysis. The form is a visible or sonorous configuration (or even a configuration which is prior to the distinction of the senses) in which the sensory value of each element is determined by its function in the whole and varies with it. The thresholds of chromatic perception are different for the same spot of color depending on whether it is perceived as "figure" or "ground." [87] This same notion of form will permit us to describe the mode of existence of the primitive objects of perception. They are lived as realities, we have said, rather than known as true objects.

Certain states of adult consciousness permit us to comprehend this distinction. For the player in action the football field is not an "object," that is, the ideal term which can give rise to an indefinite multiplicity of perspectival views and remain equivalent under its apparent transformations. It is pervaded with lines of force (the "yard lines"; those which demarcate the "penalty area") and articulated in sectors (for example, the "openings" between the adversaries) which call for a certain mode of action and which initiate and guide the action as if the player were unaware of it. The field itself is not given to him, but present as the immanent term of his practical intentions; the player becomes one with it and feels the direction of the "goal," for example, just as immediately as the vertical and the horizontal planes of his own body. It would not be sufficient to say that consciousness inhabits this milieu. At this moment consciousness is nothing other than the dialectic of milieu and action. Each maneuver undertaken by the player modifies the character of the field and establishes in it new lines of force in which the action in turn unfolds and is accomplished, again altering the phenomenal field.

But one might be tempted to say that these characteristics pose no special problems. That perception is first a perception of human actions or of use-objects would be explained simply by the actual presence of people and artifacts in the child's milieu. That perception reaches objects only through words would be the effect of language as a social phenomenon. That social structures are carried over into the knowledge of nature itself by perception would be only one further argument in favor of a sociology of knowledge. Finally, that perception opens on a reality which solicits our action rather than on a truth, an object of knowledge, would result from the reverberation in consciousness of its motor accompaniment. In other words, we would have brought to light the social and physiological determinants of perception; we would have described, not an original form of consciousness, but the social or kinesthetic contents which are imposed on it by the existence of the body or the integration into a society and which would not oblige us to modify our conception of its proper structure. On the contrary, we propose to show that the descriptive dimension of nascent perception demands a reformulation of the notion of consciousness.

The simple *de facto* presence of other human beings and of use-objects or cultural objects in the infantile milieu cannot explain the forms of primitive perception as a cause explains its effect. Consciousness is not comparable to a plastic material which would receive its privileged structure from the outside by the action of a sociological or physiological causality. If these structures were not in some way prefigured in the consciousness of the child, the use-object or the "other" would be expressed in it only by constructions of sensation, a progressive interpretation of which would slowly disengage the human meaning. If language did not encounter some predisposition for the act of speech in the child who hears speaking, it would remain for him a sonorous phenomenon among others for a long time; it would have no power over the mosaic of sensations possessed by infantile consciousness; one could not understand how it could play the guiding role which psychologists agree in granting to it in the constitution of the perceived world.[88] In other words, it cannot be in virtue of the fact that it *exists* around the child that the human world can immediately acquire a privileged importance in infantile consciousness; it is in virtue of the fact that the consciousness of the child, who sees human objects used and begins to use them in his turn, is capable of discovering immediately in these acts and in these objects the intention of which they are the visible testimony. To use a human object is always more or less to embrace and assume for one's self the meaning of the work which produced it.

It is not a question of upholding the absurd thesis of an innateness of these fundamental structures of conduct. Aside from the fact that innatism accords poorly with the facts—the influence of the milieu in the formation of the mind is sufficiently evident; it is clear that a child who had never seen an article of clothing would not know how to act with clothing; nor would he be able to speak or to envisage other persons if he had always been absolutely alone—it bypasses the difficulty: it limits itself to putting the contents which empiricism derives from external experience "in" consciousness, that is, in brief, to putting them in an internal experience. Rather, the child would understand the human meaning of bodies and of use-objects or the signifying value of language before any logical elaboration because he himself would sketch the acts which give their meaning to words and gestures. It is evident that this is not a solution: we have already seen that the child understands attitudes which he has never had the occasion of assuming; above all, it is difficult to see why these attitudes—actualized in him in the form of innate structures and presented to him in an internal view—would be more immediately understood than when they are given to him in a view from the outside.

Whether the child contemplates their external and visual appearance or whether he grasps their motor actualization in his own body, the question still remains of knowing how an irreducible unity of meaning is apprehended through these materials. Beyond the artificial opposition between the innate and the acquired, therefore, it is a question of describing the emergence of an indecomposable signification in the moment of experience itself: whether it be precocious or retarded, internal or external, motor or sensory. For a child, language which is understood or simply sketched, the appearance of a face or that of a use-object, must from the beginning be the sonorous, motor or visual envelope of a significative intention coming from another.

The organization and the sense of understood language can be very minimal at first; it will be the inflection of the voice, the intonation, which will be understood rather than the verbal material.[89] But from the beginning the sonorous phenomena—whether I speak or another speaks—will be integrated into the structure: expression-expressed; the face—whether I touch my own or I see that of another—will be integrated into the structure: alter-ego.

In other words, as soon as nascent consciousness is taken as the object of analysis one realizes that it is impossible to apply to it the celebrated distinction between *a priori* form and empirical content.[90] Reduced to what is incontestable about it, the *a priori* is that which cannot be conceived part by part and must be conceptualized all at once as an indecomposable essence; the *a posteriori,* on the contrary, designates what can be constructed vis-à-vis thought, piece by piece, by an assembling of external parts. The essence of Kantianism is to admit only two types of experiences as possessing an *a priori* structure: that of a world of external objects, that of states of the inner sense; and to relate all other specifications of experience, for example, linguistic consciousness or consciousness of other persons, to the variety of *a posteriori* contents. Thus, a word can be only a sonorous phenomenon, a moment of external experience to which a signification, that is, a concept, is secondarily adjoined and associated. Another person can consist only of the coordination of a multitude of phenomena of external experience subsumed under a concept which is taken from the inner sense.

The fact that Kant has gone beyond the empiricist notion of the association of states by discovering consciousness as the condition of this association does not change the fact that the relation of meaning to word remains a conceptualized contiguity, the act of speaking, a banal conceptual operation accompanied by a phonation mechanism which is contingent with regard to it. Finally, it does not change the fact that another person remains a derived notion by means of which I coordinate certain aspects of external experience.

But child psychology precisely proposes the enigma of a linguistic consciousness and a consciousness of others which is almost pure and which is prior to that of sonorous and visual phenomena—as is sufficiently shown by the magical and animistic beliefs of the child. Speech and other persons, therefore, cannot derive their meaning from a systematic interpretation of sensory phenomena and the "multiple given." They are indecomposable structures and in that sense are *a prioris*. But a double consequence with regard to the definition of consciousness follows from this. Since the distinction between sensible content and *a priori* structure is a secondary distinction—justified in the universe of natural objects known by adult consciousness, but impossible in infantile consciousness—and since there do exist "material *a prioris*," [91] the conception of consciousness which we must formulate is profoundly modified. It is no longer possible to define it as a universal function for the organization of experience which would impose on all its objects the conditions of logical and physical existence which are those of a universe of articulated objects and which would owe its specifications only to the variety of its contents. There will be sectors of experience which are irreducible to each other.

At the same time that one abandons the notion of the "multiple given" as the source of all specifications one will doubtless be obliged to abandon the notion of mental activity as the principle of all coordinations. Indeed, as soon as one refuses to separate the relation from the different concrete structures which appear in experience, it is no longer possible to found all relation on the activity of the "epistemological subject"; and, at the same time as the perceived world is fragmented into discontinuous "regions," [92] consciousness is divided into different types of acts of consciousness. [93] In particular, the fact that primitive perception is, as it were, haunted by human presence and lacunary for all the rest obliges us to accept the fact that "others," although they may be reached in adults through "sensations" or "images," can also be known by means of very impoverished representational contents: therefore, there must be several ways for consciousness to intend its object and several sorts of intentions in it. To possess and contemplate a "representation" and to coordinate a mosaic of sensations—these are special attitudes which cannot account for all the life of consciousness and which probably apply to its more primitive modes, as a translation applies to a text. Desire could be related to the object desired, will to the object willed, fear to the object feared, without this reference—even if it always includes a cognitive nucleus—being reduced to the relation of representation to represented. Acts of thought would not be alone in having a signification, of containing in them the prescience of what they are seeking; there would be a sort of blind recognition of the object desired by the desire, and of the good by the will. This is the means by which a person can be "given" to a child as the pole of his desires and fears before the long work of interpretation which would arrive at the person as a conclusion from a universe of representations. This is also the means by which confused sensory ensembles can nevertheless be very precisely identified as the bases of certain human intentions. It may happen that, in entering a room, we perceive a poorly localized disorder before discovering the reason for this impression: for example, the asymmetrical position of a picture frame. In entering an apartment we can perceive the character of those who live there without being capable of justifying this impression by an enumeration of remarkable details, and certainly well before having noted the color of the furniture.[94] To actualize these justifications ahead of time in the form of "latent content" or "unconscious knowing" is to postulate that nothing is accessible to consciousness which is not present to it in the form of representation or content.

The implicit conception of consciousness to which these remarks lead will have to be made more precise. What we have said is sufficient to show that the possession of a representation or the exercise of a judgment is not coextensive with the life of consciousness. Rather, consciousness is a network of significative intentions which are sometimes clear to themselves and sometimes, on the contrary, lived rather than known. Such a conception will permit us to link consciousness with action by enlarging our idea of action. Human action can be reduced to vital action only if one considers the intellectual analysis by which it passes for a more ingenious *means* of achieving animal ends. But it is this completely external relation of end and means which becomes impossible from the point of view which we are adopting. It imposes itself as long as consciousness is defined by the possession of certain "representations," for then the consciousness of the act is necessarily reduced to representation of its goal on the one hand and possibly to that of the bodily mechanisms which assure its execution on the other. The relation of means to end can be only external under these conditions.

But if, as we have just said, representative consciousness is only one of the forms of consciousness and if this latter is defined more generally by reference to an object—whether it be willed, desired, loved, or represented—the felt movements will be linked together by a practical intention which animates them, which makes of them a directed melody; and it becomes impossible to distinguish the goal and the means as separable elements, impossible to treat human action as another solution to the problems which instinct resolves: if the problems were *the same,* the solutions would be identical. An analysis of the immanent meaning of action and its internal structure is substituted for an analysis of the goals of action and their means.

From this new point of view one realizes that, although all actions permit an adaptation to life, the word "life" does not have the same meaning in animality and humanity; and the conditions of life are defined by the proper essence of the species. Doubtless, clothing and houses serve to protect us from the cold; language helps in collective work and in the analysis of the "unorganized mass." But the act of dressing becomes the act of adornment or also of modesty and thus reveals a new attitude toward oneself and others. Only men see that they are nude. In the house that he builds for himself, man projects and realizes his preferred values. Finally, the act of speaking expresses the fact that man ceases to adhere immediately to the milieu, that he elevates it to the status of spectacle and takes possession of it mentally by means of knowledge properly so called.[95]

The conception which we are outlining will also allow us to integrate into consciousness the coefficient of reality which psychologists seek to introduce from the outside when they speak of a "reality function" or of a feeling of present reality. Consciousness of reality cannot be reduced to the reverberation in us of a motor accompaniment of our thoughts. And it is difficult to see how the adjunction of kinesthetic contents (which recalls the mental alchemy of associationism) could be sufficient to constitute the spectacle of a real world in which consciousness grasps itself as involved. There is a motor accompaniment of our thoughts without any doubt, but how the brute existence which it is supposed to make us feel is related to the perceived object must still be explained; clearly something in the visual spectacle itself must solicit this transfer. The fact is that every alteration of individual existences in consciousness manifests itself in a modification of the concrete appearance of the objects. A schizophrenic says: "See these roses; my wife would have found them beautiful; for me, they are a pile of leaves, petals, thorns and stems." [96] The same thing is true of the "reality function" as of "reflex nativism," which thinks it is explaining the precocious perception of space by basing it on the fact of our becoming conscious of certain localizing reflexes, and of the classical theories, which would engender visual space from tactile space.

All of these hypothetical constructions presuppose what they want to explain since how and according to what criteria consciousness recognizes the correspondent of such and such a tactile or motor given in this or that visual given, for example, must still be explained—which implies finally a visual and even an inter-sensory organization of space. Likewise, awareness of an individual existence is not explained by the coupling of judgments which concern only an object of thought with a motor accompaniment charged with transforming the object into reality. It is in the phenomenal dimension of the perceived and in its intrinsic meaning that the existential index must be found, since *it is this* which appears to be real.

But this lived consciousness does not exhaust the human dialectic. What defines man is not the capacity to create a second nature—economic, social or cultural—beyond biological nature; it is rather the capacity of going beyond created structures in order to create others. And this movement is already visible in each of the particular products of human work. A nest is an object which has a meaning only in relation to the possible behavior of the organic individual; if a monkey picks a branch in order to reach a goal, it is because it is able to confer a functional value on an object of nature. But monkeys scarcely succeed at all in constructing instruments which would serve only for preparing others; we have seen that, having become a stick for the monkey, the tree branch is eliminated as such—which is the equivalent of saying that it is never possessed as an instrument in the full sense of the word. Animal activity reveals its limits in the two cases: it loses itself in the real transformations which it accomplishes and cannot reiterate them. For man, on the contrary, the tree branch which has become a stick will remain precisely a tree-branch-which-has-become-a-stick, the same *thing* in two different functions and visible *for him* under a plurality of aspects.

This power of choosing and varying points of view permits man to create instruments, not under the pressure of a *de facto* situation, but for a virtual use and especially in order to fabricate others. The meaning of human work therefore is the recognition, beyond the present milieu, of a world of things visible for each "I" under a plurality of aspects, the taking possession of an indefinite time and space; and one could easily show that the signification of speech or that of suicide and of the revolutionary act is the same.[97] These acts of the human dialectic all reveal the same essence: the capacity of orienting oneself in relation to the possible, to the mediate, and not in relation to a limited milieu; they all reveal what we called above, with Goldstein, the categorial attitude. Thus, the human dialectic is ambiguous: it is first manifested by the social or cultural structures, the appearance of which it brings about and in which it imprisons itself. *But its use-objects and its cultural objects would not be what they are if the activity which brings about their appearance did not also have as its meaning to reject them and to surpass them.*

Correlatively, perception, which until now has appeared to us to be the assimilation of consciousness into a cradle of institutions and a narrow circle of human "milieus," can become, especially by means of art, perception of a "universe." The knowledge of a truth is substituted for the experience of an immediate reality. "Man is a being who has the power of elevating to the status of objects the centers of resistance and reaction of his milieu . . . among which animals live entranced." [98] But the knowledge of a universe will already be prefigured in lived perception, just as the negation of all the milieus is prefigured in the work which creates them. More generally, the life of consciousness outside of self which we have described above, on the one hand, and, on the other, the consciousness of self and of a universe, which we are reaching now—in Hegelian terms, consciousness in-itself (*en soi*) and consciousness in-and-for-itself (*en et pour soi*)—cannot be purely and simply juxtaposed. The problem of perception lies completely in this duality.

In the preceding pages we have attempted to describe the advent of human action and of human perception and to show that they are irreducible to the vital dialectic of the organism and its milieu, even when modified by the contributions of a sociological causality. But it is not sufficient to oppose a description to reductive explanations since the latter could always challenge these descriptive characteristics of human action as being only apparent. It would be necessary to bring to light the abuse of causal thinking in explanatory theories and at the same time to show positively how the physiological and sociological dependencies which they rightly take into account ought to be conceived. Here we can neither treat this point completely nor leave it aside altogether. Since nascent perception is an emotional contact of the infant with the centers of interest of its milieu much more than a cognitive and disinterested operation, we would like to make more precise the relations of the properly human dialectic with the vital dialectic by using the example of the Freudian system.

One could have believed that Freud proposed to distinguish these two dialectics since he had protested against the physiological theories of dreams which, according to him, furnish only their most general conditions and since he sought their explanation in the individual life of the dreamer and in its immanent logic. But the proper meaning of a dream is never its manifest meaning. It has been clearly shown how, faced with the contrast between the subject's first recital of the dream and the second recital which analysis reveals, Freud believed it necessary to actualize the latter in the form of latent content within an ensemble of unconscious forces and mental entities which enter into conflict with the counter-forces of the censor; the manifest content of the dream would result from this sort of energic action.[99]

Without calling into question the role which Freud assigns to the erotic infrastructure and to social regulations, what we should like to ask is whether the conflicts themselves of which he speaks and the psychological mechanisms which he has described—the formation of complexes, repression, regression, resistance, transfer, compensation and sublimation—really require the system of causal notions by which he interprets them and which transforms the discoveries of psychoanalysis into a metaphysical theory of human existence. For it is easy to see that causal thinking is not indispensable here and that one can use another language. Development should be considered, not as the fixation of a given force on outside objects which are also given, but as a progressive and discontinuous structuration (*Gestaltung, Neugestaltung*)[100] of behavior. Normal structuration is one which reorganizes conduct in depth in such a way that infantile attitudes no longer have a place or meaning in the new attitude; it would result in perfectly integrated behavior, each moment of which would be internally linked with the whole. One will say that there is repression when integration has been achieved only in appearance and leaves certain relatively isolated systems subsisting in behavior which the subject refuses both to transform and to assume. A complex is a segment of behavior of this kind, a stereotyped attitude, an acquired and durable structure of consciousness with regard to a category of stimuli. A situation which could not be mastered at the time of an initial experience and which gave rise to the anguish and the disorganization which accompanies failure is no longer experienced directly: the subject perceives it only through the physiognomy that it assumed at the time of the traumatic experience. In these conditions each new experience, which in reality is not a new experience, repeats the result of the preceding ones and renders its return even more probable in the future.

The complex is not like a thing which would subsist deep within us and produce its effects on the surface from time to time. Exclusive of the times when it is manifested, it is present only in the way in which the knowledge of a language is present when we are not speaking it.[101] Certain objective stimuli have been clothed with a meaning from which we do not extricate them, have given rise to a rigid and stable structure. Doubtless this adhesiveness, this inertia, of certain structures of behavior (as, moreover, the acts which put an end to them) poses a problem in turn. It will be a question of understanding how certain separated dialectics and, changing the meaning of the word, certain mental automatons— gifted with an internal logic—can be constituted in the flux of consciousness and provide an apparent justification to the causal thinking, to Freud's "explanations in the third person." [102] But the problem is not resolved by attributing to complexes a reality and an efficacy of their own, as if the existence of this fragment of isolated conduct were not conditioned by the whole attitude of the consciousness which avoids thinking about it in order not to have to integrate and be responsible for it.[103]

The childhood memory which provides the key to a dream and the traumatic event which provides the key to an attitude (and which analysis succeeds in laying bare) are not therefore the *causes* of the dream or of the behavior.[104] They are the means for the analyst of understanding a present structure or attitude.[105] Consciousness *becomes* infantile consciousness in the dreamer or disassociated consciousness in the cases in which one speaks of a complex.

What is required by the facts which Freud describes under the name of repression, complex, regression or resistance is only the possibility of a fragmented life of consciousness which does not possess a unique significance at all times. This weakening, which allows a partial conduct to have an apparent autonomy, which brings back the stereotyped attitudes and thus conditions the alleged efficacy of the complex, at the same time allows it to remain equivocal.

The catastrophic attitude or that of the dreamer is not bound up with historical antecedents which would explicitate their true meaning. At that moment the subject lives after the manner of children, who are guided by the immediate feeling of the permitted or the forbidden, without looking for the meaning of the prohibitions. Thus, the pretended unconsciousness of the complex is reduced to the ambivalence of immediate consciousness.[106] The regression of the dream, the efficacy of a complex acquired in the past and, finally, the unconsciousness of the repressed only manifest the return to a primitive manner of organizing conduct, a yielding of the more complex structures and a withdrawal toward more facile ones. But then mental functioning as Freud has described it, the conflicts of force and the energic mechanisms which he imagined, would represent (in a very approximative way, moreover) only fragmentary behavior, that is, behavior which is pathological.

The possibility of constructing a causal explanation of behavior is exactly proportional to the inadequacy of the structurations accomplished by the subject. The work of Freud constitutes, not a tableau of human existence, but a tableau of anomalies—however frequent they may be. Along with mechanisms of compensation, sublimation and transfer which presuppose the same energic metaphors and which are thus the solutions of the sick, a true development, a transformation of human existence would be possible. To the extent that sublimation is only a derivation of unemployed biological forces, new activity must conserve the fluctuating character, the lability characteristic of non-integrated behavior; in cases in which sublimation and transfer have succeeded, on the contrary, it is because vital energies are no longer the motor forces of behavior; they have been really integrated into a new whole and eliminated as biological forces.

From this we see that it should be possible and necessary to distinguish cases in which Freudian mechanisms function from others in which they have been transcended. There would be people whose whole conduct is explicable by the history of the libido and all of whose acts would be related only to the universe of biology. Through the human world which they do not see they aim at vital objects just as others, prisoners of a parental complex, believe they "are marrying" when in reality they are seeking a maternal protection. This is because the reorganization, the new birth of the adult or the man, is accomplished in them in word and not in reality. Others, by mechanisms of sublimation properly so called, would believe they were transcending the vital and social dialectic and would be able only to distract themselves from it.

There is a vague love which attaches itself to the first object which it accidentally encounters; there is an art and a religion the whole true meaning of which is to compensate in a virtual world for real failures or constraints; there is finally, as Nietzsche said, an adherence to values of sacrifice which is only a form of vital impotence and of "impoverished life." These pseudo-solutions are recognizable from the fact that the being of the person never coincides with what he says, what he thinks, or even with what he does. False art, false sanctity and false love which *seek,* like the seminary companions of Julien Sorel, to "perform significant acts" [107] give to human life only a borrowed significance, effect only an ideal transformation, a flight into transcendent ideas.

But there are other men, capable of integrating into their existence, by unifying it, what in the preceding ones was only ideological pretext, and these *would be* truly men. With respect to them, the causal explanations of Freud would always be anecdotal; they would account only for the most external aspects of a true love just as, according to Freud himself, physiological explanations do not exhaust the content of a dream. Mental acts would have their own proper meaning and their own internal laws.

But neither the psychological with respect to the vital nor the rational (*spirituel*) with respect to the psychological can be treated as substances or as new worlds. The relation of each order to the higher order is that of the partial to the total. A normal man is not a body bearing certain autonomous instincts joined to a "psychological life" defined by certain characteristic processes—pleasure and pain, emotion, association of ideas—and surmounted with a mind which would unfold its proper acts over this infrastructure. The advent of higher orders, to the extent that they are accomplished, eliminate the autonomy of the lower orders and give a new signification to the steps which constitute them. This is why we have spoken of a human order rather than of a mental or rational order. The so frequent distinction of the mental and the somatic has its place in pathology but cannot serve for the knowledge of normal man, that is, of integrated man, since in him the somatic processes do not unfold in isolation but are integrated into a cycle of more extensive action. It is not a question of two *de facto* orders external to each other, but of two types of relations, the second of which integrates the first. The contrast between what is called mental life and what are called bodily phenomena is evident when one has in view the body considered part by part and moment by moment.

But, as we have seen, biology already refers to the phenomenal body, that is, to the center of vital actions which are extended over a segment of time, respond to certain concrete stimulus wholes and effect the collaboration of the whole organism. These modes of behavior do not even subsist as such in man. Reorganized in its turn in new wholes, vital behavior as such disappears. This is what is signified, for example, by the periodicity and monotony of sexual life in animals, by its constancy and its variations in man. Thus, one cannot speak of the body and of life in general, but only of the animal body and animal life, of the human body and of human life; and the body of the normal subject—if it is not detached from the spatio-temporal cycles of behavior of which it is the support— is not distinct from the psychological.

Remarks of the same kind would be possible concerning the notion of mind. We are not defending a mentalism which would distinguish mind and life or mind and the psychological as two "powers of being." [108] It is a question of a "functional opposition" which cannot be transformed into a "substantial opposition." [109] Mind is not a specific difference which would be added to vital or psychological being in order to constitute a man. Man is not a rational animal. The appearance of reason and mind does not leave intact a sphere of self-enclosed instincts in man. Cognitive disorders which affect the categorial attitude are expressed by a loss of sexual initiatives.[110] The alteration of higher functions reaches as far as the so-called instinctive structures; the ablation of the higher centers entails death, although decerebrate animals can subsist after a fashion. "If man had the senses of an animal, he would not have reason." [111] Man can never be an animal: his life is always more or less integrated than that of an animal. But if the alleged instincts of man do not exist *apart* from the mental dialectic, correlatively, this dialectic is not conceivable outside of the concrete situations in which it is embodied. One does not act with mind alone. Either mind is nothing, or it constitutes a real and not an ideal transformation of man. Because it is not a new sort of being but a new form of unity, it cannot stand by itself.

What is artificial in the alternatives of psychology can be seen from the point of view which we have adopted. After the psychology as a science of the facts of consciousness has come the psychology without consciousness of Watson. But it is not realized that a partitive analysis, which decomposes behavior into reflexes and conditioned reflexes, does not succeed in furnishing laws of natural behavior. Therefore, it is said, "determinants" or "functional variables" must be introduced as conditions of behavior in addition to the "stimuli," [112] which variables confer a value and a meaning on the stimuli. But no more in Tolman than in his critics is the philosophical status of the determinants ever correctly conceptualized: they are compared to the ideal components of the phenomena which physics formulates and it is added that, being abstractions like speed, output and energy, they should no more be considered real than these latter. But while the ideal variables of science constitute reality itself for it, psychologists conserve the realistic distinction of causes and conditions: "Only stimuli and responses are realities. The determinants of behavior, that is, the mental phenomena, are *only* traits, or relations between traits and phases of behavior." [113] Thus, "purposive behaviorism" [114] remains "materialistic" and tries to gain acceptance only for the rights of a description of behavior which does not divide it into atoms, does not reduce it to physiological terms but considers it "in its unity and originality." [115] But either the determinants which the description introduces admit somatic equivalents and then the description spoken of has only a provisional value and there is nothing essential to be changed in physiological behaviorism, whose inadequacy is nevertheless recognized; or else these determinants are irreducible and then, it is asserted, they bring back finalism.[116] Thus, one does not escape from the classical debate between "mentalists" and "materialists." The negation of materialistic realism seems possible only to the benefit of mentalistic realism, and conversely. It is not seen that, from the moment behavior is considered "in its unity" and in its human meaning, one is no longer dealing with a material reality nor, moreover, with a mental reality, but with a significative whole or a structure which properly belongs neither to the external world nor to internal life. It is realism in general which must be called into question.

The obscurity comes from the old antithesis between external

and internal perception and from the privilege generally accorded
the latter. But it is a fact that it was possible to constitute a psychology which owes nothing to introspection. A purely objective
method can delineate the structure of the universe of "colors" in
butterflies by comparing the reactions which are evoked in them
by the different colored stimuli—precisely on the condition of limiting oneself strictly to the identity or difference of the responses in
the presence of such and such given stimuli and of not projecting
our lived experience of colors into the consciousness of the butterfly.
There is an objective analysis and an objective definition of perception, intelligence and emotion as structures of behavior,[117] and we
have attempted a description of this kind in the preceding chapter.

The mental thus understood is comprehensible from the outside. Even more, introspection itself is a procedure of knowledge
which is homogeneous with external observation. For what it gives
us, as soon as it is communicated, is not the lived experience itself,
but an account in which language plays the role of a general preparation—acquired once and for all—which does not differ essentially
from the preparation of the circumstances employed by the objective
method. The child who is supposed to say which colors appear
similar to him and the monkey which has been trained to put all
the slugs of the same color in a saucer are in the same situation.
Nothing is changed when the subject is charged with interpreting
his reactions himself, which is what is proper to introspection. When
he is asked if he can read the letters inscribed on a panel or distinguish the details of a shape, he will not trust a vague "impression
of legibility." He will attempt to read or to describe what is presented
to him. "Introspection, as soon as it is translated into language,
affirms something completely other than the existence of certain
inner qualities. The state of consciousness is the consciousness of a
state. Consciousness is always consciousness of something (consciousness of . . . , consciousness that . . .), that is, of a function . . . ,
these functions are part of the real; the consciousness which we
have of them can be correct or incorrect." [118] The object which is
intended by both external observation and introspection is then a
structure or a signification which is reached in both cases through
different materials.

There is no reason either to reject introspection or to make it
the privileged means of access to a world of psychological facts. It

is one of the possible perspectives of the structure and immanent meaning of conduct, which latter constitute the only psychological "reality."

Conclusion

In the preceding chapters we have considered the birth of behavior in the physical world and in an organism; that is, we have pretended to know nothing of man by reflection and have limited ourselves to developing what was implied in the scientific representation of his behavior. Aided by the notion of structure or form, we have arrived at the conclusion that both mechanism and finalism should be rejected and that the "physical," the "vital" and the "mental" do not represent three powers of being, but three dialectics. Physical nature in man is not subordinated to a vital principle, the organism does not conspire to actualize an idea, and the mental is not a motor principle *in* the body; but what we call nature is already consciousness of nature, what we call life is already consciousness of life and what we call mental is still an object vis-à-vis consciousness. Nevertheless, while establishing the ideality of the physical form, that of the organism, and that of the "mental," and *precisely because we did it,* we could not simply superimpose these three orders; not being a new substance, each of them had to be conceived as a retaking and a "new" structuration of the preceding one. From this comes the double aspect of the analysis which both liberated the higher from the lower and founded the former on the latter. It is this double relation which remains obscure and which now induces us to situate our results with respect to the classical solutions and in particular with respect to critical idealism. At the beginning we considered consciousness as a region of being and as a particular type of behavior. Upon analysis one finds it presupposed everywhere as the place of ideas and everywhere interconnected as the integration of existence. What then is the relation between consciousness as universal milieu and consciousness enrooted in the subordinated dialectics? Must the point of view of the "outside spectator" be abandoned as illegitimate to the benefit of an unconditioned reflection?

IV. THE RELATIONS OF THE SOUL AND THE BODY AND THE PROBLEM OF PERCEPTUAL CONSCIOUSNESS

The Classical Solutions

That naive consciousness is realistic has been affirmed too much. Or at least a distinction should be made in this regard between the opinions of common sense, the manner in which it verbally accounts for perception,[1] and the perceptual experiences themselves; verbalized perception should be distinguished from lived perception. If we return to objects as they appear to us when we live in them without speech and without reflection and if we try to describe their mode of existence faithfully, they do not evoke any realistic metaphor. If I adhere to what immediate consciousness tells me, the desk which I see in front of me and on which I am writing, the room in which I am and whose walls enclose me beyond the sensible field, the garden, the street, the city and, finally, the whole of my spatial horizon do not appear to me to be causes of the perception which I have of them, causes which would impress their mark on me and produce an image of themselves by a transitive action. It seems to me rather that my perception is like a beam of light which reveals the objects there where they are and manifests their presence, latent until then. Whether I myself perceive or consider another subject perceiving, it seems to me that the gaze "is posed" on objects and reaches them from a distance—as is well expressed by the use of the Latin *lumina* for designating the gaze.

Doubtless I know that my present experience of this desk is not complete, that it shows me only some of its aspects: be it the color, the form or the size, I know very well that they would vary under another lighting, from another point of view and standing in another place; I know that "the desk" is not reducible to the determinations with which it is presently clothed. But in immediate consciousness this perspectival character of my knowledge is not conceived as an accident in its regard, as an imperfection relative to the existence of my body and its proper point of view; and knowledge by "profiles"[2] is not treated as the degradation of a true knowledge which would grasp the totality of the possible aspects of the object all at once.

Perspective does not appear to me to be a subjective deformation of things but, on the contrary, to be one of their properties, perhaps their essential property. It is precisely because of it that the perceived possesses in itself a hidden and inexhaustible richness, that it is a "thing." In other words, when one speaks of the perspectival character of knowledge, the expression is equivocal. It can signify that only the perspectival projection of objects would be given to primitive knowledge; and in this sense the expression is inexact since the first reactions of an infant are adapted, for example, to the distance of objects[3]—a fact which excludes the idea of a phenomenal world originally without depth. From the beginning the perspectival character of knowledge is known as such and not something to which we are subjected. Far from introducing a coefficient of subjectivity into perception, it provides it on the contrary with the assurance of communicating with a world which is richer than what we know of it, that is, of communicating with a real world. The profiles of my desk are not given to direct knowledge as appearances without value, but as "manifestations" of the desk.

Although naive consciousness never confuses the thing with the manner which it has of appearing to us, and precisely because it does not make this confusion, it is the thing itself which naive consciousness thinks it is reaching, and not some inner double, some subjective reproduction. It does not imagine that the body or that mental "representations" function as a screen between itself and reality. The perceived is grasped in an indivisible manner as "in-itself" (*en soi*), that is, as gifted with an interior which I will never have finished exploring; and as "for-me" (*pour moi*), that is, as given "in person" through its momentary aspects. Neither this me-

tallic spot which moves while I glance toward it, nor even the
geometric and shiny mass which emerges from it when I look at
it, nor finally, the ensemble of perspectival images which I have
been able to have of it *are* the ashtray; they do not exhaust the
meaning of the "this" by which I designate it; and, nevertheless,
it is the ashtray which appears in all of them.

This is not the place to analyze further the parodoxical relation
of the "aspects" to the thing, of the "manifestations" [4] to that which
is manifested by them and beyond them. But what we have said
is sufficient to show that this relation is original and founds a consciousness of reality in a specific manner. The perspectival appearance of the ashtray is not to the "ashtray itself" what one event
is to another event which it announces, or what a sign is to that
which it signifies. Neither the sequence of "states of consciousness"
nor the logical organization of thought accounts for perception:
the first, because it is an external relation while the perspectival
appearances of the ashtray are representative of each other; the
second, because it presupposes a mind in possession of its object
while my will is without direct action on the unfolding of the
perceived perspectives and because their concordant multiplicity is
organized of itself. A "cube" is not what I see of it since I see only
three sides at a time; but no more is it a judgment by which I link
together the successive appearances. A judgment, that is, a coordination conscious of itself, would be necessary only if the isolated
appearances were given beforehand, which is counter to the hypothesis of intellectualism. Something of the empiricism which it
surmounts always remains in intellectualism—something like a repressed empiricism. Thus, to do justice to our direct experience of
things it would be necessary to maintain at the same time, against
empiricism, that they are beyond their sensible manifestations and,
against intellectualism, that they are not unities in the order of
judgment, that they are embodied in their apparitions. The "things"
in naive experience are evident as *perspectival beings:* it is essential
to them, both to offer themselves without interposed milieu and
to reveal themselves only gradually and never completely; they are
mediated by their perspectival appearances; but it is not a question
of a logical mediation since it introduces us to their bodily reality;
I grasp *in* a perspectival appearance, which I know is only one of
its possible aspects, the thing itself which transcends it. A transcendence which is nevertheless open to my knowledge—this is the

very definition of a thing as it is intended (*visée*) by naive consciousness.

Whatever difficulty one may find in conceptualizing perception described in this way, it is for us to accommodate ourselves to it; this is the way that we perceive and that consciousness lives in things. Nothing is more foreign to perception therefore than the idea of a universe which would produce in us representations which are distinct from it by means of a causal action. To speak Kantian language, the realism of naive consciousness is an empirical realism—the assurance of an external experience in which there is no doubt about escaping "states of consciousness" and acceding to solid objects—and not a transcendental realism which, as a philosophical thesis, would posit these objects as the ungraspable causes of "representations" which alone are given.

The bodily mediation most frequently escapes me: when I witness events that interest me, I am scarcely aware of the perpetual breaks which the blinking of the eyelids imposes on the scene, and they do not figure in my memory. But after all, I know very well that I am able to interrupt the view by closing my eyes, that I see by the intermediary of my eyes. This knowledge does not prevent my believing that I see things themselves when I look at them. This is because the body proper and its organs remain the bases or vehicles of my intentions and are not yet grasped as "physiological realities." The body is *present* to the soul as external things are present; in neither case is it a question of a causal relation between the two terms. The unity of man has not yet been broken; the body has not been stripped of human predicates; it has not yet become a machine; and the soul has not yet been defined as existence for-itself (*pour soi*). Naive consciousness does not see in the soul the *cause* of the movements of the body nor does it put the soul in the body as the pilot in his ship. This way of thinking belongs to philosophy; it is not implied in immediate experience.

Since the body itself is not grasped as a material and inert mass or as an external instrument but as the living envelope of our actions, the principle of these actions has no need of being a quasi-physical force. Our intentions find their natural clothing or their embodiment in movements and are expressed in them as the thing is expressed in its perspectival aspects. Thus, thinking can be "in the throat," as the children questioned by Piaget say it is,[5] without any contradiction or confusion of the extended and the non-extended, because the throat is not yet an ensemble of vibrating cords capable of producing the sonorous phenomena of language, because it remains that privileged region of a qualitative space where my signifying intentions manifest themselves in words. Since the soul remains coextensive with nature, since the perceiving subject does not grasp himself as a microcosm into which messages of external events would make their way mediately and since his gaze extends over the things themselves, to act upon them is not for him to get outside the self and provoke a local movement in a fragment of extension; it is to make an intention explode in the phenomenal field in a cycle of significative gestures, or to join to the things in which he lives the actions which they solicit by an attraction comparable to that of the first unmoved mover.

One can say, if you like, that the relation of the thing perceived to perception, or of the intention to the gestures which realize it, is a magical relation in naive consciousness; but it would still be necessary to understand magical consciousness as it understands itself and not to reconstruct it from subsequent categories. The subject does not live in a world of states of consciousness or representations from which he would believe himself able to act on and know external things by a sort of miracle. He lives in a universe of experience, in a milieu which is neutral with regard to the substantial distinctions between the organism, thought and extension; he lives in a direct commerce with beings, things and his own body. The ego as a center from which his intentions radiate, the body which carries them and the beings and things to which they are addressed are not confused: but they are only three sectors of a unique field. Things are things, that is, transcendent with respect to all that I know of them and accessible to other perceiving subjects, but intended precisely as things; as such they are the indispensable moment of the lived dialectic which embraces them.

But on the other hand consciousness discovers, particularly in illness, a resistance of the body proper. Since an injury to the eyes is sufficient to eliminate vision, we must then see through the body. Since an illness is sufficient to modify the phenomenal world, it must be then that the body forms a screen between us and things. In order to understand this strange power of the body to upset the entire view of the world, we are obliged to renounce the image of it which direct experience gives us. The phenomenal body, with the human determinations which permitted consciousness not to be distinguished from it, is going to take on the status of appearance; the "real body" will be the one which we know through anatomy or, more generally, through the isolating methods of analysis: an ensemble of organs of which we have no notion in immediate experience and which interpose their mechanisms, their unknown powers, between ourselves and things. One could still conserve the favorite metaphor of naive consciousness and admit that the subject perceives *in conformity with* his body—as a colored glass modifies what the beam illuminates—without denying him access to the things themselves or putting them outside him.

But the body appears capable of fabricating a pseudo-perception. Thus certain phenomena of which it is the seat must be the necessary and sufficient condition for perception; the body must be the necessary intermediary between the real world and perception which are henceforth disassociated from each other. Perception can no longer be a taking-possession of things which finds them in their proper place; it must be an event internal to the body and one which results from their action on it. The world is doubled: there will be the real world as it is outside my body and the world as it is for me, numerically distinct from the first; the external cause of perception and the internal object which it contemplates will have to be separated. The body proper has become a material mass and, correlatively, the subject withdraws from it to contemplate its representations within himself.

Instead of the three inseparable terms bound together in the living unity of an experience which a pure *description* reveals, one finds oneself in the presence of three orders of events which are external to each other: the events of nature, the organic events and those of thought, which will explain each other. Perception will result from an action of the thing on the body and of the body on the soul. First it is the sensible, the perceived itself, to which the functions of extra-mental things are attributed; then the problem is to understand how a duplicate or an imitation of the real is aroused in the body, then in thought. Since a picture makes us think of what it represents, it will be supposed—based on the privileged case of the visual apparatus—that the senses receive "little pictures" of real things which excite the soul to perceive them.[6] The Epicurean "simulacra" or the "intentional species," "all those little images fluttering through the air"[7] which bring the sensible appearance of things into the body, only transpose the ideal presence of the thing to the perceiving subject into terms of causal explanation and real operations. It is the former, as we have seen, which is an evidence for naive consciousness. In default of a numerical identity the philosopher seeks to maintain a specific identity between the perceived and the real, to have the distinctive characteristic of the perceived come from the things themselves; this is why perception is understood as an imitation or a duplication in us of sensible things, or as the actualization in the soul of something which was in potency in an external sensible thing.

The difficulties which this explanatory mythology encounters would not have to be mentioned if they issued only from the realism of the sensible which has been abandoned since Descartes. In fact they are the permanent difficulties of any causal explanation applied to perception. The Descartes of the *Dioptrics* rejects the transitive action by means of which sensible things, identical with perceived objects, would impress their image in the body, where the soul would find it. Since light is only a movement, there is no need to suppose any resemblance between the things external to the body, the physiological phenomena and what the soul perceives. And, moreover, even if the perceived object resembled the bodily phenomena which condition perception or their external causes, perception would still not have been explained. "Even if this painting, by passing into the interior of our head in this way, still retains something of a resemblance to the objects from which it proceeds, one must still not be persuaded . . . that it is by means of this resemblance that it causes us to sense them, as if there were other eyes over again in our brain with which we could apperceive; one should hold rather that it is the movements which compose it which, acting immediately on the soul inasmuch as it is united to our body, are constituted by nature to cause the soul to have such feelings." [8]

The external thing and the bodily impression do not act therefore as exemplar causes; they are the occasional causes[9] of the feelings of the soul. But all the difficulties are not removed; if the cerebral impressions are only the occasional causes of perception there must still be a regulated correspondence between certain cerebral impressions and certain perceptions. One has indeed gotten rid of the myths which made the idea of a real transference of sensible things into the mind inevitable; but one is obliged to construct physiological schemata which make comprehensible how sensory impressions are prepared in the brain to become the adequate occasions of our perceptions. Since we perceive only one object in spite of the two images which it forms on our retina, only one space in which the givens of the different senses are distributed, it will be necessary to imagine a bodily operation which combines these multiple elements and provides the soul with the occasion of forming a single perception.[10] Thus the substitution of occasional causes for exemplar causes does not eliminate the necessity of placing some physiological representation of the perceived object in the brain. This necessity is inherent in the realist attitude in general.

It is found again in the pseudo-Cartesianism of scientists and psychologists. Both consider perception and its proper objects as "internal" or "mental phenomena," as functions of certain physiological and mental variables. If by nature one means a group of events bound by laws, perception would be a part of nature, the perceived world a function of the real world of primary qualities. Then the problem is to designate in the body the adequate conditions of perception. Just as Descartes is obliged to reserve the mediation of the body and perception to the pineal gland [11] as seat of the common sense, so physiologists have had to give up designating fixed spatial and chromatic values in the periphery of the nervous system and to make those which in perception are distributed over the different points of the visual field depend on the assimilation of the corresponding excitations into variable associative circuits. Descartes' pineal gland plays the role of the association zone of modern physiologists.

As soon as one accepts as given, as realism wants it, that the soul "sees immediately only by the interposition of the brain," [12] this mediation, even if it is not a transitive action, necessitates looking in the body for a physiological equivalent of the perceived. But the nerve functioning which distributes their spatial or chromatic values to the different points of the sensory field, and which in normal cases, for example, renders diplopia impossible, is not itself conceivable without reference to the phenomenal field and its laws of internal equilibrium; it is a process of form, the notion of which is borrowed in the final analysis from the perceived world.

"It is the soul that sees and not the eyes," Descartes said [13] in order to get rid of the "little images fluttering through the air." The evolution of modern physiology shows that this expression must be taken absolutely literally and turned back against Descartes himself. It is the soul which sees and not the brain; it is by means of the perceived world and its proper structures that one can explain the spatial value assigned to a point of the visual field in each particular case. The coordinate axes of the phenomenal field, the direction which at each moment receives the value of "vertical" or "horizontal" and "frontal" or "lateral," the ensembles to which are assigned the index "immobile" and with respect to which the remainder of the field appears "in movement," the colored stimuli which are seen as "neutral" and determine the distribution of the apparent colors in the rest of the field, and the contexts of our spatial and chromatic perception—none of these result as effects from an intersection of mechanical actions; they are not a function of certain physical variables. Gestalt theory believed that a causal explanation, and even a physical one, remained possible on the condition that one recognized processes of structuration in physics in addition to mechanical actions.

But, as we have seen, physical laws do not furnish an explanation *of* the structures, they represent an explanation *within* the structures. They express the least integrated structures, those in which the simple relations of function to variable can be established. They are already becoming inadequate in the "acausal" domain of modern physics. In the functioning of the organism, the structuration is constituted according to new dimensions—the typical activity of the species or the individual—and the preferred forms of action and perception can be treated even less as the summative effect of partial interactions. Thus the properties of the phenomenal field are not expressible in a language which would owe nothing to them. The structure of the "thing perceived" now offers a new support to this conclusion.

The relation of the perspectival aspects to the thing which they present to us is not reducible to any of the relations which exist within nature. As we have seen, it is neither the relation of effect to cause, nor that of function to corresponding variable. All the difficulties of realism arise precisely from having tried to convert this original relation into a causal action and to integrate perception into nature. As soon as the presence or the presentation of a "thing" to consciousness—instead of remaining an ideal relation, as in naive experiences—is interpreted as a real operation of the thing on the body and on the perceiving subject, it becomes impossible to reconstitute the descriptive content of perception, the actual view of the world, as an effect. The difficulty was evident in the theory of "simulacra" or in that of "intentional species" since, as copies of the thing itself, these "little pictures" which were transported into the body could not assume the variable perspectival aspects through which we nevertheless perceive things. Perspectival variation becomes understandable, on the contrary, once optics and the theory of light have excluded the idea of a resemblance between the real thing and the perceived.

But, inversely, it is the constancy of perceived things under their variable perspectival aspect which is going to become a problem. How are retinal images—so different depending on the points of view—going "to provide the soul with a means" of perceiving the same thing under several profiles? It would be necessary to suppose some association of present cerebral impressions with traces left by past impressions. But modern physiology has precisely given up the supposition of stores of cerebral traces, of "image centers" distinct from "perception centers"; and the physiological substrate of our perception is conceived as an indecomposable coordinating process in which the influence of prior excitations is not separately assignable. Most often one tries to "explain" the constancy of the phenomenal thing by a psychological process, by some "projection" [14] of memories which will complete or correct the present lacunary givens. To the extent that this "psychological explanation" is only a new kind of causal thinking we can reject it as we can every "explanation." Whether it is a question of memories or of cerebral traces, only a real transformation of sensible givens can be obtained by the real operations of a psychological or physiological causality: it will be shown how the "mental image" of an object does not follow exactly the perspectival variations of its "retinal image," how its phenomenal size when it is at some distance represents a mean between the size of the retinal image for a short distance and the size of the retinal image for a long one. But even if it could be established (which is false) that the mental image remains constant for variable distances, one would still not have explained the presentation of an identical thing under variable aspects since one would have purely and simply eliminated the perspectival variation by replacing it with the inertia of a constant "conscious content," with an immutable "mental image." The view of a thing seen through its "profiles," this original structure, is nothing which can be "explained" by some real physiological or psychological process. When I see an object at a distance I do not contemplate a *mental image of a determinate size,* as a sensitive plate can receive a physical image. I grasp in and by the perspectival aspect a constant thing which it mediates. The phenomenal object is not spread out on a plane, as it were; it involves two layers: the layer of perspectival aspects and that of the thing which they present. This ideal reference, this ambiguous mode of organization, can be described or understood, but not explained— with the help of a psycho-physiological law, for example—as if the "mental image" were another retinal image the size of which could be measured and related to certain variables.

But until now we have spoken only of a pseudo-Cartesianism. The *Dioptrics,* the *Treatise on Man,* and the *Treatise on the Passions* are situated in a ready-made world in which they delineate the human body and into which the soul is finally introduced. This is evidently not the principal undertaking of Cartesianism. Descartes' first step was to abandon the extra-mental things which philosophical realism had introduced in order to return to an inventory, to a description, of human experience without presupposing anything at first which explains it from the outside. With regard to perception, the radical originality of Cartesianism is to situate itself within perception itself, not to analyze vision and touch as functions of our body, but "only the thought of seeing and touching." [15] Beyond causal explanations which constitute the appearance of perception as an effect of nature, Descartes, in search of the internal structure, makes its meaning explicit and disengages the grounds which assure naive consciousness that it is acceding to "things"; that, beyond the transitory appearances, it is grasping a solid being in a piece of wax, for example. If, as is always said, methodic doubt concerning sensible things is distinguished from sceptical doubt—the one finding in itself that which brings it to an end, the other being a state of uncertitude which does not admit of a solution—this difference in the results should stem from a difference in the operations which lead to them. Sceptical doubt is insurmountable because it is not radical; it presupposes extra-mental things as the ideal term of knowledge and it is in relation to this inaccessible reality that dreams and perception take on the character of equivalent appearances.

The Cartesian doubt necessarily carries its solution within itself precisely because it presupposes nothing—no realist idea of knowledge—and because—bringing attention back in this way from the vision or touch which lives in things to the "thought of seeing and touching" and laying bare the internal meaning of perception and of acts of knowledge in general—it reveals to thought the indubitable domain of significations. Even if I see and touch nothing which exists outside my thought, it is still a fact that I think I am seeing and touching something and that certain judgments are possible concerning the meaning of this thought considered as such. The *cogito* not only discloses to me the certitude of my existence, but more generally it provides me with access to a whole field of knowledges by giving me a general method: the method of searching, by reflection, for the pure thought in each domain which defines it; with regard to perception, for example, of analyzing the thought of perceiving and the meaning of the perceived which are immanent in the sight of a piece of wax, which animate it and sustain it internally.

One can say that here Descartes was very close to the modern notion of consciousness understood as the center in which all the objects about which man can speak and all the mental acts which intend them take on an indubitable clarity. With the help of this notion Kant was able to go definitively beyond scepticism and realism by recognizing the descriptive and irreducible characteristics of external and internal experience as the sufficient foundation of the world. From this point of view perception could no longer appear to be the effect in us of the action of an external thing, nor the body as the intermediary of this causal action; the external thing and the body, defined as the "thought of" the thing and the "thought of" the body, as the "signification thing" and the "signification body," became indubitable as they present themselves to us in a lucid experience at the same time that they lost the occult powers that philosophical realism had given them.

But Descartes does not follow this path to the end. The analysis of the piece of wax gives us only the essence of the thing, only the intelligible structure of dream objects or of perceived objects.[16] The imagination already contains something which this analysis does not take into account: it gives us the pentagon as "present."[17] In perception, the object "presents" itself without having been willed.[18] There is an existential index which distinguishes the perceived or imaginary object from the idea and which manifests "something" in them "which differs from my mind,"[19] whatever this "other" may be in other respects.[20] Thus the experience of a sensible presence is explained by a real presence; the soul, when it perceives, is "excited" to think such and such an existing object by means of a bodily event to which it "applies itself" and which "represents" to it an event from the real extension.[21] The body ceases to be what it was vis-à-vis the understanding—a fragment of extension in which there are no real parts and in which the soul could not have a special seat[22]—to become, like the cubic foot of which Malebranche will speak,[23] a real individual. As such, it could be the occasional cause of perceptions and it could even be so in only one of its parts to which the soul is immediately connected.[24] The experience of my body as "mine" [25]— which discredits the Aristotelian metaphor of the soul as a pilot of his ship[26]—is explained in turn by a real "mixture" of "the mind with the body."

Thus the universe of consciousness revealed by the *cogito* and in the unity of which even perception itself seemed to be necessarily enclosed was only a universe of thought in the restricted sense: it accounts for the thought of seeing, but the fact of vision and the ensemble of existential knowledges remain outside of it. The intellection which the *cogito* had found in the heart of perception does not exhaust its content; to the extent that perception opens out on an "other," to the extent that it is the experience of an existence, it arises from a primary and original notion which "can only be understood in its own terms," [27] from an order of "life" in which the distinctions of the understanding are purely and simply annulled.[28] Thus Descartes did not attempt to integrate the knowledge of truth and the experience of reality, intellection and sensation.[29] It is not in the soul, it is in God that they are linked with each other. But after Descartes this integration was to appear to be the solution of the problems posed by philosophical realism. It would permit abandoning the action of the body or of things on the mind and allow them to be defined as the indubitable objects of a consciousness; it would permit surpassing the alternatives of realism and scepticism by associating, following Kant's terms, a transcendental idealism and an empirical realism.

The conception of sensible knowledge which was taught by Descartes is taken up again by a philosophy in the critical tradition. To know something is not only to find oneself in the presence of a compact ensemble of givens and to live in it as it were; this "conascence," [30] this blind contact with a singular object and this participation in its existence would be as nothing in the history of a mind and would leave no more acquisitions and available memories in the mind than would a physical pain or a fainting spell if the contrary movement by which I detach myself from the thing in order to apprehend the meaning were not already contained in them. Red, as sensation, and red, as *quale,* must be distinguished; the quality already includes two moments: the pure impression of red and its function, which for example is to cover a certain extension of space and of time.[31] To know therefore is always to grasp a given in a certain function, in a certain relation, "in as much" as it signifies to me or presents to me such or such a structure.

Psychologists often speak as if the whole question were to know where the signification of the perceived *comes from;* they treat it as an aggregate of additional givens and explain it by means of a projection of images over the brute givens of the senses. They do not see that the same problem poses itself with respect to the images introduced. If they are the simple copy of old perceptions, "little pictures" which are less clear, the becoming aware of these new "things" will still have to be analyzed once they have been brought back under the gaze of the mind by some psychological or physiological mechanism. And even if a "dynamic plan" presides over the evocation of memories, it remains an operation in the third person as long as *I* do not recognize an illustration of the plan in the memory evoked.

One does not construct perception as one does a house: by assembling the material gotten from the senses and the material gotten from memory; one does not explain it as an event of nature by situating it at the confluence of several causal series—sensory mechanisms and mnemonic mechanisms. Even if the search for physiological and psychological determinants were to make possible the establishment of a relation of function to variable between them and the view perceived—we have seen that this is not at all the case—this explanation would give us only the conditions of existence of the view; since it connects the view with bodily and mental events situated in space and time, this explanation would make it a mental event also. But there is something else. If I look steadily at an object in front of me, the psychologist will say that—external conditions remaining the same—the mental image of the object has remained the same. But it would still be necessary to analyze the act by which at each instant I recognize this image as identical in its meaning to that of the preceding instant.

The mental image of the psychologist is one thing; what the consciousness of that thing is must still be understood. The act of knowing is not of the order of events; it is a taking-possession of events, even internal ones, which is not mingled with them; it is always an internal "re-creation" of the mental image and, as Kant and Plato have said, a recognizance, a recognition. It is not the eye, not the brain, but no more is it the "psychism" of the psychologist which can accomplish the act of vision. It is a question of an inspection of the mind in which events are known in their meaning at the same time as they are lived in their reality. No matter how evident the determination of the perceived contents by natural conditions may be in each particular case, perception, by its general structure at least, eludes natural explanation and admits of only an internal analysis.

It follows from this that the moments of knowledge in which I grasp myself as determined to perceive a thing by that thing itself should be considered as derived modes of consciousness, founded in the final analysis on a more original mode of consciousness. Since the grounds for our affirmations can only be sought within their proper sphere (*sens*), the experience of a real thing cannot be explained by the action of that thing on my mind: the only way for a thing to act on a mind is to offer it a meaning, to manifest itself to it, to *constitute* itself vis-à-vis the mind in its intelligible articulations. The analysis of the act of knowing leads to the idea of a constituting or naturizing thought which internally subtends the characteristic structure of objects. In order to indicate both the intimacy of objects to the subject and the presence in them of solid structures which distinguish them from appearances, they will be called "phenomena"; and philosophy, to the extent that it adheres to this theme, becomes a phenomenology, that is, an inventory of consciousness as milieu of the universe.

Thus philosophy returns to the evidences of naive consciousness. Transcendental idealism, by making the subject and the object inseparable correlatives, guarantees the validity of perceptual experience in which the world appears in person and nonetheless as distinct from the subject. If knowledge, instead of being the presentation to the subject of an inert tableau, is the apprehension of the meaning of this tableau, the distinction of the objective world and subjective appearances is no longer that of two sorts of beings, but of two significations; as such, it is unchallengeable. It is the thing itself which I reach in perception since everything of which one can think is a "signification of thing" and since the act in which this signification is revealed to me is precisely called perception. One must go back, not to Bergson, but to Kant for this idea that the perception of point "o" is at point "o." [32] It follows immediately from a notion of consciousness as universal life in which every affirmation of object finds its grounds.

The body becomes one of the objects which is constituted vis-à-vis consciousness; it is integrated into the objective world; and, since any nature is conceivable only as the correlate of a naturizing knowledge, there is no longer any question of treating knowledge as a fact of nature. Doubtless consciousness itself recognizes that natural laws determine the order of its perceptual events in terms of the position of the body and of bodily phenomena. In this sense it manifests itself as a part of the world, since it can be integrated into the relations which constitute it. It seems to include two aspects: on the one hand it is milieu of the universe, presupposed by every affirmation of a world; on the other hand it is conditioned by it. Thus, the first moment of critical philosophy will be to distinguish, on the one hand, a general form of consciousness which cannot be derived from any bodily or psychological event, in order to do justice to its analysis of knowledge; and, on the other, the empirical contents whose actual existence could be related to such and such external events or to this or that particularity of our psycho-physical constitution, in order to account for the external conditions which govern perception as well as the passivity which we grasp in it. Such is approximately the meaning of the *Transcendental Esthetic*.[33] But this attitude can be only provisional, as is shown by the second edition of the *Critique of Pure Reason*.

How, as a matter of fact, are we to conceive the relations of the "given" and "thought," the operation of consciousness on inert "things" which pure sensations would be, the connection of "affection" and knowledge and the connection of sensible and intellectual consciousness? In the final analysis, then, there will be no sensible consciousness, no hiatus between the esthetic and the analytic, and no naturized consciousness.[34] An analysis which would try to isolate the perceived content would find nothing; for all consciousness of something, as soon as this thing ceases to be an indeterminate existence, as soon as it is identifiable and recognizable, for example, *as* "a color" or even as "this unique red," presupposes the apprehension of a meaning through the lived impression which is not *contained* in consciousness and is not a real part of it. The matter of knowledge becomes a borderline-notion posed by consciousness in its reflection upon itself, and not a component of the act of knowing. But from then on perception is a variety of intellection and, in all its positive aspects, a judgment.

Critical philosophy would resolve the problems posed by the relations of form and matter, given and thought, and soul and body by terminating in an intellectualist theory of perception.[35] If as a matter of fact an incipient science, a first organization of experience which is completed only by scientific coordination, could be shown in perception, the alleged sensible consciousness would no longer pose any problem, since the "original" characteristics of perceptual experience would be nothing but privation and negation: "The universe of immediate experience contains, not *more* than what is required by science, but *less;* for it is a superficial and mutilated world; it is, as Spinoza says, the world of *conclusions without premises.*" [36] The problem of the relations of the soul and the body would be posed only at the level of a confused thought which adheres to the products of consciousness instead of rediscovering in them the intellectual activity which produces them. Put back into the intellectual context which alone gives it a meaning, "sensible consciousness" is eliminated as a problem. The body rejoins the extension whose action it undergoes and of which it is only a part; perception rejoins judgment, which subtends it. Every form of consciousness presupposes its completed form: the dialectic of the epistemological subject and the scientific object.

Is There Not a Truth of Naturalism?

Are we compelled in this direction by the preceding analyses? At least they lead to the transcendental attitude, that is, to a philosophy which treats all conceivable reality as an object of consciousness. It has seemed to us that matter, life, and mind could not be defined as three orders of reality or three sorts of beings, but as three planes of signification or three forms of unity. In particular, life would not be a force which is added to physico-chemical processes; its originality would be that of modes of connection without equivalent in the physical domain, that of phenomena gifted with a proper structure and which bind each other together according to a special dialectic. In a living being, bodily movements and moments of behavior can be described and understood only in a specially tailored language and in accordance with the categories of an original experience. And it is in this same sense that we have recognized a psychological order and a mental order. But these distinctions then are those of different regions of experience. We have been moved from the idea of a *nature* as *omnitudo realitatis* to the idea of objects which could not be conceived in-themselves (*en soi*), *partes extra partes,* and which are defined only by an idea in which they participate, by a signification which is realized in them. Since the relations of the physical system and the forces which act upon it and those of the living being and its milieu are not the external and blind relations of juxtaposed realities, but dialectical relations in which the effect of each partial action is determined by its signification for the whole, the human order of consciousness does not appear as a third order superimposed on the two others, but as their condition of possibility and their foundation.

The problem of the relations of the soul and the body seems to disappear from the point of view of this absolute consciousness, milieu of the universe, as it did from the critical point of view. There can be no question of a causal operation between three planes of signification. One says that the soul "acts" on the body when it happens that our conduct has a rational signification, that is, when it cannot be understood by any play of physical forces or by any of the attitudes which are characteristic of the vital dialectic. In reality the expression is improper: we have seen that the body is not a self-enclosed mechanism on which the soul could act from the outside. It is defined only by its functioning, which can present all degrees of integration. To say that the soul acts on the body is wrongly to suppose a univocal notion of the body and to add to it a second force which accounts for the rational signification of certain conducts. In this case it would be better to say that bodily functioning is integrated with a level which is higher than that of life and that the body has truly become a human body. Inversely one will say that the body has acted on the soul if the behavior can be understood without residue in terms of the vital dialectic or by known psychological mechanisms.

Here again one does not, properly speaking, have the right to imagine a transitive action from substance to substance, as if the soul were a constantly present force whose activity would be held in check by a more powerful force. It would be more exact to say that the behavior had become disorganized, leaving room for less integrated structures. In brief, the alleged reciprocal action is reducible to an alternation or a substitution of dialectics. Since the physical, the vital and the mental individual are distinguished only as different degrees of integration, to the extent that man is completely identified with the third dialectic, that is, to the extent that he no longer allows systems of isolated conduct to function in him, his soul and his body are no longer distinguished.

If one supposes an anomaly of vision in El Greco, as has sometimes been done, it does not follow that the form of the body in his paintings, and consequently the style of the attitudes, admit of a "physiological explanation." When irremedial bodily peculiarities are integrated with the whole of our experience, they cease to have the dignity of a cause in us. A visual anomaly can receve a universal signification by the mediation of the artist and become for him the occasion of perceiving one of the "profiles" of human existence. The accidents of our bodily constitution can always play this revealing role on the condition that they become a means of extending our knowledge by the consciousness which we have of them, instead of being submitted to as pure facts which dominate us. Ultimately, El Greco's supposed visual disorder was conquered by him and so profoundly integrated into his manner of thinking and being that it appears finally as the necessary expression of his being much more than as a peculiarity imposed from the outside. It is no longer a paradox to say that "El Greco was astigmatic because he produced elongated bodies." [37] Everything which was accidental in the individual, that is, everything which revealed partial and independent dialectics without relationship to the total signification of his life, has been assimilated and centered in his deeper life. Bodily events have ceased to constitute autonomous cycles, to follow the abstract patterns of biology and psychology, and have received a new meaning. It is nevertheless the body, it will be said, which in the final analysis explains El Greco's vision; his liberty consisted only in justifying this accident of nature by infusing it with a metaphysical meaning. Unity does not furnish an adequate criterion of the liberty which has been won, since a man dominated by a complex, for example, and subject to the same psychological mechanism in all his undertakings, realizes unity in slavery. But here it is only a question of an apparent unity, of a stereotyped unity, which will not withstand an unexpected experience. It can be maintained only in a chosen milieu which the sick person has constructed for himself precisely by avoiding all situations in which the apparent coherence of his conduct would be disorganized. True unity on the contrary is recognized from the fact that it is not obtained by a restriction of the milieu. The same sensory or constitutional infirmity can be a cause of slavery if it imposes on man a type of vision and monotonous action from which he can no longer escape, or the occasion of a greater liberty if he makes use of it as an instrument. This supposes that he knows it instead of obeys it. For a being who lives at the simply biological level, it is a fatality.

For a being who has acquired the consciousness of self and his body, who has reached the dialectic of subject and object, the body is no longer the cause of the structure of consciousness; it has become the object of consciousness. Then one can no longer speak of a psycho-physiological parallelism: only a disintegrated consciousness can be paralleled with physiological processes, that is, with a partial functioning of the organism. By acceding to true knowledge, by going beyond the dialectic of the living or the social being and its circumscribed milieu, by becoming the pure subject who knows the world objectively, man ultimately realizes that absolute consciousness with respect to which the body and individual existence are no longer anything but objects; death is deprived of meaning. Reduced to the status of object of consciousness, the body could not be conceived as an intermediary between "things" and the consciousness which knows them; and since consciousness, having left the obscurity of instinct, no longer expresses the vital properties of objects but their *true* properties, the parallelism here is between consciousness and the true world which it knows directly. All the problems seem to be eliminated: the relations of the soul and the body—obscure as long as the body is treated in abstraction as a fragment of matter—are clarified when one sees in the body the bearer of a dialectic. Since the physical world and the organism can be conceptualized only as objects of consciousness or as significations, the problem of the relations of consciousness and its physical or organic "conditions" would exist only at the level of a confused thought which adheres to abstractions; it would disappear in the domain of truth in which the relation of the epistemological subject and its object alone subsists as original. This would constitute the only legitimate theme of philosophical reflection.

Let us consider a subject who turns his eyes toward a sensible object placed in front of him. Our preceding remarks permit us to say that the consecutive modification of his perceptual field is not an "effect" of the physical phenomenon of excitation or of the corresponding physiological phenomenon. We have shown that the most remarkable characteristics of the perceived object—its distance, its size, its apparent color—cannot be deduced from the physiological antecedents of perception. The modern theory of nerve functioning relates them to "transverse phenomena" of which there is neither a physical nor a physiological definition and which are conceived precisely by borrowing from the perceived world and the image of its descriptive properties. It becomes impossible to assign a *somatic* substrate of perception. The elaboration of stimuli and the distribution of motor influxes are accomplished according to articulations proper to the phenomenal field; what is introduced under the name of "transverse phenomena" is in reality the perceived field itself. For us this signifies that the living body and the nervous system, instead of being like annexes of the physical world in which the occasional causes of perception would be prepared, are "phenomena" emerging from among those which consciousness knows. Perceptual behavior, as science studies it, is not defined in terms of nerve cells and synapses; it is not in the brain or even in the body; science has not been able to construct the "central sectors" of behavior from the outside like something which is enclosed within a cranial box; it can understand it only as a dialectic, the moments of which are not stimuli and movements but phenomenal objects and actions. The illusion of a transitive operation of stimuli on the sensory apparatus and of the latter "against" consciousness comes from the fact that we actualize separately the physical body, the body of the anatomists or even the organism of the physiologists, all of which are abstractions, snapshots taken from the functional body.

When its existence is accepted, the hallucinatory image is no longer treated in recent works as an isolated phenomenon which could be explained by some irritation of centers: it is connected with the whole of organic-vegetative functioning;[38] which is to say that, rather than a perception without object, hallucination is a global conduct related to a global alteration of nerve functioning. It supposes a complete structure the description of which, like that of normal functioning, cannot be given in somatic terms. The somatic events do not act directly. Section of the optic nerve can be called the cause of blindness only in the sense in which Beethoven's deafness "explains" his last works. It provokes a change of the phenomenal field only by rendering impossible the functioning of the whole of the cortex under the action of luminous excitants. Is it this functioning itself which can be considered as a cause? No, if it is understood as the sum of the nerve events which are produced in each point of the cortex. This whole can be only the *condition of existence* of such and such a sensible scene; it accounts for the *fact that* I perceive but not for *that which* I perceive,[39] not for the scene as such since this latter is presupposed in a complete definition of the nerve process. Everything takes place as if my perception opened out on a network of original significations. The passage of nerve influx in such and such conductors does not produce the visible scene; it does not even determine its structure in a univocal manner since it is organized according to laws of equilibrium which are neither those of a physical system nor those of the body considered as such. The somatic substrate is the passage point, the base of a dialectic. In the same way, nobody thinks of explaining the content of a delirium by its physiological conditions even though this form of consciousness presupposes *in existendo* some alteration of the brain.

Speaking generally, it seems that we are rejoining the critical idea. Whatever the external conditions may be—bodily, psychological, social—upon which the development of consciousness depends and even if it is only gradually constituted in history, the history itself out of which it comes is only a view which consciousness gives itself with regard to the acquired consciousness of self. A reversal of perspective is produced vis-à-vis adult consciousness: the historical becoming which prepared it was not *before* it, it is only *for* it; the time during which it progressed is no longer the time *of* its constitution, but a time which it constitutes; and the series of events is subordinated to its eternity. Such is the perpetual reply of critical thought to psychologism, sociologism and historicism.

This discussion of causal thinking has seemed valid to us and we have pursued it at all levels of behavior. It leads, as we have just said, to the transcendental attitude.[40] This is the first conclusion which we have to draw from the preceding chapters. It is not the only one, and it would even be necessary to say that this first conclusion stands in a relation of simple homonymy with a philosophy in the critical tradition.[41] What is profound in the notion of "Gestalt" from which we started is not the idea of signification but that of *structure,* the joining of an idea and an existence which are indiscernible, the contingent arrangement by which materials begin to have meaning in our presence, intelligibility in the nascent state. The study of the reflex has shown us that the nervous system is the place in which an order without anatomical guarantee is realized by means of a continuing organization. It already permitted us to establish a rigorously reciprocal relation between function and substrate; there was not an area which was not linked in its functioning to the global activity of the nervous system, but also not a function which was not profoundly altered by the subtraction of a single one of these areas; and function was nothing outside the process which is delineated at each instant and which, based on the nerve mass, organizes itself.[42]

The study of the "central sector" of behavior confirmed this ambiguity of bodily nature. On the one hand it appeared that absolutely no function could be localized, since each region plays a role only in the context of a global activity and since the diverse movements which it governs correspond to several modes of qualitatively distinct functioning rather than to several locally differentiated devices. On the other hand, it was equally clear that certain parts of the nerve substance are indispensable for the reception of certain stimuli, that the execution of certain movements are assigned to certain receptive regions or to some muscular ensemble, and that, even when nerve substance is not the depository of any special power of this kind, there can be no substitution for the nerve substance in each place. Thus, we were dealing less with two types of localization than with an inextricable intersecting of "horizontal" and "vertical" localizations—without the body being anywhere pure thing, *but also without it being anywhere pure idea.*[43] It is not possible to designate separate contributions of the visual and auditive regions of the brain; both function only with the center; and integral thinking transfigures the hypothetical "visual contents" and "auditive contents" to the point of rendering them unrecognizable; but also the alteration of one of these regions is manifested in thought by a determinate deficit: it is the intuition of simultaneous wholes or that of successive wholes which becomes impossible.[44] Thus the integration of the optic or auditive regions in a functional whole, although it infuses the corresponding "contents" with a new signification, does not annul their specificity; it uses and sublimates it.

For life, as for the mind, there is no past which is absolutely past; "the moments which the mind seems to have behind it are also borne in its present depths."[45] Higher behavior retains the subordinated dialectics in the present depths of its existence, from that of the physical system and its topographical conditions to that of the organism and its "milieu." They are not recognizable in the whole when it functions correctly, but the disintegration in case of partial lesion attests to their imminence. There is no essence of thinking which would receive the particular forms of "visual thought" and "auditive thought" by a contingency of our nerve organization and as a condition of existence. The alleged conditions of existence are indiscernible in the whole with which they collaborate *and reciprocally the essence of the whole cannot be concretely conceptualized without them and without its constitutive history*. Consequently, the relations of matter and form in the object-organism and the relations of the soul and body were found to be conceived differently than in critical thought.

While critical philosophy, having step by step repressed quality and existence—residues of its ideal analysis—to place them finally in a matter about which nothing can be thought and which is for us therefore as if it were not, deploys a homogeneous activity of the understanding from one end of knowledge to the other; each "formation" (*mise en forme*) appears to us on the contrary to be an event in the world of ideas, the institution of a new dialectic, the opening of a new region of phenomena, and the establishment of a new constitutive layer which eliminates the preceding one as isolated moment, but conserves and integrates it. While critical thought pushed the problem of the relations of the soul and body back step by step by showing that we never deal with a body in-itself (*en soi*) but with a body for-a-consciousness and that thus we never have to put consciousness in contact with an opaque and foreign reality, for us consciousness experiences its inherence in an organism at each moment; for it is not a question of an inherence in material apparatuses, which as a matter of fact can be only *objects* for consciousness, but of a presence to consciousness of its proper history and of the dialectical stages which it has traversed.

Therefore, we could not accept any of the materialistic models to represent the relations of the soul and body—but neither could we accept the mentalistic models, for example, the Cartesian metaphor of the artisan and his tool.[46] An organ cannot be compared to an instrument, as if it existed and could be conceived apart from integral functioning, nor the mind to an artisan who uses it: this would be to return to a wholly external relation like that of the pilot and his ship which was rightly rejected by Descartes. The mind does not use the body, but realizes itself through it while at the same time transferring the body outside of physical space. When we were describing the structures of behavior[47] it was indeed to show that they are irreducible to the dialectic of physical stimulus and muscular contraction and that in this sense behavior, far from being a thing which exists in-itself (*en soi*), is a whole significative for a consciousness which considers it; but it was at the same time and reciprocally to make manifest in "expressive conduct" the *view of a consciousness* under our eyes, to show a mind which *comes into the world*.

Doubtless it is understood why we cannot even accept without reservations a relation of expression between the soul and the body comparable to that of the concept and the word, nor define the soul as the "meaning of the body," the body as the "manifestation of the soul."[48] These formulae have the inconvenience of evoking two terms, solidary perhaps, but external to each other and the relation of which would be invariable. But sometimes our body manifests externally an intention arising from a dialectic which is higher than biology; sometimes, by a play of mechanisms which its past life has built up, it limits itself to mimicking intentions which it *does not have* any longer, as do the movements of a dying person for example;[49] from one case to the other the relation of the soul and the body and even the terms themselves are modified depending on whether the "formation" succeeds or fails and whether the inertia of the subordinated dialectics allows itself to be surmounted or not. Our body does not always have meaning, and our thoughts, on the other hand—in timidity for example—do not always find in it the plenitude of their vital expression. In these cases of disintegration, the soul and the body are apparently distinct; and this is the truth of dualism. But the soul, if it possesses no means of expression—one should say rather, no means of actualizing itself—soon ceases to be *anything whatsoever* and in particular ceases to be the soul, as the thought of the aphasic weakens and becomes dissolved; the body which loses its meaning soon ceases to be a living body and falls back into the state of a physico-chemical mass; it arrives at non-meaning only by dying. The two terms can never be distinguished absolutely without ceasing to be; thus their empirical connection is based on the original operation which establishes a meaning in a fragment of matter and makes it live, appear and be in it. In returning to this *structure* as the fundamental reality, we are rendering comprehensible both the distinction and the union of the soul and the body.

There is always a duality which reappears at one level or another: hunger or thirst prevents thought or feelings; the properly sexual dialectic ordinarily reveals itself through a passion; integration is never absolute and it always fails—at a higher level in the writer, at a lower level in the aphasic. There always comes a moment when we divest ourselves of a passion because of fatigue or self-respect. This duality is not a simple fact; it is founded in principle—all integration presupposing the normal functioning of subordinated formations, which always demand their own due.

But it is not a duality of substances; or, in other words, the notions of soul and body must be relativized: there is the body as mass of chemical components in interaction, the body as dialectic of living being and its biological milieu, and the body as dialectic of social subject and his group; even all our habits are an impalpable body for the ego of each moment. Each of these degrees is soul with respect to the preceding one, body with respect to the following one. The body in general is an ensemble of paths already traced, of powers already constituted; the body is the acquired dialectical soil upon which a higher "formation" is accomplished, and the soul is the meaning which is then established.[50] The relations of the soul and the body can indeed be compared to those of concept and word, but on the condition of perceiving, beneath the separated products, the constituting operation which joins them and of rediscovering, beneath the empirical languages—the external accompaniment or contingent clothing of thought—the living *word* which is its unique actualization, in which the meaning is formulated for the first time and thus establishes itself as meaning and becomes available for later operations.

In this way our analyses have indeed led us to the ideality of the body, but it was a question of an idea which proffers itself and even constitutes itself in the contingency of existence. By a natural development the notion of "Gestalt" led us back to its Hegelian meaning, that is, to the concept before it has become consciousness of self. Nature, we said, is the exterior of a concept.[51] But precisely the concept as concept has no exterior and the Gestalt still had to be conceptualized as unity of the interior and exterior, of nature and idea.[52] Correlatively the consciousness *for* which the Gestalt exists was not intellectual consciousness but perceptual experience.[53] Thus, it is perceptual consciousness which must be interrogated in order to find in it a definitive clarification. Let us limit ourselves here to indicating how the status of the object, the relations of form and matter, those of soul and body, and the individuality and plurality of consciousnesses are founded in it.

I cannot simply identify what I perceive and the thing itself. The real color of the object which I look at in and will always remain known to myself alone. I have no means whatsoever of knowing if the colored impression which it gives to others is identical to my own. Our intersubjective confrontations bear only upon the intelligible structure of the perceived world: I can assure myself that another viewer employs the same word as I to designate the color of this object and the same word, on the other hand, to qualify a series of other objects which I also call red objects. But, the relationships being conserved, it could happen that the scale of colors which he sees is completely different from mine. However, it is when objects give me the unique impression of the "sensed," when they have that direct manner of taking hold of me, that I say they are existing. It follows from this that perception, as knowledge of existing things, is an individual consciousness and not the consciousness in general of which we were speaking above. This sensible mass in which I live when I stare at a sector of the field without trying to recognize it, the "this" which my consciousness wordlessly intends, is not a signification or an idea, although subsequently it can serve as base for acts of logical explicitation and verbal expression. Already when I name the perceived or when I recognize it *as* a chair or tree, I substitute the subsumption under a concept for the experience of a fleeting reality; even when I pronounce the word "this," I already relate a singular and lived existence to the essence of lived existence. But these acts of expression or reflection intend an original text which cannot be deprived of meaning.

The signification which I find in a sensible whole was already adherent in it. When I "see" a triangle, my experience would be very poorly described by saying that I conceive or comprehend the triangle with respect to certain sensible givens. The signification is embodied. It is here and now that I perceive this triangle as such, while conception gives it to me as an eternal being whose meaning and properties, as Descartes said, owe nothing to the fact that I perceive it. It is not only the matter of perception which comes off the thing as it were and becomes a content of my individual consciousness. In a certain manner, the form also makes up a part of the psychological individual, or rather is related to it; and *this reference is included in its very meaning,* since it is the form *of* this or that thing which presents itself to me here and now and since this encounter, which is revealed to me by perception, does not in the least concern the proper nature of the thing and is, on the contrary, an episode of my life. If two subjects placed near each other look at a wooden cube, the total structure of the cube is the same for both; it has the value of intersubjective truth and this is what they both express in saying that there is a cube there. But it is not the same sides of the cube which, in each of them, are strictly seen and sensed.

We have said that this "perspectivism" of perception is not an indifferent fact, since without it the two subjects would not be aware of perceiving an existent cube subsisting beyond the sensible contents. If all the sides of the cube could be known at once, I would no longer be dealing with a thing which offers itself for inspection little by little, but with an idea which my mind would truly possess. This is what happens when I think of objects which I hold to be existent without actually perceiving them. In affirming that they continue to exist, I mean that a properly placed psycho-physical subject would see this or that sensible sight, articulated in this or that way and connected with the view which I perceive here and now by such and such objective transitions.

But this *knowing about* the world must not be confused with my *perception of* this or that segment of the world and its immediate horizon. The objects which do not belong to the circle of the perceived exist in the sense in which truths do not cease to be true when I am not thinking about them: their mode of being is one of logical necessity and not of "reality." For I certainly suppose a "perspectivism" in them also, and it is essential to them to present themselves to a viewer through a multiplicity of "profiles." But since I do not perceive them, it is a question of a perspectivism in idea and of an essence of the viewer; the relation of the one to the other is itself a relation of significations. These objects belong therefore to the order of significations and not to that of existences.[54] A perception which would be coextensive with sensible things is inconceivable; and it is not physically but logically that it is impossible. For there to be perception, that is, apprehension of an existence, it is absolutely necessary that the object not be completely given to the look which rests on it, that aspects intended but not possessed in the present perception be kept in reserve. A seeing which would not take place from a certain point of view and which would give us, for example, all the sides of a cube at once is a pure contradiction in terms; for, in order to be visible all together, the sides of a wooden cube would have to be transparent, that is, would cease to be the sides of a wooden cube. And if each of the six sides of a transparent cube were visible as square, it is not a cube which we would be seeing. Thus the Bergsonian idea of a "pure perception," that is, adequate to the object or identical with it, is inconsistent. It is the cube as signification or geometrical idea which is made of six equal sides. The relation—unique and characteristic of existing things—of the "aspects" to the total object is not a logical relation like that of sign to signification: the sides of the chair are not its "signs," but precisely the sides.

In the same way the phenomena of my body should be distinguished from purely logical significations. What differentiates it from external things even as they are presented in lived perception is the fact that it is not, like them, accessible to an unlimited inspection. When it is a question of an external thing, I know that by changing place I could see the sides which are hidden from me; by occupying the position which was that of my neighbor a moment ago, I could obtain a new perspectival view and give a verbal account which would concur with the description of the object which my neighbor gave a moment ago. I do not have the same liberty with my body. I know very well that I will never see my eyes directly and that, even in a mirror, I cannot grasp their movement and their living expression. For me, my retinas are an absolute unknowable. This is, after all, only a particular case of the perspectival character of perception.

To say that I have a body is simply another way of saying that my knowledge is an individual dialectic in which intersubjective objects appear, that these objects, when they are given to knowledge in the mode of actual existence, present themselves to it by successive aspects which cannot coexist; finally, it is a way of saying that one of them offers itself obstinately "from the same side" without my being able to go around it. Reservation made for its image which mirrors give me (but *this image moves* as soon as I try to see it from different points of view, by leaning the head to the right and left; it is not a true "thing"), my body as given to me by sight is broken at the height of the shoulders and terminates in a tactile-muscular object. I am told that an object is visible for others in this lacuna in which my head is located; science teaches that organs, a brain and —each time that I perceive an external thing—"nerve influxes" in this visible object would be found by means of analyses. I will never see anything of all that. I could never make an actually present experience of my body adequately correspond to the signification, "human body," as it is given to me by science and witnesses. There are entities which will always remain pure significations for me under some of their aspects and which will never be offered to other than lacunary perception. In itself, this structure is not much more mysterious than that of external objects with which, moreover, it is one: how could I receive an object "in a certain direction" if I, the perceiving subject, were not in some way hidden in one of my phenomena, one which envelops me since I cannot go around it? Two points are necessary for determining a direction.

We have not completely described the structure of the body proper, which also includes an affective perspective, the importance of which is evident. But the preceding is sufficient to show that there is no enigma of "my body," nothing inexpressible in its relation to myself. It is true that, by describing it, we are transforming into signification the lived perspective which by definition is not one. But this alogical essence of perceived beings can be clearly designated: one will say, for example, that to offer themselves through profiles which I do not possess as I possess an idea is included in the idea of perceived being and of the body.

Reduced to its positive meaning, the connection of the soul and body signifies nothing other than the *ecceitas* of knowledge by profiles; it appears to be a marvel only if, by a dogmatic prejudice, it is posited that all entities which we experience should be given to us "completely," as significations pretend to be. Thus the obscure causality of the body is reducible to the original structure of a phenomenon; and we do not dream of explaining perception as an event of an individual consciousness "by means of the body" and in terms of causal thinking. But if it is still not a question of externally connecting my consciousness to a body whose point of view it would adopt in an inexplicable manner, and if, in order to remain faithful to this phenomenon, it all comes back in brief to accepting the fact that some *men see things which I do not see,* the zone of individual perspectives and that of intersubjective significations must be distinguished in my knowledge. This is not the classical distinction between sensibility and intelligence, since the horizon of the perceived extends beyond the perimeter of vision and encloses, in addition to the objects which make an impression on my retina, the walls of the room which are behind me, the house and perhaps the town in which I am, arranged perspectively around the "sensible" nucleus. Nor are we returning to the distinction of matter and form since, on the one hand, the very form of perception participates in the *ecceitas* and since, inversely, I can bring acts of recognition and denomination to bear on the sensible content which will convert it into signification.

The distinction which we are introducing is rather that of the lived and the known. The problem of the relations of the soul and body is thus transformed instead of disappearing: now it will be the problem of the relations of consciousness as flux of individual events, of concrete and resistant structures, and that of consciousness as tissue of ideal significations. The idea of a transcendental philosophy, that is, the idea of consciousness as constituting the universe before it and grasping the objects themselves in an indubitable external experience, seems to us to be a definitive acquisition as the first phase of reflection. But is one not obliged to re-establish a duality within consciousness which is no longer accepted between it and external realities? The objects as ideal unities and as significations are grasped through individual perspectives. When I look at a book placed in front of me, its rectangular form is a concrete and embodied structure. What is the relation between this rectangular "physiognomy" and the signification, "rectangle," which I can make explicit by a logical act?

Every theory of perception tries to surmount a well-known contradiction: on the one hand, consciousness is a function of the body—thus it is an "internal" event dependent upon certain external events; on the other hand, these external events themselves are known only by consciousness. In another language, consciousness appears on one hand to be part of the world and on the other to be co-extensive with the world. In the development of methodical knowledge, of science, that is, the first observation seems initially to be confirmed: the subjectivity of the secondary qualities seems to have as a counterpart the reality of the primary qualities. But a deeper reflection on the objects of science and on physical causality finds relations in them which cannot be posited in-themselves (*en soi*) and which have meaning only before the inspection of mind.

The antinomy of which we are speaking disappears along with its realistic thesis at the level of reflexive thought (*la pensée réfléchie*); it is in perceptual knowledge that it has its proper location. Until now critical thought seemed to us to be incontestable. It shows marvelously that the problem of perception does not exist for a consciousness which adheres to objects of reflexive thought, that is, to significations. It is subsequently that it seems necessary to leave it. Having in this way referred the antinomy of perception to the order of life, as Descartes says, or to the order of confused thought, one pretends to show that it has no consistency there: if perception conceptualizes itself ever so little and knows what it is saying, it reveals that the experience of passivity is also a construction of the mind. Realism is not even based on a coherent appearance, it is an *error*. One wonders then what can provide consciousness with the very notion of passivity and why this notion is confused with its body if these natural errors rest on no authentic experience and *possess strictly no meaning whatsoever*. We have tried to show that, as a matter of fact, to the extent that the scientific knowledge of the organism becomes more precise, it becomes impossible to give a coherent meaning to the alleged action of the world on the body and of the body on the soul. The body and the soul are significations and have meaning, then, only with regard to a consciousness.

From our point of view also, the realistic thesis of common sense disappears at the level of reflexive thought, which encounters only significations in front of it. The experience of passivity *is not explained* by an actual passivity. But it should have a meaning and be able *to be understood*. As philosophy, realism is an error because it transposes into dogmatic thesis an experience which it deforms or renders impossible by that very fact. But it is a motivated error; it rests on an authentic phenomenon which philosophy has the function of making explicit. The proper structure of perceptual experience, the reference of partial "profiles" to the total signification which they "present," would be this phenomenon. Indeed, the alleged bodily conditioning of perception, taken in its actual meaning, requires nothing more—and nothing less—than this phenomenon in order to be understood. We have seen that excitations and nerve influxes are abstractions and that science links them to a total functioning of the nervous system in the definition of which the phenomenal is implied. The perceived is not an effect of cerebral functioning; it is its signification.

All the consciousnesses which we know present themselves in this way through a body which is their perspectival aspect. But, after all, each individual dialectic has cerebral stages, as it were, of which it itself knows nothing; the signification of nerve functioning has organic bases which do not figure in it. Philosophically, this fact admits of the following translation: each time that certain sensible phenomena are actualized in my field of consciousness, a properly placed observer would see certain other phenomena in my brain which cannot be given to me myself in the mode of actuality. In order to understand these phenomena, he would be led to grant them (as we did in Chapter II) a signification which would concur with the content of my perception. Inversely, I can represent for myself in the virtual mode, that is, as pure significations, certain retinal and cerebral phenomena which I localize in a virtual image of my body on the basis of the actual view which is given to me. The fact that the spectator and myself are both bound to our bodies comes down in sum to this: that that which can be given to me in the mode of actuality, as a concrete perspective, is given to him only in the mode of virtuality, as a signification, and conversely. In sum, my total psycho-physical being (that is, the experience which I have of myself, that which others have of me, and the scientific knowledge which they and I apply to the knowledge of myself) is an interlacing of significations such that, when certain among them are perceived and pass into actuality, the others are only virtually intended. But this structure of experience is similar to that of external objects. Even more, they mutually presuppose each other. If there are things for me, that is, perspectival beings, reference to a point from which I see them is included in their perspectival character itself.

But to be situated within a certain point of view necessarily involves not seeing that point of view itself, not possessing it as a visual object except in a virtual signification. Therefore, the existence of an external perception, that of my body and, "in" this body, the existence of phenomena which are imperceptible for me are rigorously synonymous. There is no relation of causality between them. They are *concordant phenomena*. One often speaks as if the perspectival character of perception were explained by the projection of objects on my retina: I see only three sides of a cube *because* I see with my eyes, where a projection of only these three sides is possible; I do not see objects which are behind me *because they* are not projected on my retina. But the converse could be said just as well. Indeed, what are "my eyes," "my retina," "the external cube" in itself, and "the objects which I do not see"? They are logical significations which are bound up with my actual perception on valid "grounds" [55] and which explicitate its meaning, but which get *the index of real existence from it*. These significations do not have in themselves therefore the means to explain the actual existence of my perception. The language which one habitually uses is nevertheless understandable: my perception of the cube presents it to me as a complete and real cube, my perception of space, as a space which is complete and real beyond the aspects which are given to me. Thus it is natural that I have a tendency to detach the space and the cube from the concrete perspectives and to posit them in-themselves (*en soi*).

The same operation takes place with respect to the body. And as a consequence I am naturally inclined to engender perception by an operation of the cube or of objective space on my objective body. This attempt is natural, but its failure is no less inevitable: as we have seen, one cannot reconstitute the structure of perceptual experience by combining ideal significations (stimuli, receptors, associative circuits). But if physiology does not explain perception, optics and geometry do not explain it either. To imagine that I see my image in the mirror *because* the light waves form a certain angle in reaching my eyes and because I situate their origin at their point of coincidence is to make the use of mirrors during so many centuries when optics was not yet invented mysterious indeed. The truth is that man first sees his image "through" the mirror, without the word yet having the signification which it will take on vis-à-vis the geometrical mind. Then he constructs a geometrical representation of this phenomenon which is *founded* on the concrete articulations of the perceived field, which makes them explicit and accounts for them—without the representation ever being able to be the cause of the concrete articulations, as realism wants to do, and without our being able to substitute it for them, as critical idealism does.

Access to the proper domain of perception has been rendered difficult for all philosophies which, because of a retrospective illusion, actualized a natural geometry in perception on the pretext that it has been possible to construct a geometry of perceived objects. The perception of a distance or a size is not the same as the quantitative estimations by which science makes distance and size precise.

All the sciences situate themselves in a "complete" and real world without realizing that perceptual experience is constituting with respect to this world. Thus we find ourselves in the presence of a field of lived perception which is prior to number, measure, space and causality and which is nonetheless given only as a perspectival view of objects gifted with stable properties, a perspectival view of an objective world and an objective space. The problem of perception consists in trying to discover how the intersubjective world, the determinations of which science is gradually making precise, is grasped through this field. The antinomy of which we spoke above is based upon this ambiguous structure of perceptual experience. The thesis and the antithesis express the two aspects of it: it is true to say that my perception is always a flux of individual events and that what is radically contingent in the lived perspectivism of perception accounts for the realistic appearance. But it is also true to say that my perception accedes to things themselves, for these perspectives are articulated in a way which makes access to inter-individual significations possible; they "present" a world.

Thus there are things *exactly in the sense in which I see them,* in my history and outside it, and inseparable from this double relation. I perceive things directly without my body forming a screen between them and me; it is a phenomenon just as they are, a phenomenon (gifted, it is true, with an original structure) which precisely presents the body to me as an intermediary between the world and myself although it *is not* as a matter of fact. I see with my eyes, which are not an ensemble of transparent or opaque tissues and organs, but the instruments of my looking. The retinal image, to the extent that I know it, is not yet produced by the light waves issuing from the object; but these two phenomena resemble and correspond to each other in a magical way across an interval which is not yet space.

We are returning to the givens of naive consciousness which we were analyzing at the beginning of this chapter. The philosophy of perception is not ready made in life: we have just seen that it is natural for consciousness to misunderstand itself precisely because it is consciousness of things. The classical discussions centering around perception are a sufficient testimony to this natural error. The constituted world is confronted with the perceptual experience of the world and one either tries to engender perception from the world, as realism does, or else to see in it only a commencement of the science of the world, as critical thought does. To return to perception as to a type of original experience in which the real world is constituted in its specificity is to impose upon oneself an inversion of the natural movement of consciousness;[56] on the other hand every question has not been eliminated: it is a question of understanding, without confusing it with a logical relation, the lived relation of the "profiles" to the "things" which they present, of the perspectives to the ideal significations which are intended through them.[57] The problem which Malebranche tried to resolve by occasionalism or Leibnitz by pre-established harmony is carried over into human consciousness.

Conclusion

Yet until now we have considered only the perspectivism of true perception. Instances in which lived experience appears clothed with a signification which breaks apart, so to speak, in the course of subsequent experience and is not verified by concordant syntheses would still have to be analyzed. We have not accepted the causal explanation which naturalism provides in order to account for this subjectivity in the second degree. What is called bodily, psychological or social determinism in hallucination and error has appeared to us to be reducible to the emergence of imperfect dialectics, of partial structures. But why, *in existendo,* does such a dialectic at the organic-vegetative level break up a more integrated dialectic, as happens in hallucination? Consciousness is not only and not always consciousness of truth; how are we to understand the inertia and the resistance of the inferior dialectics which stand in the way of the advent of the pure relations of impersonal subject and true object and which affect my knowledge with a coefficient of subjectivity? How are we to understand the adherence of a fallacious signification to the lived, which is constitutive of illusion?

We have rejected Freud's causal categories and replaced his energic metaphors with structural metaphors. But although the complex is not a thing outside of consciousness which would produce its effects in it, although it is only a structure of consciousness, at least this structure tends as it were to conserve itself. It has been said that what is called unconsciousness[58] is only an inapperceived signification: it may happen that we ourselves do not grasp the true meaning of our life, not because an unconscious personality is deep within us and governs our actions, but because we understand our lived states only through an idea which is not adequate for them.

But, even unknown to us, the efficacious law of our life is constituted by its true signification. Everything happens as if this signification directed the flux of mental events. Thus it will be necessary to distinguish their ideal signification, which can be true or false, and their immanent signification, or—to employ a clearer language which we will use from now on—their ideal *signification* and their actual *structure*. Correlatively, it will be necessary to distinguish in development an ideal liberation, on the one hand, which does not transform us in our being and changes only the consciousness which we have of ourselves, and, on the other, a real liberation which is the *Umgestaltung* of which we spoke, along with Goldstein. We are not reducible to the ideal consciousness which we have of ourselves any more than the existent thing is reducible to the signification by which we express it.

It is easy to argue in the same way, in opposition to the sociologist, that the structures of consciousness which he relates to a certain economic structure are in reality the consciousness of certain structures. This argument hints at a liberty very close to mind, capable by reflection of grasping itself as spontaneous source, and naturizing from below the contingent forms with which it has clothed itself in a certain milieu. Like Freud's complex, the economic structure is only one of the objects of a transcendental consciousness. But "transcendental consciousness," the full consciousness of self, is not ready made; it is to be achieved, that is, realized in existence. In opposition to Durkheim's "collective consciousness" and his attempts at sociological explanation of knowledge, it is rightly argued that consciousness cannot be treated as an effect since it is that which constitutes the relation of cause and effect. But beyond a causal thinking which can be all too easily challenged, there is a truth of sociologism. Collective consciousness does not produce categories, but neither can one say that collective representations are only the objects of a consciousness which is always free in their regard, only the consciousness in a "we" of an object of consciousness in an "I."

The mental, we have said,[59] is reducible to the structure of behavior. Since this structure is visible from the outside and for the spectator at the same time as from within and for the actor, another person is in principle accessible to me as I am to myself; and we are both objects laid out before an impersonal consciousness.[60] But just as I can be mistaken concerning myself and grasp only the apparent or ideal signification of my conduct, so can I be mistaken concerning another and know only the envelope of his behavior. The perception which I have of him is never, in the case of suffering or mourning, for example, the equivalent of the perception which he has of himself unless I am sufficiently close to him that our feelings constitute together a single "form" and that our lives cease to flow separately. It is by this rare and difficult consent that I can be truly united with him, just as I can grasp my natural movements and know myself sincerely only by the decision to belong to myself. Thus I do not know myself because of my special position, but neither do I have the innate power of truly knowing another. I communicate with him by the signification of his conduct; but it is a question of attaining its structure, that is of attaining, beyond his words or even his actions, the region where they are prepared.

As we have seen,[61] the behavior of another expresses a certain manner of existing before signifying a certain manner of thinking. And when this behavior is addressed to me, as may happen in dialogue, and seizes upon my thoughts in order to respond to them—or more simply, when the "cultural objects" which fall under my regard suddenly adapt themselves to my powers, awaken my intentions and make themselves "understood" by me—I am then drawn into a *coexistence* of which I am not the unique constituent and which founds the phenomenon of social nature as perceptual experience founds that of physical nature. Consciousness can *live* in existing things without reflection, can abandon itself to their concrete structure, which has not yet been converted into expressible signification; certain episodes of its life, before having been reduced to the condition of available memories and inoffensive objects, can imprison its liberty by their proper inertia, shrink its perception of the world, and impose stereotypes on behavior; likewise, before having conceptualized our class or our milieu, we *are* that class or that milieu.

Thus, the "I think" can be as if hallucinated by its objects. It will be replied (which is true) that it "should be able" to accompany all our representations and that it is presupposed by them, if not as term of an act of actual consciousness at least as a possibility

in principle. But this response of critical philosophy poses a problem. The conversion of seeing which transforms the life of consciousness into a pure dialectic of subject and object, which reduces the
thing in its sensible density to a bundle of significations, the traumatic reminiscence into an indfferent memory, and submits the
class structure of my consciousness to examination—does this conversion make explicit an eternal "condition of possibility" or does
it bring about the appearance of a new structure of consciousness?
It is a problem to know what happens, for example, when consciousness disassociates itself from time, from this uninterrupted
gushing forth at the center of itself, in order to apprehend it as
an intellectual and manipulable signification. Does it lay bare only
what was implicit? Or, on the contrary, does it not enter as into
a lucid dream in which indeed it encounters no opaqueness, not
because it has clarified the existence of things and its own existence,
but because it lives at the surface of itself and on the envelope of
things? Is the reflexive passage to intellectual consciousness an adequation of our knowing to our being or only a way for consciousness to create for itself a separated existence—a quietism? These
questions express no empiricist demand, no complaisance for "experiences" which would not have to account for themselves. On the
contrary, we want to make consciousness equal with the whole of
experience, to gather into consciousness for-itself (*pour soi*) all
the life of consciousness in-itself (*en soi*).

A philosophy in the critical tradition founds moral theory on
a reflection which discovers the thinking subject in its liberty behind
all objects. If, however, one acknowledges—be it in the status of
phenomenon—an existence of consciousness and of its resistant
structures, our knowledge depends upon what we are; moral theory
begins with a psychological and sociological critique of oneself;
man is not assured ahead of time of possessing a source of morality;
consciousness of self is not given in man by right; it is acquired
only by the elucidation of his concrete being and is verified only
by the active integration of isolated dialectics—body and soul—between which it is initially broken up. And finally, death is not
deprived of meaning, since the contingency of the lived is a perpetual menace for the eternal significations in which it is believed
to be completely expressed. It will be necessary to assure oneself
that the experience of eternity is not the unconsciousness of death,
that it is not on this side but beyond; similarly, moreover, it will

be necessary to distinguish the love of life from the attachment to biological existence. The sacrifice of life will be philosophically impossible; it will be a question only of "staking" one's life, which is a deeper way of living.

If one understands by perception the act which makes us know existences, all the problems which we have just touched on are reducible to the problem of perception. It resides in the duality of the notions of structure and signification. A "form," such as the structure of "figure and ground," for example, is a whole which has a meaning and which provides therefore a base for intellectual analysis. But at the same time it is not an idea: it constitutes, alters and reorganizes itself before us like a spectacle. The alleged bodily, social and psychological "causalities" are reducible to this contingency of lived perspectives which limit our access to eternal significations. The "horizontal localizations" of cerebral functioning, the adhesive structures of animal behavior and those of pathological behavior are only particularly striking examples of this. "Structure" is the philosophical truth of naturalism and realism. What are the relations of this naturized consciousness and the pure consciousness of self? Can one conceptualize perceptual consciousness without eliminating it as an original mode; can one maintain its specificity without rendering inconceivable its relation to intellectual consciousness? If the essence of the critical solution consists in driving existence back to the limits of knowledge and of discovering intellectual signification in concrete structure, and if, as has been said, the fate of critical thought is bound up with this intellectualist theory of perception, in the event that this were not acceptable, it would be necessary to define transcendental philosophy anew in such a way as to integrate with it the very phenomenon of the real. The natural "thing," the organism, the behavior of others and my own behavior exist only by their meaning; but this meaning which springs forth in them is not yet a Kantian object; the intentional life which constitutes them is not yet a representation; and the "comprehension" which gives access to them is not yet an intellection.

[Original French manuscript completed in 1938.]

NOTES

Except where indicated, all notes, citations and quotations are those of the author. All quotations in the text of the work have been given in English. In the notes the following policy has been adopted: quotations from works which appeared originally in French have not been translated; quotations from works appearing first in another language, but when a French edition has been used by the author, are left in French—when possible, however, the equivalent citation in the original and in existing English translations has been given. When the author has retained a quotation in another language than French in his own work, this same policy has been followed. When the author has translated quotations from another language into French, these have been translated into English in the notes—from the original if possible and from the author's French translation where necessary. When the author quotes original English sources—in the text or in the notes—the original English version has been used whenever possible.

INTRODUCTION

1. L. Brunschvicg, *Spinoza et ses contemporains*, 3rd ed., Paris, Alcan, 1923
2. Bergson
3. One says of a man or of an animal that he behaves; one does not say it of an acid, an electron, a pebble or a cloud except by metaphor. In the present work we have attempted to elucidate directly the notion of behavior and not to follow its development in American psychology. We will justify briefly this direct procedure by calling to mind the ideological disorder in which the notion of behavior has been developed in the country of its origin. As is shown in the recent work of Tilquin (*Le Behaviorisme, origine et développement de la psychologie de réaction en Amérique*, Paris, Vrin, 1942)—which comes to us at the moment when ours is in galley proofs—the notion of behavior had a difficult time making its way among philosophies which did not succeed in conceptualizing it. Even with its principal initiator, Watson, it found only an insufficient philosophical articulation. It was said that behavior was not localized in the central nervous system (A. Tilquin, *Le Behaviorisme*, pp. 72 and 103), that it resides between the individual and the environment (*ibid.*, p. 34), that consequently the study of behavior can be made without a word about

physiology (*ibid.*, e.g., p. 107), and finally that it is concerned with a stream of activity which the living being projects around itself (*ibid.*, pp. 180, 351) and which impresses upon the stimuli a particular meaning (*ibid.*, p. 346). But what is healthy and profound in this intuition of behavior — that is, the vision of man as perpetual coming to terms with and "explication" of a physical and a social world — found itself compromised by an impoverished philosophy. In reaction against the shadows of psychological intimacy, behaviorism for the most part seeks recourse only in a physiological or even a physical explanation, without seeing that this amounts to putting behavior back into the nervous system. In our opinion (which is not that of Tilquin), when Watson spoke of behavior he had in mind what others have called *existence;* but the new notion could receive its philosophical status only if causal or mechanical thinking were abandoned for dialectical thinking.

CHAPTER I

1. R. Dejean, *Étude psychologique de la "Distance" dans la vision*, Paris, Presses Universitaires de France, 1926, p. 109
2. Cf. the *"Nativisme réflex"* of H. Piéron, "Du rôle des réflexes localisateurs dans les perceptions spatiales," *Journal de Psychologie*, XVIII, 10 (1921), pp. 804-817
3. The facts which will be mentioned in this chapter are almost all very well known. But they are understood by such German authors as Weizsäcker or Goldstein by means of original categories which correspond to a new conception of explanation in physiology. It is this which justifies the present chapter.
4. V. F. von Wiezsäcker, "Reflexgesetze," in Bethe (ed.), *Handbuch der normalen und pathologischen Physiologie*, X, pp. 38-39
5. *Idem.*
6. *Ibid.*, p. 44
7. R. Ruyer, "Un modèle mécanique de la conscience," *Journal de Psychologie*, XXIX (1932), p. 552
8. Cf. *infra*, Chapter II
9. Weizsäcker, "Reflexgesetze," p. 45. "The organism," says Weizsäcker, "is *Reizgestaller.*"
10. *Idem.*
11. *Idem.*
12. K. Goldstein, *Der Aufbau des Organismus*, The Hague, Martinus Nijhoff, 1934, p. 58 (cf. *The Organism*, Boston, Beacon Press, 1963, p. 88). There is no "vitalism" here at all. These descriptions should be taken for what they are. The interpretation will come afterward.
13. "Querfunktionen" of Wertheimer. Cf. "Experimentelle Studien über das Sehen von Bewegung," *Zeitschrift für Psychologie*, LXI (1912), p. 247
14. Weizsäcker, "Reflexgesetze," p. 50
15. *Ibid.*, p. 45
16. The law is contested, but it is not our object to discuss its exactitude.
17. "Nociceptors"
18. Goldstein, *Der Aufbau des Organismus*, pp. 46 sqq. (cf. *The Organism*, pp. 70 sqq.)
19. Weizsäcker, "Reflexgesetze," p. 40
20. *Idem.*
21. H. Piéron has already drawn a parallel between the advances made in the theory of the conditioned reflex and in the theory of perception (cf. "Les Problèmes de la perception et la psychophysiologie," *Année psychologique*, XXVII (1926), pp. 1 sqq.). We will soon have occasion to show the unity of nerve functioning in its motor part and in its sensory sector.
22. Sanders, Ezn, Ludwig, cited by Weizsäcker, "Reflexgesetze," p. 42
23. A. Lalande, *Les Théories de l'induction et de l'expérimentation*, Paris, Boivin, 1929

24. All these results have been summarized by Goldstein, in *Der Aufbau des Organismus*, pp. 46 sqq. (cf. *The Organism*, pp. 68 sqq.).
25. Weizsäcker, "Reflexgesetze," p. 51
26. *Ibid.*, p. 53
27. F. Buytendijk, "Das Verhalten von Octopus nach teilweiser Zerstörung des Gehirns," *Archives néerlandaises de physiologie*, XVIII (1933), pp. 52-53
28. Weizsäcker, "Reflexgesetze," p. 53
29. Goldstein, *Der Aufbau des Organismus*, pp. 90 sqq. (cf. *The Organism*, pp. 135 sqq. and p. 482)
30. *Ibid.*, pp. 307-308 (cf. *The Organism*, pp. 482 sqq.)
31. A later chapter will show (cf. Ch. II) that the two types of localization exist, that corporal space is ambivalent. It is precisely this which renders its study important for us. The organism is at the same time a machine in which the total activity is the sum of local activity, and a whole in which the local activities are not isolable. What mode of existence does it possess then? How does it achieve the transition from *partes extra partes* to unity? How can it be a thing according to the first point of view, an idea according to the second?
32. Goldstein, for example, shows that certain cortical lesions do not leave sexual behavior intact: "Es bedarf bei solchen Kranken z. B. schon ganz besonderer Hilfe von aussen um einen Sexualverkehr in Gang zu bringen" (*Der Aufbau des Organismus*, p. 301 (cf. *The Organism*, p. 475). The author continues, "Von einem besonders starken Trieb ist im allgemeinen nicht die Rede; im Gegenteil erst wenn durch rein äusserliche Manipulation die Einführung des Sexualorgans stattgefunden hat, kommt die sexuelle Entladung überhaupt in Gang."
33. Weizsäcker, "Reflexgesetze," p. 76
34. Goldstein, *Der Aufbau des Organismus*, pp. 175-183 (cf. *The Organism*, pp. 271 sqq.)
35. *Ibid.*, pp. 175-183 (cf. *The Organism*, pp. 278 sqq.)
36. *Ibid.*, pp. 45-46 (cf. *The Organism*, p. 72)
37. *Idem.*
38. *Ibid.*, passim and for example pp. 175 sqq. (cf. *The Organism*, pp. 275 sqq.)
39. We are translating the German *Rückschlag* (cf. in particular Weizsäcker, "Reflexgesetze," p. 71).
40. *Idem.*, "Here again the physiologists have sought to explain the facts by joining part to part when perhaps it is a question of a single total reflex characterized by a diphasic form, with the effects successively oriented in two opposed directions."
41. In a sense this phenomenon could be considered as a borderline case of the substitutions which are produced when a motor response is prevented: it is known that, if one immobilizes the leg with which an animal scratches itself, the opposite leg takes upon itself the movement which has become impossible for the first; if one makes an animal lie down on the scratched side (Weizsäcker, p. 93), it scratches the free side; later on we will have to study still more striking examples of reflex transferences or substitutions in certain insects. Finally, the influence of the effector apparatus itself on the form of the reflex which has just been pointed out is a particular case of the same process of derivation.
42. Weizsäcker, "Reflexgesetze," p. 80
43. *Ibid.*, p. 78
44. *Ibid.*, p. 79
45. Sherrington, cited by Weizsäcker, *idem.*
46. Weizsäcker, "Reflexgesetze," p. 79
47. *Ibid.*, p. 82 (cf. L. Lapicque, "Physiologie générale du système nerveux," in G. Dumas, *Nouveau Traité de Psychologie*, Paris, Presses Universitaires de France, 1930, I, p. 201). Prolonged excitation always goes beyond one member toward the one which is connected with it in habitual functioning: the exten-

sion of one leg will be followed by the extension of the other in the frog, which in general advances by symmetrical movements: but in the case of a dog, whose ordinary movements are alternating, the excitation, having evoked the extension of one paw, will evoke the flexion of the other.

48. Immediately after having remarked that irradiation follows the vital movements of each animal instead of conforming to the anatomical distribution of the motor commands, Lapicque adds: "But this relation is not fatal as it would be if it depended on only one structure: here again we find the general law of variable switching."

49. Irradiation in the old sense of the word, i.e., the overflow of an excitation which invades the closest nerve paths, can be observed in only one particular case, that of very painful and excessive excitations. This provides the first occasion for remarking that the older conception of nerve functioning expresses certain pathological phenomena or certain laboratory experiments, rather than the normal activity of the living thing (cf. Weizsäcker, "Reflexgesetze," p. 82). We will have to consider these particular cases themselves and explain how an organism can behave according to different laws in an artificial milieu and in its vital milieu.

50. Cf. *infra,* Chapter III

51. We have in mind here only the vaguest and least contestable formulation of the law, which opposes the discontinuous variations of sensation to the continuous variations of the stimulus.

52. K. Koffka, "Perception. An Introduction to the Gestalt Theory," *Psychological Bulletin,* XIX (1922), pp. 537-553. Cf. W. Koehler, *Die physischen Gestalten in Ruhe und im stationären Zustand,* Erlangen Braunschweig, 1920, p. 6 and pp. 211, sqq.

53. Concerning the facts which, in the physiology of perception, justify this hypothesis, cf. *infra,* Chapter II.

54. Weizsäcker, "Reflexgesetze," p. 41

55. F. Buytendijk, "Versuche über die Steuerung der Bewegungen," *Archives néerlandaises de physiologie,* XVII (1932), pp. 63-69

56. Cited by Buytendijk, *ibid.,* p. 94

57. *Ibid.,* p. 94

58. *Idem.*

59. *Idem.*

60. *Bewegungsentwurf*

61. P. Schilder, *Das Körperschema,* Berlin, Springer, 1923, p. 65

62. Goldstein, *Der Aufbau des Organismus,* p. 61 (cf. *The Organism,* p. 91)

63. Weizsäcker, "Reflexgesetze," p. 75, and Goldstein, *Der Aufbau des Organismus,* p. 59 (cf. *The Organism,* p. 89)

64. Cf. *supra,* pp. 1 sqq.

65. Cf. for example, Bühler, *Die geistige Entwickelung des Kindes,* 4th ed., Jena, Fischer, 1924, pp. 103 sqq.

66. K. Koffka, *The Growth of the Mind,* New York, Harcourt, Brace, 1925, p. 79

67. K. Koffka, "Mental Development," in C. Murchison (ed.), *Psychologies of 1925,* Worcester, Mass., Clark University Press, 1928, p. 130

68. Koffka, *The Growth of the Mind,* p. 79

69. Von Kries, *Über die materiellen Grundlagen der Bewusztseinserscheinungen,* Tübingen u. Leipzig, 1901, cited by Koffka, *The Growth of the Mind,* p. 272

70. M. W. Shinn, "Notes on the Development of a Child," in *University of California Studies,* I (1893), p. 99

71. Koffka, *The Growth of the Mind,* p. 71

72. *Ibid.,* p. 81

73. W. Koehler, "An Aspect of Gestalt Psychology," in Murchison (ed.), *Psychologies of 1925,* p. 192

74. Marina, "Die Relationen des Palaeencephalon sind nicht fix," *Neurol. Centralbl.,* 1915, 34, pp. 338-345. Cf. Koffka, *The Growth of the Mind,* pp. 271 sqq.

clear vision is not necessarily situated in the center of the sensitive zone but in the center of the efficacious retinal stimulations, that is, of those which are represented in the phenomenal visual field. It would be premature, in the present state of knowledge, to formulate these hypothetical laws with a rigor which is not justified. The essential point is that clear and confused vision can be grossly correlated with the enveloped and enveloping parts of the visual processes and that the central regions of the sensitive zone can be understood as a "figure-sense" (Koffka, *Principles of Gestalt Psychology*, pp. 202 sqq.), its peripheral regions as a "ground-sense."

82. We could just as well say: "expressed in verbal behavior." It is not necessary to introduce consciousness here and we do so only in order to be brief.
83. Koffka himself only does it conjecturally (*Principles of Gestalt Psychology*, p. 207).
84. Goldstein, *Der Aufbau des Organismus*, p. 34 (cf. *The Organism*, p. 49)
85. Cf. W. Koehler, *Die physischen Gestalten*, pp. 156 sqq.
86. Goldstein, *Der Aufbau des Organismus*, pp. 106 sqq. (cf. *The Organism*, pp. 157 sqq.)
87. *Ibid.*, p. 112 (cf. *The Organism*, p. 166)
88. *Ibid.*, p. 106 (cf. *The Organism*, pp. 157 sqq.)
89. Goldstein, *Der Aufbau des Organismus*, p. 111 (cf. *The Organism*, p. 166)
90. *Idem.*
91. Cf. Buytendijk, "Le Cerveau et l'Intelligence," *Journal de Psychologie*, XXVIII (1931), p. 357
92. We have had occasion to indicate (cf. *supra*, p. 40) that with hemianopics the measure of the perimeter of vision and the observation of the visual function in its natural use also give discordant results. In the second attitude, a functional reorganization occurs which is not produced in the laboratory examination because in the latter situation a response to punctual stimuli is demanded of the organism. The laws of reflexology can be transformed by those of psycho-physiology and, as we will soon see, by those of psychology.
93. The same conflict between the demands of realistic analysis and those of the phenomena studied will be encountered with respect to the notion of sensation. Far from being a primitive and elementary content of consciousness, sensation —that is, the apprehension of a pure quality—is a late and exceptional mode of organization of human consciousness; doctrines which attempt to compose consciousness out of sensations are anthropocentric illusions. What is chronologically first in behavior as well as in perception is neither a mosaic of external parts nor the precise unity which makes analysis possible; as has often been said, it is a syncretism.
94. Weizsäcker, "Reflexgesetze," p. 37
95. "The quantity of energy capable of work should be a minimum for the system taken as a whole, the entropy a maximum, and the . . . vectors whose grouping constitutes the system should not receive, in each part taken separately, values and positions determined for themselves: by means of their total grouping and relatively to each other they must produce a durable whole. For this reason the state or event in each place depends in principle upon the given conditions in all the other sectors of the system. If on the contrary the laws [of the state of equilibrium] can be formulated separately for each part of a physical complex taken by itself, then the parts do not constitute a physical system and each one taken by itself is a system of this kind in its own right" (Koehler, *Die physischen Gestalten*, p. xvi).
96. *Ibid.*, p. xix
97. Wertheimer, "Experimentelle Studien über das Sehen von Bewegung"
98. This is the first criterion of Ehrenfels; cf. Koehler, *Die physischen Gestalten*, pp. 35-37.
99. The second criterion of Ehrenfels
100. "Les fibres nerveuses sensitives d'une région cutanée donnée, fût-elle fort petite,

75. P. Guillaume, *L'Imitation chez l'Enfant*, Paris, Alcan, 1925, p. 123
76. Koffka, *The Growth of the Mind*, p. 85
77. Concerning all these points, cf. Goldstein, *Der Aufbau des O:* 146 sqq. (cf. *The Organism*, pp. 226 sqq.). We have already h call attention to the phenomenon of transference of habits: a pers(hand has been amputated does not need, properly speaking, to with the left hand; our handwriting possesses constant characte we write on a piece of paper with only the finger muscles or oi with the muscles of a whole arm. The permanence in the brair structures or "forms" capable of being expressed in different m(will be studied in Chapter II. There will also be occasion to mak(between reflex substitutions and the movements by which on(Goldstein's subjects ("Zur Psychologie des optischen Warhrn Erkennungsvorganges," *Psychologische Analysen Hirnpatholc* Leipzig, J. A. Barth, 1920, I, pp. 1-142) imitated the contours of ot to his view and which for him took the place of the deficient ceiving visual wholes. The essential point is that the subject neither the visual deficit nor the motor substitute which masked 24). Thus all the transitions between the so-called higher nerve the functions improperly called lower are represented. The not is the only one so far which allows one to explain at the same ti is already intentional in the latter, that which remains blind in also takes account of the striking parallelism which obtains betw behavior and higher behavior, particularly in illness. We will ha describe, following Buytendijk and Plessner ("Die psysiologis des Verhaltens, eine Kritik an der Theorie Pawlows," *Acta Bioth* A, I (1935), pp. 151-171), a genuine "experimental neurosis" p: peated experiments in one of the dogs which Pavlov worked ν attitudes of negativism, of caprice, or the lability of behavior known in human pathology. Goldstein has himself indicated a *Aufbau der Organismus*, pp. 24 sqq., cf. *The Organism*, p. 40 behavior of animals which avoid hot air and drafts after a s (Cannon), and that of subjects with brain injuries who avoid al which they would be incapable of mastering and who consequent vital milieu; between the attitude of the animal who "plays dead" sick person who is always "occupied," never available for one of t the milieu might unexpectedly propose to him. Perhaps one m in the "forms" of behavior the reason for the analogies pointed (lois ("La Mante religieuse, recherche sur la nature et la significati *Mesures,* April, 1937) between certain dramas of animal life and most tenacious of human myths. There is no longer anything of morphic about these comparisons, which in any case pose a prob an orientation, a structure, is recognized in the so-called ele phenomena.
78. Cf. W. Fuchs, "Eine Pseudofovea bei Hemianopikern," *Psych schung,* I (1922), pp. 157-186. The results of Fuchs are summ terpreted by Goldstein, *Der Aufbau des Organismus*, pp. 32-38 (*ism,* pp. 47-66).
79. Reported by K. Koffka, *Principles of Gestalt Psychology*, New Y Brace, 1935, pp. 202-208. These experiments anticipate the foll where perceptual behavior will be considered more particularly. here to show the unity of the physiological phenomenon of ' which the "oculo-motor reflexes" cannot be isolated. The organiz influxes depends upon that of the afferent excitations and this explicable part by part.
80. Goldstein, *Der Aufbau des Organismus,* p. 37 (cf. *The Organism,*
81. The experiments reported above show, nevertheless, that the r

se dispersent dans plusieurs faisceaux radiculaires, même dans deux ou trois racines adjacentes et font ainsi leur entrée dans la moelle en face de toute une série de fibres motrices appartenant aussi bien à des extenseurs qu'à des fléchisseurs. Pour que le mouvement observé puisse s'accomplir, s'amplifiant de fléchisseur en fléchisseur sans jamais atteindre un extenseur, faut-il donc admettre, se demande-t-il [Sherrington] que les fibres sensitives plantaires sont allées, dans la substance grise de la moelle, à la recherche des cellules motrices des fléchisseurs, laissant soigneusement de côté les cellules motrices des autres muscles, notamment des extenseurs?" (Lapicque, "Physiologie générale du système nerveux," p. 149)

101. As a matter of fact, the relationship of which we are speaking is not rigid and it is precisely the chronaxic connection which easily explains its flexibility. Let us recall that the chronaxic of an isolated nerve (called the constitutional chronaxie) is modified when the nerve is integrated into the nervous system. "Dans le système nerveux à l'état normal, c'est-à-dire constituant effectivement un système fonctionnel, il y a sans doute partout des interventions de ce genre, la chronaxie de constitution, celle du neurone isolé et en repos, fait place à une chronaxie de subordination réglable suivant des influences diverses" (ibid., p. 152). In particular (idem), "L'encéphale a réellement le pouvoir de modifier les chronaxies motrices périphériques." The notion of inhibition is in this way made considerably more precise and simple: it is the disjunction of nerve paths by simple modification of chronaxie. The phenomena of reflex stopping and reflex reversal can be readily represented in the same language.

102. Ibid., p. 151
103. Idem.
104. Ibid., p. 153
105. Idem.
106. Ibid., p. 148
107. Idem.

CHAPTER II

1. ". . . les réflexes congénitaux ne sont pas suffisants pour la vie animale. La vie journalière exige des rapports plus détaillés, plus spéciaux de l'animal avec le monde environnant . . . les faits se passent de la façon suivante: une multitude d'agents de la nature donnent par leur présence le signal . . . aux agents relativement peu nombreux qui conditionnent les réflexes congénitaux. De cette façon est obtenu l'équilibre précis et fin de l'organisme avec le monde environnant. J'ai appelé cette activité des hémisphères, activité de signalement" (I. P. Pavlov, Leçons sur l'activité du cortex cérébral, Paris, A. Legrand, 1929).
2. "Cette signalisation," Pavlov continued, "montre toutes les caractéristiques de l'acte nerveux nommé réflexe. Il sera juste d'appeler ces réflexes acquis réflexes conditionnels ou réflexes de contact" (ibid.).
3. Pavlov, Die höchste Nerventätigkeit von Tieren, München, Bergmann, 1926, p. 311
4. Drabovitch, "Les Réflexes conditionnés et la chronaxie," Revue philosophique, CXXIII (1937), p. 104
5. Pavlov, Les Réflexes conditionnels, Paris, Alcan, 1932, pp. 78-87. Cf. H. Piéron, "Les Réflexes conditionnés," in Dumas, Nouveau Traité de Psychologie, Paris, Presses Universitaires de France, II, pp. 35 sqq.
6. Pavlov, Les réflexes conditionnels, p. 83, cited by Piéron, "Les Réflexes conditionnés," p. 35
7. Pavlov, Leçons sur l'activité du cortex cérébral, pp. 349 sqq.
8. Inhibition as well as excitation tends to be irradiated in time and space. Beyond a certain temporal or spatial distance this action gives place to that of reciprocal induction, which also functions in time as well as space.

9. "Tout le langage de Pavlov et de ses élèves est déjà imprégné de théorie et les faits pourraient être exprimés sous d'autres formes" (Piéron, "Les Réflexes conditionnés," p. 33).

10. Piéron, "Les Problèmes de la perception et la psychophysiologie," *Année psychologique,* XXVII (1926), pp. 6-7

11. Doubtless Pavlov took into account the syncretic character of infantile and animal reactions in particular (law of irradiation). But Pavlov's irradiation is a sort of drainage by which a strong excitation attracts all the simultaneous excitations into its exit paths. Thus it explains why any one of these latter can subsequently evoke the reaction studied but not why this power belongs to certain determined constellations (for example, $L + S + M$) and to them alone ($L + S + M + X$ is not reflexogenic). Syncretic reactions correspond to confused ensembles, while conditioning experiments present us with reactions which are tied to a precise *structure*.

12. Piéron, "Les Réflexes conditionnés," p. 28

13. Piéron, "Recherches sur les lois de variation," *Année psychologique,* XX (1913), pp. 182-185; cf. *ibid.,* XXVII (1926), p. 1

14. Piéron, "Les Problèmes de la perception et la psychophysiologie," p. 6

15. Pavlov, *Leçons sur l'activité du cortex cérébral,* pp. 100-101, cited by Piéron, "Les Réflexes conditionnés," p. 34, n. 1

16. H. Piéron points out that Pavlov, following his meeting with Koehler in 1929 at the Congress of Psychology in New Haven, was inclined to recognize the proper role of complexes and structures.

17. ". . . Ce n'est pas la psychologie qui doit aider la physiologie des hémisphères, mais, tout au contraire, l'étude physiologique de ces organes chez les animaux qui doit servir de base à l'analyse précise et scientifique de monde subjectif de l'homme" (Pavlov, *Leçons sur l'activité du cortex cérébral*).

18. Pavlov, *Ein Beitrag zur Physiologie des hyponotischen Zustandes beim Hunde* (unter Mitarbeit von Dr. Petrova), pp. 183 sqq. This work is criticized by Buytendijk and Plessner ("Die physiologische Erklärung des Verhaltens, eine Kritik an der Theorie Pawlows," *Acta Biotheoretica,* Series A, I (1935), pp. 160 sqq.), from whom we borrow the following evaluations.

19. Buytendijk and Plessner, "Die physiologische Erklärung des Verhaltens," pp. 164-165

20. *Ibid.,* p. 166

21. "What would one think of a physicist who, convinced of the existence of ether, would, like Michelson, undertake research in order to demonstrate it and who would try to explain the negative result of the experiment by a particular property of ether or by a counter force which removes its effect?" (Buytendijk and Plessner, "Die Physiologische Erklärung des Verhaltens," p. 167)

22. *Ibid.,* p. 166

23. K. Goldstein, "Die Lokalisation in der Grosshirnrinde," in Bethe (ed.), *Handbuch der normalen und pathologischen Physiologie,* X, p. 639

24. Goldstein, *Der Aufbau des Organismus,* pp. 81-86 (cf. *The Organism,* pp. 121, 129). Cf. Buytendijk and Plessner, "Die physiologische Erklärung des Verhaltens": "If we say: excitation is the modification of the superficial tension of a nerve cell, not only is nothing gained in this way with regard to the understanding of the phenomenon itself but, further, excitation as a physiological phenomenon is lost from view. In exactly the same way the definition of sound as a vibration of the air doubtless makes physical acoustics possible, but precludes access to the immediacy of the phenomenon and thus to the theory of music" (p. 163).

25. In Pavlov's own school, Ivanov-Smolinsky has indicated the necessity of a process of cortical integration in the reception of stimuli (cited by Piéron, "Les Réflexes conditionnés," p. 34).

26. Pavlov, *Die höchste Nerventätigkeit von Tieren,* p. 311, cited by Buytendijk and Plessner, "Die Physiologische Erklärung des Verhaltens," p. 158

27. Buytendijk and Fischel, "Ueber die akustische Wahrnehmung des Hundes," *Archives néerlandaise de physiologie*, XVII (1933), p. 267
28. Buytendijk and Plessner, *art. cit.*, pp. 163-164
29. Piéron, "Les Réflexes conditionnés," p. 35
30. *Idem.*
31. Cf. for example, the convergent conclusions of H. Piéron, *Le Cerveau et la pensée*, Paris, Alcan, 1923, and K. Goldstein, "Die Lokalisation in der Grosshirnrinde"
32. A lesion can extend or more as far removed from those where it is anatomically discoverable. It can render a function impossible without our having the right to localize this function in the injured area. It is certainly necessary that specialized pathways introduce stimulations issuing from the sensory apparatus to the brain or carry the centrifugal excitations to the muscles (cf. Goldstein, "Die Lokalisation in der Grosshirnrinde," p. 636). Thus there will be an anatomical projection from the periphery of the organism toward the cerebral cortex. But it should not be concluded from this that, in functioning, the alleged centers of the zone of projection behave like autonomous governments. The anatomical distinction between "projection" and "association" has no physiological value. An occipital lesion produces blindness, but this does not signify that we see "with" the occipital lobe.
33. Goldstein, *Der Aufbau des Organismus*, pp. 9-11 (cf. *The Organism*, pp. 15-21)
34. *Ibid.*
35. Elective disorders are produced only "in case of circumscribed lesion of the pathways which connect the cortex to the periphery or in lesions of cortical regions in immediate relation to these pathways" (Goldstein, "Die Lokalisation in der Grosshirnrinde," p. 631). In addition to the circumscribed deficiencies, every injury and even certain concussions involve general disorders of cerebral functioning (lowering of the level of effort, of attention or of "nervous tension") (Piéron, *Le Cerveau et la pensée*, p. 54).
36. A. Gelb and K. Goldstein, "Ueber Farbennamenamnesie," *Psychologische Forschung*, VI (1925), pp. 127-186
37. In the subject studied by Goldstein amnesia of the names of color is accompanied by disorders in the capacity for sorting colors according to a given principle of classification (sometimes clarity, sometimes basic tint). This is because this operation, in order to be correctly accomplished, demands the same categorial attitude which is necessary for naming an object. A sample must be taken as the representative of a category of color. The patient can classify only according to concrete impressions of resemblance which are more formed in him than directed by him. Thus he classifies without principle; and this is why, left to his impressions of coherence and no matter what the directive given, the patient sometimes groups together samples which resemble each other in relation to clarity; sometimes and unexpectedly he groups together those which have nothing in common except the fundamental tint (Gelb and Goldstein, "Ueber Farbennamenamnesie," pp. 149 sqq.
38. Goldstein, *Der Aufbau des Organismus*, p. 18 (cf. *The Organism*, p. 29)
39. *Idem.* (*ibid.*, p. 30)
40. *Ibid.*, p. 19 (*ibid.*, p. 30), and "Die Lokalisation in der Grosshirnrinde," p. 666
41. Goldstein, *Der Aufbau des Organismus*, p. 18 (cf. *The Organism*, pp. 28-34)
42. *Ibid.*, p. 20 (*ibid.*, p. 33)
43. Goldstein, "Die Lokalisation in der Grosshirnrinde," p. 667
44. A. Gelb and K. Goldstein, "Zur Psychologie des optischen Wahrnehmungs und Erkennungsvorganges," in Gelb and Goldstein (eds.), *Psychologische Analysen Hirnpathologischer Fälle*, Leipzig, J. A. Barth, 1920, I, pp. 1-142
45. *Ibid.*, pp. 157-250, Chapter II: "Ueber den Einflusz des vollständigen verlustes des optischen Vorstellungsvermögens auf das taktile Erkennen." Cf. Goldstein, "Ueber die Abhängigkeit der Bewegungen von optischen Vorgängen," *Monatschrift für Psychiatrie und Neurologie*, LIV-LV (1923-1924), pp. 141-194

46. Gelb and Goldstein (eds.), *Psychologische Analysen Hirnpathologischer Fälle*, LIV; W. Benary, "Studien zur Untersuchung der Intelligenz bei einem Fall von Seelerblindheit," *Psychologische Forschung*, II (1922), pp. 209 sqq.; and Hochheimer, "Analyse eines Seelerblinden von der Sprache aus," *Psychologische Forschung*, XVI (1932), pp. 1 sqq. All of these studies have been carried out with the same subject, S . . ., either by Gelb and Goldstein or by their students; the observation of this patient—initially in a hospital for patients suffering from brain injuries, then submitted to periodic examinations in a dispensary in Frankfurt am Main—which was carried out over a period of years and which was concerned with all aspects of his behavior (including his sexual behavior: cf. Steinfeld, "Ein Beitrag Zur Analyze der Sexualfunktion," *Zeitschrift für das gesamte Neurologie und Psychiatrie*, 187 (1927), pp. 172 sqq.) constitutes the material for a unique document. In another work we will have occasion to utilize the admirable descriptions of the school of Gelb and Goldstein and concerning the relations which exist between properly perceptive disorders and disorders of thought. Here we retain from these works only what is necessary for posing the problem of localization and of the significance of place in the nerve substance.

47. In their first work (cf. n. 44) Gelb and Goldstein had diagnosed a *Gestaltblindheit* or blindness for forms. The subsequent studies enlarge the diagnosis.

48. Goldstein, "Die Lokalisation in der Grosshirnrinde," p. 665

49. Sir Henry Head, "Speech and Cerebral Localization," *Brain*, vol. 42 (1923), p. 355

50. "Experimentellpsychologische Untersuchungen zur Aphasie und Paraphasie," *Zeitschrift für das gesamte Neurologie und Psychiatrie*, XCVI (1925), pp. 481 sqq; cf. Goldstein, "Die Lokalisation in der Grosshirnrinde"

51. It is known that these are the characteristics of infantile perception, which is at the same time more syncretic and sometimes more minute than that of an adult.

52. Cf. for example, Gelb and Goldstein, "Zur Psychologie des optischen Wahrnehmungs und Erkennungsvorganges," pp. 69 sqq.

53. Goldstein, "Die Lokalisation in der Grosshirnrinde," p. 668

54. "Ueber Störungen im Denken bei Aphasiepatienten," *Monatschrift für Psychiatrie und Neurologie*, LIX (1925), pp. 256 sqq.

55. Cf. Benary, "Studien zur Untersuchung der Intelligenz bei einem Fall von Seelenblindheit," pp. 209-297, and in particular, pp. 222-224

56. Goldstein, "Die Lokalisation in der Grosshirnrinde," pp. 670-672

57. K. S. Lashley, *Brain Mechanisms and Intelligence*, Chicago, University of Chicago Press, 1929

58. F. Buytendijk, "An Experimental Investigation into the Influence of Cortical Lesions on the Behavior of Rats," *Archives néerlandaises de physiologie*, XVII (1932), pp. 370-434; cf. "Le Cerveau et l'intelligence," *Journal de Psychologie*, 1931, pp. 345-371

59. Cf. Buytendijk and Fischel, "Strukturgemäszes Verhalten von Ratten," *Archives néerlandaises de physiologie*, XVI (1931), pp. 55 sqq.

60. "Most of the observed disorders are perfectly analogous to the changes of conduct in human subjects presenting cortical lesions, such as they have been described by Grunbaum, Goldstein, Head and others" (F. Buytendijk, "An Experimental Investigation into the Influences of Cortical Lesions on the Behavior of Rats")

61. It goes without saying that in all the preceding discussions, and in spite of the anthropomorphic language which we have used in order to be brief, consciousness is not supposed in the animal. One limits oneself to noting objectively the difference between the stimuli capable of influencing the normal and the operated animal: in the first case the form of the situation is reflexogenic; in the second, only the individual and material properties of the stimuli are efficacious.

62. Buytendijk, *ibid.*

63. K. S. Lashley, *Brain Mechanisms and Intelligence*

64. K. S. Lashley, "Cerebral Control versus Reflexology," *Journal of Genetic Psychology*, V (1931), p. 3
65. "Oblique" attitude and cross-shaped movements, asymmetrical coloration of the animal in the initial period following the operation; position of defense with arms bent back in half of the body. (Buytendijk, "Das Verhalten von Octopus nach teilweiser Zerstörung des Gehirns," *Archives néerlandaises de physiologie*, XVIII (1933), pp. 24-70 and pp. 55 sqq.)
66. *Ibid.*, p. 52
67. *Ibid.*, p. 53
68. Goldstein, "Die Lokalisation in der Grosshirnrinde," p. 672
69. Goldstein excludes the conception of a "diffuse activity of the whole cortex" (*ibid.*, p. 673). "The activity [of different sectors of the cortex] contributes certain determined elements to the whole" (*ibid.*, p. 672). Piéron rejects the thesis "d'après laquelle le cerveau ne jouerait dans le fonctionnement mental qu'un certain rôle banal, comme réservoir d'énergie ou comme substrat indifférencié" (*Le Cerveau et la pensée*, p. 61).
70. Piéron, *Le Cerveau et la pensée*, p. 55
71. Goldstein, "Die Lokalisation in der Grosshirnrinde," pp. 684 sqq.
72. *Ibid.*, p. 693
73. *Ibid.*, p. 687
74. It is true that, in the hemianopic, the different points of the intact calcarine area which by construction had no determined value have assumed new chromatic and "spacial values" (cf. *supra*, p. 41). We will return in a moment to this superimposition of a mosaic and structural functioning in the brain.
75. Goldstein, "Die Lokalisation in der Grosshirnrinde," pp. 686-687
76. The simultaneous contraction of the two superior members following an electrical excitation of only one of them; the indifferent use of either hand; the appearance of aphasic symptoms as a result of a lesion at the source of either hemisphere, followed by a rapid restoration
77. Goldstein, *ibid.*, p. 661
78. Cf. *supra*, p. 65, and Gelb and Goldstein, "Zur Psychologie des optischen Wahrnehmungs und Erkennungsvorganges"
79. Cf. *supra*, p. 65-66, and Benary, "Studien zur Untersuchung des Intelligenz bei einem Fall von Seelenblindheit," pp. 290 sqq.
80. Piéron, *Le Cerveau et la pensée*, pp. 61-66
81. *Ibid.*, pp. 66-67
82. Goldstein, *Der Aufbau des Organismus*, p. 166 (cf. *The Organism*, p. 259)
83. The conception of Goldstein, from whom we borrow much here, agrees entirely with the conclusions of M. Ombredane. "Le langage doit être envisagé à la fois . . . sur le plan *horizontal* des éléments sensoriels et moteurs qui concourent à en assurer le jeu, et sur le plan *vertical* des degrés de complexité et de différenciation des opérations expressives effectuées. Une destruction cérébrale en foyer peut entraîner des dissociations dans les deux plans. Autant dire qu'une explication de l'aphasie ne saurait prétendre à l'unité rationnelle d'une doctrine purement psychologique, mais qu'à côté des considérations sur le niveau des opérations expressives inhibées, elle doit admettre des éléments empiriques irréductibles qui tiennent aux relations dans l'espace, étrangères à toute logique, des appareils sensoriels et moteurs dont le fonctionnement solidaire fournit au langage ses instruments matériels" ("Le Langage," *Revue Philosophique*, 1931, pp. 217-271, 424-453 and p. 252). Thus all the transitions will exist between the limiting case of amimia and anarthria, where the deficit largely affects certain contents, and at the opposite pole, the case of a global deficit which leaves perception and the utilization of concrete situations intact, depending on whether the lesion is situated at the level of the "cerebral terminations of the sensory and motor apparatuses" or is removed from them and approaches the center (*ibid.*, pp. 252-254).
84. *Le Cerveau et la pensée*, pp. 94-95

85. *Ibid.*, p. 151
86. *Ibid.*, p. 147
87. Concerning all the localizations mentioned, cf. *ibid.*, pp. 213-214, and pp. 248 sqq.
88. *Ibid.*, p. 242
89. *Ibid.*, p. 243
90. *Ibid.*, p. 245
91. The physiological support for the evocation of a word is "le complexus des processus d'évocation qui met en jeu, dans un *ensemble spécifique,* des éléments servant à toutes les combinaisons possibles: *l'ordre* des phonèmes successifs constitue l'image auditive d'un mot, les mêmes phonèmes, dans un autre ordre, donnant un autre mot" (*ibid., p.* 243).
92. Goldstein, "Die Lokalisation in der Grosshirnrinde," p. 641: "The mistake of the classical doctrine did not reside in its effort to make psychology the basis of the theory of localizations, but in the inadequacy of its psychological analysis. Neither did this mistake consist in the postulation of homogeneous laws for the neurological and the psychological event, nor in the hypothesis according to which it would be possible to understand the psychological from the neurological, but rather in the inadequacy of its representation of the neurological event." *Ibid.*, p. 659: "Perception, representation, motor processes or thought is not a fortuitous juxtaposition of partial contents; each mental ensemble reveals a systematic structure in which the partial contents emerge more or less according to their signification for the global process of the moment, but always in the framework of the whole . . . I believed I could localize the purely qualitative and the purely motor elements of the whole-process in the motor and sensory fields. But I believed it necessary to make the whole cortex and, above all, the sector situated between the motorium and the sensorium come into play for that process which alone gives to these qualitative and motor elements a mental character properly so-called and which manifests itself in the construction of the consciousness of object . . . of the concept, of thought or of authentic linguistic consciousness." Cf. Piéron, *Le Cerveau et la pensée,* p. 60: ". . . les notions de facultés conçues comme des individualités indépendantes ou des collections d'états psychiques qu'il n'y aurait plus qu'à loger dans les compartiments de l'âme ou dans ceux du cerveau ne se prêtaient guère à un rapprochement du fonctionnement nerveux et du fonctionnement mental. . . . Mais les notions dynamiques auxquelles a conduit l'étude expérimentale de l'esprit se sont singulièrement rapprochées des notions dynamiques que l'étude expérimentale des fonctions nerveuses impose aux anatomistes eux-mêmes, qui ne peuvent plus limiter leur pensée aux individualités morphologiques artificielles des lobes du cerveau, ni aux collections de cadavres, embaumés par des liquides fixateurs, qui se montrent dans le champ du microscope."
93. We will have to raise the question as to whether, from this point of view, one ought still to speak of parallelism; whether we can expect, for example, the discovery in the future of a determined physiological substrate for all the structures of behavior which psychology describes, for all the complexes known to psychoanalysis for instance. We do not think so (cf. *infra,* Chapter IV). But here only the points on which the authors agree should be retained; for the moment it is sufficient for us to have shown that physiological, like psychological, analysis is an ideal analysis. It is from this point of view that we can investigate later whether a physiological "idea" can be made to correspond to each psychological "idea."
94. *Le Cerveau et la pensée,* p. 152, n. 3
95. Koffka, "Some Problems of Space Perception," in C. Murchison (ed.), *Psychologies of 1930,* Worcester, Mass., Clark University Press, 1930, p. 179
96. *Ibid.;* E. R. Jaensch, "Ueber die Wahrnehmung des Raumes," *Zeitschrift für Psychologie,* VI (1911)

97. Goldstein, "Die Lokalisation in der Grosshirnrinde," p. 685; cf. *supra*, Chapter I.

98. Goldstein, "Die Lokalisation in der Grosshirnrinde," *ibid.*, pp. 683-684

99. We leave open for the moment the question of whether this apparent finality of nerve functioning is carried by a physiological phenomenon of structure, as is thought by Gestalt psychology, or whether (cf. *infra*, Chapter III) it must be admitted very simply that there is no physiological analysis of the constitution of the spatial field.

100. Piéron, *Le Cerveau et la pensée*, p. 154

101. *Idem.*

102. Piéron adds (*idem*): "Cette évocation délicate des nuances chromatiques exige . . . une intégrité complète des neurones transmettant les influx, et surtout des neurones synchronisés du clavier chromatique, car le coefficient propre du neurone est modifié par la moindre atteinte qu'il subit." Clearly the reintroduction of considerations of quality is being sought. But it remains true that the work is effected in anatomical apparatuses distinct from those in which, for example, the distribution of local signs is effected.

103. K. Koffka, *Principles of Gestalt Psychology*, New York, Harcourt, Brace, 1935, p. 133

104. K. Koffka, "Some Remarks on the Theory of Colour Constancy," *Psychologische Forschung*, XVI (1932), pp. 334-335. The experiment is taken up again with more precision in *Principles of Gestalt Psychology*, pp. 255 sqq.

105. Koffka, "Some Remarks on the Theory of Colour Constancy," p. 335

106. *Ibid.*, pp. 304-342

107. Koffka, *Principles of Gestalt Psychology*, p. 259

108. Such as Piéron perhaps conceived it when he brought into play "la longueur d'onde prédominante" of excitants (*Le Cerveau et la pensée*, p. 134)

109. Koffka, *Principles of Gestalt Psychology*, p. 134

110. W. Fuchs, "Experimentelle Untersuchungen über das simultane Hintereinander auf derselben Sehrichtung," *Zeitschrift für Psychologie*, XCI, pp. 145-235

111. Koffka, *Principles of Gestalt Psychology*, p. 262

112. G. Heider, "New Studies in Transparency, Colour and Form," *Psychologische Forschung*, XVII (1933), pp. 13-56

113. B. Tudor-Hart, "Studies in Transparency, Form and Colour," *Psychologische Forschung*, X (1928), pp. 255-298 and especially pp. 263-264

114. In case of lesion, "ce n'est donc pas l'utilisation d'une image cliché qui est atteinte, c'est la *réalisation* de l'image, dynamisme associatif" (Piéron, *Le Cerveau et la pensée*, p. 243).

115. *Ibid.*, p. 237, n. 2

116. *Ibid.*, pp. 246-247

117. *Ibid.*, p. 256

118. *Ibid.*, p. 254, n. 2

119. *Ibid.*, pp. 246-247

120. *Ibid.*, p. 247, n. 1

121. Cf. *supra*, p. 81

122. The expression is from H. Wallon, *Stades et troubles du développement psychomoteur et mental chez l'enfant*, Paris, Alcan, 1925 (republished under the title: *L'Enfant turbulent*, 1925)

123. "Il est classique de désigner la zone calcarine de *l'area striata* comme le centre de la vision. Mais l'expression est impropre. L'acte de vision ne s'effectue pas en entier dans cette station de connexion réceptrice, il comporte la mise en jeu de circuits associatifs qui . . . s'étendent parfois jusqu'à l'autre pôle du cerveau" (Piéron, *Le Cerveau et la pensée*, p. 154).

124. Goldstein, "Die Lokalisation in der Grosshirnrinde," p. 758

125. *Ibid.*, p. 650

126. Goldstein, *Der Aufbau des Organismus*, p. 166 (cf. *The Organism*, pp. 259-260)

127. Koffka, *Principles of Gestalt Psychology,* preface
128. Cf. *supra,* p. 87
129. E. C. Tolman, "Sign-Gestalt or Conditioned Reflex?" *Psychological Review,* XL (1933), p. 246
130. Koffka, *The Growth of the Mind,* New York, Harcourt, Brace, 1925, pp. 174 sqq.
131. P. Guillaume, *La Formation des habitudes,* Paris, Alcan, 1936, p. 51
132. Cf. Koehler, *L'Intelligence des singes supérieurs,* Paris, Alcan, 1927, *passim*
133. Tolman, "Sign-Gestalt or Conditioned Reflex?"
134. Koffka, *The Growth of the Mind,* pp. 174 sqq.
135. *Idem.*
136. *Idem.*
137. F. Buytendijk, *Psychologie des animaux,* Paris, Payot, 1928, pp. 202-205
138. Koehler, *Intelligenzprüfungen an Menschenaffen,* 2nd ed., Berlin, 1921, pp. 140 sqq. (Cf. English edition, *The Mentality of Apes,* trans. by E. Winters, London, Routledge & Kegan Paul, 1925, pp. 194 sqq.)
139. Koehler, *L'Intelligence des singes supérieurs,* pp. 219-223 (cf. *The Mentality of Apes,* pp. 226-229)
140. Guillaume, *La Formation des habitudes,* pp. 53 and 55
141. Koehler, *L'Intelligence des singes supérieurs,* pp. 142-143 and pp. 145-146 (cf. *The Mentality of Apes,* pp. 135-152)
142. Koffka, *The Growth of the Mind,* p. 219
143. Koehler, *Intelligence des singes supérieurs,* pp. 171 sqq. (cf. *The Mentality of Apes,* pp. 194 sqq.)
144. Buytendijk, "Les Différences essentielles des fonctions psychiques de l'homme et des animaux," *Cahiers de philosophie de la nature,* Vrin, IV (1930), p. 53
145. *Idem.*
146. Guillaume, *La Formation des habitudes,* p. 69
147. *Ibid.,* p. 85
148. Cf. *supra,* p. 94
149. Koffka, *The Growth of the Mind,* p. 192
150. Koehler, *L'Intelligence des singes supérieurs, passim*
151. H. A. Ruger, "Psychology of Efficiency," *Archives of Psychology,* XV (1910)
152. Cf. *supra,* pp. 97 sqq.
153. Buytendijk, "Les Différences essentielles des fonctions psychiques de l'homme et des animaux," pp. 46-47
154. Koehler, "Optische Untersuchungen am Schimpansen und am Haushuhn," *Berliner Abhandlungen,* Jahrang 1915, and "Nachweis einfacher Strukturfunktionen beim Schimpansen und beim Haushuhn," *Berliner Abhandlungen,* Jahrang 1918
155. Tolman, "Sign-Gestalt or Conditional Reflex?", pp. 246-255
156. Miller, "A Reply to 'Sign-Gestalt or Conditioned Reflex?'" *Psychological Review,* XLII (1935)
157. Miller, *ibid.,* pp. 286 sqq.
158. Tolman, "Sign-Gestalt or Conditional Reflex?" pp. 254-255
159. G. Revesz, "Experiments on Animal Space Perception," *VIIth International Congress of Psychology, Proceedings and Papers,* Cambridge, 1924, pp. 29-56
160. Koffka, *Principles of Gestalt Psychology,* p. 34
161. Revesz, "Experiments on Animal Space Perception"
162. Buytendijk, "Les Différences essentielles des fonctions psychiques de l'homme et des animaux," p. 62
163. Buytendijk, "Die Bedeutung der Feldkräfte und der Intentionalität für das Verhalten des Hundes," *Archives néerlandaises de physiologie,* XVII (1932), pp. 459-494
164. Buytendijk, Fischel and Ter Laag, "Ueber die Zieleinstellung von Ratten und Hunden," *Archives néerlandaises de physiologie,* XX (1935), pp. 446-466

165. The resistance of the partial structures to this new integration can be measured by putting them in competition with it. Between a path the elements of which form an acute angle and another path where there are only oblique angles, everything else being equal, the rats choose the second more often. It can be arranged so that the oblique angles are found on the longer path, the acute angles on the shorter. The results are scarcely modified by this apparatus.

166. Reported by Guillaume, *La Formation des habitudes*, pp. 88 sqq.

167. Buytendijk, *Psychologie der animaux*, pp. 136 sqq.

168. Koehler, *Intelligenzprüfungen an Menschenaffen*, p. 19 (cf. *The Mentality of Apes*, p. 27)

169. Buytendijk, *Psychologie des animaux*, pp. 236 sqq.

170. Cf. W. T. Shepherd, "Tests on Adaptive Intelligence in Rhesus Monkeys," *American Journal of Psychology*, XXVI (1915); H. Nellman and W. Trendelenburg, "Ein Beitrag zur Intelligenzprüfung niederer Affen," *Zeitschrift für vergleichende Physiologie*, IV (1926), pp. 180 sqq.

171. Koehler, "Nachweis einfacher Strukturfunktionen," pp. 56 sqq.

172. Koehler, *Intelligenzprüfungen an Menschenaffen*, pp. 128 sqq. (cf. *The Mentality of Apes*, pp. 178-179)

173. It must be added that our world is not constantly made up of them.

174. Nellman and Trendelenburg, "Ein Beitrag zur Intelligenzprüfung niederer Affen," pp. 155 sqq.

175. Koehler, *Intelligenzprüfungen an Menschenaffen*, p. 128 (cf. *The Mentality of Apes*, pp. 178-179)

176. Koehler, *L'Intelligence des singes supérieurs*, p. 171 (cf. *The Mentality of Apes*, pp. 179-182)

177. Koehler, *Intelligenzprüfungen an Menschenaffen*, p. 19 (cf. *The Mentality of Apes*, pp. 27-28)

178. Koehler, *L'Intelligence des singes supérieurs*, pp. 238-239 (cf. *The Mentality of Apes*, pp. 245-247)

179. Koehler, *Intelligenzprüfungen an Menschenaffen*, pp. 30 sqq. (cf. *The Mentality of Apes*, pp. 41-42)

180. Koffka, *The Growth of the Mind*, pp. 193-195; cf. *supra*

181. Cf. J. Piaget, *La Causalité physique chez l'enfant*, Paris, Alcan, 1927, *passim*

182. Koehler, *L'Intelligence des singes supérieurs*, p. 153 (cf. *The Mentality of Apes*, p. 59)

183. *Ibid.*, p. 143 (cf. *The Mentality of Apes*, p. 152)

184. *Ibid.*, p. 142 (cf. *The Mentality of Apes*, p. 151)

185. *Ibid.*, pp. 179-180 (cf. *The Mentality of Apes*, p. 190)

186. *Ibid.*, p. 94 (cf. *The Mentality of Apes*, p. 100)

187. Cf. *supra*, p. 229, n. 77 and p. 69

188. Koehler, *L'Intelligence des singes supérieurs*, p. 144, n. 1 (cf. *The Mentality of Apes*, p. 153, n. 2)

189. *Ibid.*, pp. 229-239 (cf. *The Mentality of Apes*, pp. 245-250)

190. *Ibid.*, pp. 108-109 (cf. *The Mentality of Apes*, pp. 112-114)

191. *Ibid.*, p. 143, n. 1 (cf. *The Mentality of Apes*, p. 153, n. 1)

192. The expression *dingbezogene Verhalten* is common among German writers. Cf. Buytendijk, *Psychologie des animaux*, pp. 455 sqq. Volkelt (*Die Vorstellungen der Tiere*, 1914) speaks of the insufficient *dinghafte Gliederung* of animal behavior.

193. Cf. the examples of Koehler, *L'Intelligence des singes supérieurs*, p. 224 (cf. *The Mentality of Apes*, pp. 235 sqq.)

194. *Ibid.*, pp. 153 sqq. (cf. *The Mentality of Apes*, pp. 163 sqq.)

195. Cf. *supra*, p. 37

196. In the analysis of the case S . . . , Gelb and Goldstein had also initially made the visual contents responsible, and it was little by little that they arrived at a "structural" interpretation (cf. *supra*, pp. 65 and 71) with the collaboration of

their students. In a general way, it is little by little that the notion of "form" reveals all that it implies, either in the experimental order or in the order of reflection (cf. *infra,* Chapter III).

197. Buytendijk and Fischel, "Ueber die Reaktionen des Hundes auf menschliche Wörter," *Archives néerlandaises de physiologie,* XIX (1934); cf. Buytendijk, Fischel and Ter Laag, "Ueber die Zieleinstellung von Ratten und Hunden," pp. 455 sqq.

198. Perhaps it will be thought that it is too easy, by means of these examples, to bring to light the originality of symbolic behavior since the very "stimuli" of these motor habits are symbols of writing created by man. But it could be shown just as well that any acquired aptitude with regard to a "use-object" is an adaptation of this object to human structure and consists in taking possession with our body of a type of "artificial" behavior in the image of which the object was made. It is not by chance that the analysis of symbolic behavior always brings us back to these objects created by man. We will see that symbolic behavior is the condition of all creation and of all novelty in the "ends" of conduct. Thus it is not astonishing that it is first manifested in the adaptation to objects which do not exist in nature.

199. Cf. J. Chevalier, *L'Habitude,* Paris, Bouvin, 1929

200. *Idem.*

201. "Amener le chimpanzé à une activité, à une habitude, à un mode d'abstention ou de relation avec les choses . . . qui ne lui appartiennent pas, qui ne sont pas des réactions naturelles du chimpanzé dans les circonstances considérées,— tout cela peut réussir (par des corrections ou par tout autre moyen),—pour la durée des représentations du cirque; mais faire assimiler à un chimpanzé un acte qui serait étranger à sa nature de façon qu'il l'accomplisse désormais comme une chose naturelle, cela me paraît une tâche très difficile et même presque impossible." Koehler, *L'Intelligence des singes supérieurs,* p. 63 (cf. *The Mentality of Apes,* p. 68)

202. Pavlov, *Leçons sur l'activité du cortex cérébral,* pp. 12-13

203. Piéron, "Les Réflexes conditionnés," p. 35

204. Cf. *supra.*

205. Koehler, "Nachweis einfacher Strukturfunktionen," p. 24

206. Koffka, *The Growth of the Mind,* p. 157

207. Piéron, "Les Réflexes conditionnés," p. 37.

208. Cf. Chapter III

CHAPTER III

1. K. Koffka, *Principles of Gestalt Psychology,* New York, Harcourt, Brace, 1935, p. 28

2. F. Buytendijk, *Psychologie des animaux,* Paris, Payot, 1928, pp. 106, 142.

3. Koffka's "accomplishment" (*Principles of Gestalt Psychology,* p. 37)

4. *Ibid.,* p. 38

5. Buytendijk and Plessner, "Die physiologische Erklärung des Verhaltens, eine Kritik an der Theorie Pawlows," *Acta Biotheoretica,* Series A, I: "die jedem Verhalten als solchem innewohnende Verständlichkeit" (p. 169); it is necessary to leave behaviors "in ihrem natürlichen Situationszusammenhang und damit in ihrer Ausdruckshaftigkeit und unmittelbarer Verständlichkeit" (p. 170).

6. Buytendijk, *Psychologie des animaux,* p. 142. A dog left at liberty can be trained to choose a door marked with a triangle, even if it is different or even reversed from the one which was used in training, on the condition that the difference be not too great at first. A dog kept on a leash cannot acquire any reaction at all to an immobile triangle after one thousand trials. Cf. Buytendijk, "Les Différences essentielles des fonctions psychiques de l'homme et des animaux," *Cahiers de philosophie de la nature,* IV, 50 sqq.

7. This word does not necessarily designate a world of which the animal *is aware*, but only the ensemble of original relations which define behavior.

8. Buytendijk, *Psychologie des animaux*

9. Koffka, *Principles of Gestalt Psychology*, p. 42

10. *Ibid.*, pp. 10-20

11. *Ibid.*, p. 20

12. M. Wertheimer," Ueber Gestalttheorie," *Symposion* I (1927), pp. 1-24

13. Koffka, *Principles of Gestalt Psychology*, p. 19

14. *Ibid.*, p. 48

15. *Ibid.*, pp. 56, 57

16. W. Koehler, *Gestalt Psychology*, London, G. Bell, 1930

17. Wertheimer, "Ueber Gestalttheorie," p. 20

18. Koffka, *Principles of Gestalt Psychology*, p. 65

19. *Ibid.*, p. 63

20. *Idem.*

21. One can refer to the example of changes of state, or to that of functional reorganization in hemianopsia since, as we have seen, it is produced suddenly when the two demi-retinas become blind.

22. Cf. P. Guillaume, *La Psychologie de la forme*, Paris, Flammarion, 1937

23. W. Koehler, *Die physischen Gestalten in Ruhe und im stationären Zustand*, Erlangen, Braunschweig, 1920, p. 51

24. Cournot, *Traité de l'enchaînement des idées fondamentales*, paragraphs 183 and 184, cited by L. Brunschvicg, *L'Expérience humaine et la causalité physique*, Paris, Alcan, 1922, p. 514

25. Brunschvicg, *ibid.*

26. The future could be calculated only "si nous pouvions détacher de l'ensemble cosmologique qui nous est donné une série de causes indépendantes, qui manifesteraient, chacune dans leur série, leur caractère essentiel, sans que, du fait de leur rencontre, dût jamais sortir une conséquence qui introduirait une inflexion brusque dans le cours des choses" (*ibid.*, p. 521).

27. *Ibid.*, p. 517

28. *Idem.* Brunschvicg cites the formula of Painlevé: "un élément matériel infiniment éloigné de tous les autres reste absolument fixe si sa vitesse initiale est nulle et décrit une droite s'il est animé d'une vitesse initiale . . . Le mot infiniment signifie que la proposition est d'autant plus exacte que l'élément matériel est plus éloigné de tous autres" (*De la méthode dans les sciences*, I [1909], p. 386).

29. Brunschvicg, *L'Expérience humaine et la causalité physique*, p. 513

30. With all the reservations made concerning the subsequent "composition" of reflexes, Sherrington was persuaded that he possessed, with the laws of the simple reflex, the real elements of nerve functioning. Thus there is a concordance between the criticisms which have been shown to be telling against this conception of explanation in biology and the effort which physics is making to liberate itself from the dogmatism of laws.

31. Brunschvicg, *L'Expérience humaine et la causalité physique*, pp. 518-519

32. $\sigma = \dfrac{\eta}{4\pi\, abc} \cdot \dfrac{1}{\sqrt{\dfrac{x^2}{a^4} + \dfrac{y^2}{b^4} + \dfrac{z^2}{c^4}}}$ in which x, y, z represent the coordinates of the point considered, η the total charge, and a, b, c the demi-axes of the ellipsoid

33. Koehler, *Die physischen Gestalten*, p. 105

34. *Ibid.*, p. 117

35. The example in reference to which we were just reasoning is evidently not sufficient. Contemporary science has encountered more integrated systems which have demanded the creation of more subtle mathematical instruments. One could compare the notion of form, and the notion of individuality which is implied, in wave mechanics (cf. L. de Broglie, "Individualité et interaction dans le monde physique," *Revue de Métaphysique et de Morale*, April, 1937,

pp. 353-368). Material points, gifted with an invariable mass, and particles (electrons, protons, neutrons, positrons), defined by a constant mass and electrical charge, already appeared in pre-quantum science as abstract notions; for the movement of a material point is determined by the field of forces which surrounds it, and the total mass of a system of particles in interaction—proportional, according to the theory of relativity, to its energy, which cannot be divided among the particles—is not equal therefore to the sum of masses which would belong to the particles taken separately. In classical physics itself "la réalité paraît en général intermédiaire entre le concept d'individualité entièrement autonome et celui de système totalement fondu" (*ibid.*, p. 357). With still more reason, quantum science, in which objects can no longer be localized in time and space, in which it is impossible to exclude the occupation of the same place by two particles and, finally, in which the constancy of their properties is no longer maintained, permits in turn the conclusion that "la réalité, dans tous ses domaines, paraît être intermédiaire entre ces deux idéalisations extrêmes" (*ibid.*, p. 367). "En physique quantique, le système est une sorte d'organisme dans l'unité duquel les unités élémentaires constituantes se trouvent presque résorbées" (L. de Broglie, "La Réalité physique et l'idéalisation," *Revue de Synthèse,* April-October, 1934, p. 129). These analogies could be multiplied without providing any decision to the question which concerns us. The fact that the physical system is imaginable today only with the help of biological or psychological models does not reveal relations characteristic of life or mind in physical phenomena any more than Newtonian attraction did, and does not accredit the chimera of a mentalistic physics or a materialistic psychology: henceforth we know that causality is a means of circumscribing phenomena, the success of which is not guaranteed ahead of time by an infrastructure of eternal laws, and that physical phenomena do not have any privilege over the phenomenon of life or the human phenomenon in this respect. But the structures thus laid bare lose all meaning when they are separated from the mathematical relations which, in spite of everything, the physicist succeeds in establishing indirectly. Thus both belong to a universe of thought and not to a universe of realities.

36. We are thinking of the conclusions which Brunschvicg draws from his critique of positivism and finality, *L'Expérience humaine et la causalité physique,* Chapter XLIX.
37. J. Wahl, *Vers le concret,* Paris, Vrin, 1932, preface
38. Brunschvicg, *L'Expérience humaine et la causalité physique,* p. 520
39. E. Husserl, "Ideen zu einer reinen Phänomenologie und phänomenologische Philosophie," I, in *Jahrbuch für Philosophie und phänomenologische Forschung,* Halle, M. Niemeyer, 1913, I, 72-73
40. Koehler, *Die physischen Gestalten,* p. 180
41. Brunschvicg, *L'Expérience humaine et la causalité physique,* p. 515
42. Concerning all of these points, cf. Goldstein, *Der Aufbau des Organismus,* pp. 320 sqq. (cf. *The Organism,* pp. 344 sqq.)
43. The peripheral explanation which would relate the frequency of these modes of behaviors to certain local devices can be immediately excluded: a very slightly inclined oblique position would be treated as approaching the vertical position because the vertical, coinciding with a meridian of the retina, would give rise to special physiological phenomena. But in fact it is very rare that objectively vertical positions are projected on a meridian of the retina because it is very rare that we hold our head or body rigorously vertical themselves. The preferred positions of the hand, the head and the body would be less tiring, would be the positions in which the least tension of the adductors and abductors is achieved. But the tension of the muscles depends neither solely nor principally on the local mechanics of the skeleton; it is largely determined by the position of the other parts of the body. A displacement of the preferred plane in movements of the arm is obtained by modifying the position of other parts of the

body and that of the entire organism. Thus if the deviation between the frontal plane and that in which the arm moves remains constant for widely varying gestural directions, this local constancy cannot be the effect of local causes and refers us back to a constancy of the entire bodily attitude. Cf. Goldstein, *ibid.*, pp. 228 sqq. (cf. *The Organism*, pp. 351 sqq.)

44. *Ibid.*, p. 230 (cf. *The Organism*, p. 354): "Aber das ist ja das Problem: warum ist etwas eine Gestalt."

45. *Ibid.*, p. 235 (cf. *The Organism*, p. 347 sqq.)

46. It is known that, in the same way, the apparent vertical plane is displaced by a labyrinthic or cutaneous stimulation, or by a change in the position of the members.

47. Concerning all of these points, cf. *ibid.*, pp. 231 sqq. (cf. *The Organism*, pp. 355 sqq.)

48. *Ibid.*, p. 235 (cf. *The Organism*, p. 361)

49. *Ibid.*, pp. 237 sqq. (cf. *The Organism*, pp. 365 sqq.)

50. Cf. *supra*, Chapter I, for the distinction of *Eigenreflexe* and *Fremdreflexe*.

51. Goldstein, *Der Aufbau des Organismus*, p. 310 (cf. *The Organism*, p. 485)

52. One sees them appear, for example, in the tortoise which is removed from its natural support.

53. The tendency to consider the nervous system as "higher" in itself, for example, to the sexual system should be renounced once and for all: they cannot be separated or consequently subordinated one to the other in the functioning of the organism. Normal sexual life is integrated into the whole of behavior. The fact that cortical lesions can, as we have seen, entail a fall from sexual love to plain sexuality at the same time as gnostic disorders (*ibid.*, p. 313; cf. *The Organism*, p. 489) show that the sexual system is not autonomous in the normal subject. Actions of varying levels can be accomplished through an anatomically defined organic ensemble.

54. Karl C. Schneider, *Tierpsychologie*, pp. 227-230; cf. Buytendijk, *Psychologie des animaux*, p. 60

55. H. S. Jennings, *The Behavior of the Lower Organism*, New York, Columbia University Press, 1906; cf. Buytendijk, *Psychologie des animaux*, p. 60

56. Cf. E. Rubin, *Visuell wahrgenommene Figuren*, Christiania, Gyldendalske Boghandel, 1921

57. Concerning all these points, cf. P. Guillaume, *La Psychologie de la forme*

58. Goldstein, *Der Aufbau des Organismus*, pp. 323, 325 (cf. *The Organism*, pp. 375, 378)

59. *Ibid.*, p. 351 (cf. *The Organism*, p. 412)

60. *Ibid.*, p. 242 (cf. *The Organism*, p. 401)

61. N. Bohr, "Die Atomtheorie und die Prinzipien der Naturbeschreibung," *Die Naturwissenschaften*, XVIII (1930), pp. 74-78, cited by Goldstein, *Der Aufbau der Organismus*, p. 258 (cf. *The Organism*, p. 417)

62. Goldstein, *ibid.* (cf. *The Organism*, p. 417)

63. *Ibid.*, p. 333 (cf. *The Organism*, p. 387)

64. *Ibid.*, p. 258 (cf. *The Organism*, pp. 416 sqq.)

65. Cf. for example Bohr (cf. n. 60 *supra*) and P. Jordan ("Die Quantenmechanik und die Grundprobleme der Biologie und Physiologie," *Die Naturwissenschaften*, XX (1932), pp. 815-821), cited by Goldstein, *Der Aufbau der Organismus*, p. 256 (cf. *The Organism*, pp. 416 sqq.)

66. Cf. Wolff, "Selbstbeurteilung und Frembeurteilung . . . ," *Psychologische Forschung*, XVI (1932), pp. 251-328

67. It is nevertheless striking to see that attitudes of extension, the catastrophic character of which is established by science by means of a methodical observation are perceived by a three-year-old child as an expression of terror and are realized by him when he wants to simulate terror (personal observation).

68. Buytendijk speaks of an "investigation phénoménologique des mouvements d'expression" which "isole un phénomène, le réduit à son résidu irréductible,

contemple ses traits essentiels par une intuition immédiate" ("Les Différences essentielles des fonctions psychiques de l'homme et des animaux," pp. 70 and 85). Applied to intelligent mimicry, this method finds its general meaning to consist of the "possession de quelque chose" (*ibid.*, p. 85). The word "phenomenology" is taken here in the very large sense of a description of structures.

69. This determination of essences is practiced all the time by the scientists although it is not *recognized* as such. The physiologists take it into account in their experiments with the physiognomy of behavior. They will mention in their results that the animal was "tired," and they recognize it from the general character of its behavior rather than from the physico-chemical characteristics of fatigue. It is also the norm of behavior which Pavlov came up against (cf. *supra*, p. 146) when experiments of repeated conditioning provoked genuine experimental neuroses in his subjects.

70. Cited without reference by Buytendijk, "Les Différences essentielles des fonctions psychiques de l'homme et des animaux," p. 131

71. Hegel, *Jenenser Logik* in G. Lasson (ed.), *Hegels Sammtliche Werke kritische Ausgabe,* Leipzig, Meiner (1905—), p. 113. Cf. Hyppolite, "Vie et prise de conscience de la vie dans la philosophie hégélienne d'Iena," *Revue de Métaphysique et de Morale,* January 1938, p. 47

72. Cited by Hyppolite without reference, *ibid.*

73. Husserl, "Ideen zu einer reinen Phänomenologie und phänomenologische Philosophie," *passim*

74. E. Husserl, *Méditations cartésiennes,* Paris, Colin, 1931, *passim*

75. H. Bergson, *Évolution créatice,* in *Œuvres* (notes and introduction by A. Robinet), Paris, Presses Universitaires de France, 1959

76. Cf. for example, Pierre Janet, *De l'angoisse à l'extase,* II, Paris, Alcan, 1928

77. Pierre Janet, "La Tension psychologique et ses oscillations," in G. Dumas, *Traité de Psychologie,* Paris, Presses Universitaires de France

78. Brunschvicg, *L'Expérience humaine et la causalité physique,* pp. 466-467

79. G. Politzer, *Critique des fondements de la psychologie,* Paris, Rieder, 1929, p. 212

80. François Arouet (pseudonym of G. Politzer), "La Fin d'une parade philosophique, Le Bergsonisme," Paris, *Les Revues,* 1929

81. "C'est l'herbe en général qui attire l'herbivore" (H. Bergson, *Matière et Mémoire,* in *Œuvres*).

82. It is ordinarily said that psychology is not competent concerning this point, since it is not concerned with objects of experience (for example, space or other persons), but only with the contents (visual and tactile sensations, etc.) through which they are given to us, and that the operation of consciousness cannot be known by the observation of these contingent materials and their temporal genesis, but only by a reflection on the structure of the object. In reality it is precisely this distinction of structure and contents, of psychological origin and transcendental origin, which is in question. The *a priori* is not the innate or the primitive; and although all knowledge begins with experience, it manifests laws and a necessity in experience which do not come from the latter. But psychology itself has learned to define the innate, not as that which is present from birth, but as that which the subject draws from its proper resources and projects outside (cf. for example the chapter on instinct in Guillaume, *Traité de psychologie,* Paris, Alcan, 1931). And how could the psychological and the transcendental genesis differ if the second really gives us the order in which the objects of experience depend upon each other? For example, the perception of other persons cannot be chronologically prior to the knowledge of the universe if it depends upon it for its constitution. A *complete* psychology, which develops what is included in the experience of other persons, must find in it a reference to Nature and to the universe. Thus, the task of psychological analysis and that of transcendental analysis are not distinct, at least if psychology ceases to be a blind notation of "mental events" and becomes a description

of their meaning. What is true is that psychology never pushes the explicitation of experience all the way because it considers notions as self-evident in which the whole of a sedimented knowing and an obscure becoming are enclosed by the natural attitude. For example, psychology establishes with certitude the chronological and transcendental priority of the perception of others over the perception of objects in the sense in which the natural sciences understand them. But because it also takes the word Nature in the sense of the sciences of nature, it is not in a position to apperceive that primordial Nature, that pre-objective sensible field in which the behavior of other persons appears, which is prior according to its meaning to the perception of other persons just as it is prior to the Nature of the sciences, and which transcendental reflection could discover. Thus what psychology says, taken exactly in the sense in which it can say it, is incomplete, but not false; psychological genesis poses transcendental problems. This is all that we need to accept here. A more complete explicitation must be reserved for another work.

83. Cf. Shinn, "Notes on the Development of a Child," *University of California Studies*, I, 1-4, 1893-1899
84. The use that surrealist poetry has made of these themes is known.
85. Unpublished observation of J. P. Sartre
86. Cited without reference by Eugenio d'Ors, *L'Art de Goya*, Paris, Degrave, 1928
87. Cf. for example Koffka, "Perception. An Introduction to the Gestalt Theory," *Psychological Bulletin*, XIX (1922)
88. Cf. in particular Cassirer, "Le Langage et la constitution du monde des objets," *Journal de Psychologie normale et pathologique*, January 1934
89. It is known that a dog scarcely distinguishes the words in a command which is given to it; rather it is the intonation which it obeys.
90. For Kant, the distinction of matter and of form is evidently not that of two factors or of two real elements of knowledge which would produce it as two combined forces produce a resultant. It remains no less true that total consciousness reflected upon itself discovers the distinction between judgments of relation and the empirical terms on which they bear, between space and the qualities which fill it. This ideal analysis is constitutive of critical philosophy.
91. M. Scheler, "Der Formalismus in der Ethik und die Materiale Werthethik," in *Jahrbuch für Philosophie und phänomenologische Forschung*, Halle, M. Niemeyer, 1927, I-II
92. Husserl, "Ideen zu einer reinen Phänomenologie und phänomenologische Philosophie," *passim*
93. Of course, how it recognizes itself through the structures which it assumes one after the other must still be explained.
94. Scheler, "Der Formalismus in der Ethik und die Materiale Werthethik," p. 140
95. In this sense the act of speech or of expression makes us go beyond the universe of use-objects which we have described until now. For thought, language is at the same time a principle of slavery, since it is interposed between things and thought, and a principle of liberty, since one rids oneself of a prejudice by giving it its name.
96. Reported by R. Caillois, *Procès intellectuel de l'art*, cited by J. Wahl, *Nouvelle Revue française*, Jan. 1936, p. 123
97. It has often been noted that the revolutionary phenomenon or the act of suicide are only encountered in humanity. This is because both presuppose the capacity of rejecting the given milieu and of searching for equilibrium beyond any milieu. The famous preservation instinct, which probably appears in man only in case of illness or fatigue, has been abused. The healthy man proposes to live, to attain certain objects in the world or beyond the world and not to preserve himself. We have had occasion to see how certain persons with brain injuries create a restricted milieu for themselves in which life remains possible for them by diminishing as it were the sensible surface they offer to the world. The asylum is precisely a milieu of this kind. But suicide attempts among patients

who are replaced in the old milieu too soon signify that man is capable of situating his proper being, not in biological existence, but at the level of properly human relations.

98. M. Scheler, *Die Stellung des Menschen im Kosmos*, Darmstadt, Otto Reichl, 1928, pp. 47-50
99. Politzer, *Critique des fondements de la psychologie*
100. Goldstein, *Der Aufbau des Organismus*, pp. 213 sqq. (cf. *The Organism*, pp. 326 sqq.)
101. *Ibid.*, p. 213 (cf. *The Organism*, pp. 326-327)
102. Politzer, *Critique des fondements de la psychologie*
103. *Ibid.*, p. 130
104. *Ibid.*, p. 145
105. *Ibid.*, p. 193
106. Goldstein, *Der Aufbau des Organismus*, p. 213 (cf. *The Organism*, pp. 322 sqq.)
107. Stendhal, *Le Rouge et le noir*
108. Goldstein, *Der Aufbau des Organismus*, p. 300 (cf. *The Organism*, p. 472)
109. E. Cassirer, "Geist und Leben in der Philosophie der Gegenwart," *Die neue Rundschau*, XLI, pp. 244 sqq.
110. Goldstein, *Der Aufbau des Organismus*, p. 301 (cf. *The Organism*, pp. 474 sqq.)
111. Herder, cited by Goldstein, *ibid.*, p. 305 (cf. *The Organism*, p. 478)
112. A. Tilquin, "Un behaviorisme téléologique," *Journal de Psychologie*, November-December, 1935, p. 742
113. *Idem.* (our underlining)
114. E. C. Tolman, *Purposive Behavior in Animals and Men*, New York, Century, 1932
115. *Ibid.*, p. 768
116. *Ibid.*, pp. 768 sqq.
117. Cf. P. Guillaume, "L'Objectivité en psychologie," *Journal de Psychologie*, November-December 1932, pp. 700 sqq.
118. *Ibid.*, p. 739

CHAPTER IV

1. This distinction between direct perception and verbal account remains valid even if linguistic consciousness is primary (cf. the preceding chapter) and even in regard to the latter.
2. *Abschattungen.* Cf. E. Husserl, "Ideen zu einer reinen Phänomenologie und phänomenologische Philosophie," in *Jahrbuch für Philosophie und phänomenologische Forschung*, Halle, M. Niemayer, 1913, I, *passim*
3. Cf. P. Guillaume, "Le problème de la perception de l'espace et la psychologie de l'enfant," *Journal de Psychologie*, XXI, 1924.
4. We are trying to translate the German *Erscheinung.*
5. J. Piaget, *Le Représentation du monde chez l'enfant*, Paris, Presses Universitaires de France. 1948.
6. Descartes, *Dioptrique*, "Discours quatrième," édition Cousin, Paris, 1824-1826, pp. 39-40
7. *Ibid.*, "Discours premier," pp. 7-8
8. *Ibid.*, "Discours sixième," p. 54
9. ". . . ce qui donne occasion à son âme de sentir tout autant de diverses qualités en ces corps qu'il se trouve de variétés dans les mouvements qui sont causés par eux en son cerveau" (*ibid.*, "Discours quatrième," p. 40).
10. *Traité des passions*, art. 32 and 35; *Dioptrique*, "Discours quatrième," p. 53
11. *Traité des passions*, art. 34
12. *Dioptrique*, "Discours sixième," p. 64
13. *Idem.*
14. Bergson still employs this language.

15. Descartes, *Réponses aux Cinquièmes objections*, Bridoux (ed.), *Œuvres et Lettres*, Paris, Bibliothèque de la Piéiade, N.R.F., p. 376

16. ". . . il ne s'agissait pas ici de la vue et du toucher qui se font par l'entremise des organes corporels, mais de la seule pensée de voir et de toucher qui n'a pas besoin de ces organes comme nous expérimentons toutes les nuits dans nos songes." *Réponses aux Cinquièmes objections*, p. 376

17. *Méditations touchant la Philosophie Première* in Adam and Tannery (eds.), *Œuvres de Descartes*, Paris, Cerf, 1897-1910, 12 vols., IX ("Sixième Méditation"), pp. 9, 30

18. *Ibid.*, p. 59

19. *Ibid.*, p. 58

20. *Ibid.*, p. 63

21. *Traité des passions*, Part I

22. *Ibid.*, art. 30

23. "Je sais bien qu'un pied-cube est de même nature que toute autre étendue, mais ce qui fait qu'un pied-cube est distingué de tout autre, c'est son existence." (Malebranche, *Correspondance avec Mairan*, édition nouvelle, J. Moreau (ed.), Paris, Vrin, 1947, p. 139)

24. *Traité des passions*, art. 31

25. "Ce corps lequel par un certain droit particulier, j'appelais mien. . . ." "Sixième Méditation," ed. Adam and Tannery, IX, p. 60.

26. *Ibid.*, p. 64

27. Letter: "À Élisabeth, 21 mai 1643," ed. Adam and Tannery, III, p. 666

28. "Bien qu'on veuille concevoir l'âme comme matérielle (ce qui est proprement concevoir son union avec le corps) . . ." ("À Élisabeth, 28 juin 1643," *ibid.*, p. 691)

29. The *Réponses aux Sixièmes objections* speaks, concerning the perception of size, distance and shape, of explicit reasoning in childhood and refers in this connection to the *Dioptrique*. But though it is true that the *Dioptrique* describes, with respect to the situation of objects, an "action de la pensée qui, n'etant qu'une imagination toute simple, ne laisse pas d'envelopper en soi un raisonnement" ("Discours Sixième," ed. Cousin, p. 62), Descartes accepts the fact that the soul knows directly the situation of objects without passing through that of the members, and this by an "institution de la nature" ("Discours Sixième," ed. Cousin, p. 60) which brings it about that such and such a situation is "vue" (*ibid.*, p. 63) when this or that disposition of the parts of the brain is realized. It is only when Descartes analyzes perception from within, as happens in the *Méditations*, that the "géométrie naturelle" (*Traité de l'homme*, ed. Cousin, IV, p. 380) of perception becomes a reasoning of the soul itself and perception an inspection of the mind (cf. "Sixième Méditation," ed. Adam and Tannery, IX, p. 66). The *Dioptrique* enunciates the "jugements naturels," that is, the "naturized" thought, of Malebranche ("L'âme ne fait point tous les jugements que je lui attribue: ces jugements naturels ne sont que des sensations . . ." [*Recherche de la vérité*, I, chapter IX]; "Dieu les fait en nous pour nous . . . tels que nous les pourrions former nous-mêmes si nous savions divinement l'optique et la géométrie" [*ibid.*]). The implicit reasonings of perception arise from God, not as word and place of ideas, but as creative will and legislator of occasional causes. On the other hand, the *Méditations* enunciates the "naturizing" thought of Spinoza.

30. P. Claudel, *Art poétique: Traité de la co-naissance au monde et de soi-même*, Paris, Mercure de France

31. E. Husserl, "Vorlesungen zur Phänomenologie des inneren Zeitbewusztseins," in *Jahrbuch für Phänomenologie und phänomenologische Philosophie*, IX (1928), p. 5

32. M. Wahl seems to see in it a discovery of contemporary philosophy (*Vers le concret*, Paris, Vrin, 1932, preface).

33. The *Esthétique transcendental* (tr. Barni, I, pp. 64, 68, 70, 80; cf. "The Tran-

scendental Esthetic" in *Critique of Pure Reason*, tr. N. K. Smith, London, Macmillan, 1933, pp. 65-91) goes so far as to relate, besides the empirical contents, the form of space itself to the contingencies of the human constitution.

34. It is known how the second edition of the *Critique of Pure Reason* withdraws "formal intuition" from the sensibility—the "Transcendental Esthetic" spoke of the "manner in which we are affected"—and gives it to the understanding, how it abandons the three syntheses of transcendental imagination—which, even if each one presupposed the following one, gave the appearance of a structure of the mind—in order to manifest better the presence of the "I think" at all the levels of consciousness which an abstract analysis could distinguish.

35. Brunschvicg, *L'Expérience humaine et la causalité physique*, Pairs, Alcan, 1922, p. 466

36. *Ibid.*, p. 73

37. J. Cassou, *Le Greco*, Paris, Rieder, 1931, p. 35

38. R. Mourgue, *Neurobiologie de l'hallucination*, Brussels, Lamertin, 1932

39. M. Scheler, *Die Wissensformen und die Gesellschaft*, Leipzig, Der Neue Geist, 1926, p. 394

40. "Without leaving the natural attitude one could show how the problems of totality (*Ganzheitsprobleme*) of the natural world, pursued to their root, end up instigating the passage to the transcendental attitude." E. Fink, "Vergegenwärtigung und Bild," *Jahrbuch für Philosophie und phänomenologische Forschung*, 1930, XI, p. 279

41. We are thinking of a philosophy like that of L. Brunschvicg and not of Kantian philosophy, which, particularly in the *Critique of the Judgment*, contains essential indications concerning the problems of which it is a question here.

42. Cf. Chapter I

43. Cf. Chapter I, p. 227, n. 31, and Chapter II

44. Cf. *supra.*

45. Hegel, *Vorlesungen über die Philosophie der Geschichte*, in G. Lasson (ed.), *Hegels Sammtliche Werke kritische Ausgabe*, Leipzig, Meiner, 1905—

46. ". . . on ne vous croit pas quand vous avancez si hardiment et sans aucune preuve que l'esprit croît et s'affaiblit avec le corps; car de ce qu'il n'agit pas si parfaitement dans le corps d'un enfant que dans celui d'un homme parfait, et que souvent ses actions peuvent être empêchées par le vin et par d'autres choses corporelles, il s'ensuit seulement que tandis qu'il est uni au corps il s'en sert comme d'un instrument pour faire ces sortes d'opérations auxquelles il est pour l'ordinaire occupé, mais non pas que le corps le rende plus ou moins parfait qu'il est en soi; et la conséquence que vous tirez de là n'est pas meilleure que si, de ce qu'un artisan ne travaille pas bien toutes les fois qu'il se sert d'un mauvais outil, vous infériez qu'il emprunte son adresse et la science de son art de la bonté de son instrument." ("Réponses aux Cinquièmes objections," Bridoux (ed.) *Œuvres et Lettres*, p. 371.) It is not a question of approving Gassendi, who attributed to the biological body what belongs to the phenomenal body—but this is not a reason for speaking of a perfection of the mind in-itself (*en soi*). If the body plays a role in preventing the actualization of the mind, it is because the body is involved with the mind when this actualization is achieved.

47. Cf. Chapter II, Section III

48. "The soul is the meaning of the body and the body is the manifestation of the soul; neither of the two acts on the other because neither of the two belongs to the world of things. . . . The soul is inherent in the body as the concept is inherent in speech: the former is the meaning of the word, the latter is the meaning of the body; the word is the clothing of thought and the body the manifestation of the soul. And there are no souls without manifestations any more than there are concepts without speech" (L. Klages, *Vom Wesen des Bewusztseins*, Leipzig, Barth, 1921).

49. ". . . sa main qui écartait les couvertures d'un geste qui eût autrefois signifié

que ces couvertures la gênaient et qui maintenant ne signifiait rien" (Proust, *Le Côté des Guermantes,* II, p. 27). "Dégagé par la double action de la morphine et de l'oxygène, le souffle de ma grand-mère ne peinait plus, ne geignait plus, mais vif, léger, glissait, patineur, vers le fluide délicieux. Peut-être à l'haleine, insensible comme celle du vent dans la flûte d'un roseau, se mêlait-il dans ce chant quelques-uns de ces soupirs plus humains qui, libérés à l'approche de la mort, font croire à des impressions de souffrance ou de bonheur chez ceux qui déja ne sentent plus, il venaient ajouter un accent plus mélodieux, mais sans changer son rythme, à cette longue phrase qui s'élevait, montait encore puis retombait, pour s'élancer de nouveau, de la poitrine allégée, à la poursuite de l'oxygène" (*ibid.,* p. 31).

50. Nevertheless there would be a place for investigating more thoroughly the distinction of our "natural body," which is always already there, already constituted for consciousness, and our "cultural body," which is the sedimentation of its spontaneous acts. The problem is posed by Husserl when he distinguishes "original passivity" and "secondary passivity." Cf. in particular "Formale and transzendentale Logik," in *Jahrbuch für Philosophie und phänomenologische Forschung,* X (1929), p. 287

51. Cf. p. 162

52. Cf. p. 136

53. Cf. p. 144

54. We reserve the question of whether there is not, as Heidegger suggests, a perception of the *world,* that is, a manner of acceding to an indefinite field of objects which gives them in their reality. What is certain is that the perceived is not limited to that which strikes my eyes. When I am sitting at my desk, the space is closed behind me not only in idea but also in reality. Even if the horizon of the perceived can be expanded to the limits of the world, the perceptual consciousness of the world as existing remains distinct from the intellectual consciousness of the world as object of an infinity of true judgments.

55. Husserl, "Ideen zu einer reinen Phänomenologie und phänomenologische Philosophie," p. 89

56. We are defining here the "phenomenological reduction" in the sense which is given to it in Husserl's final philosophy.

57. The notion of intentionality will be of help in this regard.

58. J.-P. Sartre, "La Transcendance de L'Ego," *Recherches philosophiques,* 1936-1937

59. Cf. *supra,* p. 184

60. This is the thesis of J.-P. Sartre, "La Transcendance de l'Ego"

61. Cf. *supra,* p. 126

STUDIES CITED IN THIS WORK

Arouet, François (pseudonym of G. Politzer), "La Fin d'une parade philosophique, LeBergsonisme," *Les Revues*, Paris, 1929

Benary, W., "Studien zur Untersuchung der Intelligenz bei einem Fall von Seelenblindheit," *Psychologische Forschung*, II (1922)

Bergson, H., *Évolution créatice* (1907) in *Œuvres* (notes and introduction by A. Robinet), Paris, Presses Universitaires de France, 1959

———, *Matière et Memoire* (1896) in *Œuvres, ibid.*

Bohr, N., "Die Atomtheorie und die Prinzipien der Naturbeschreibung," *Die Naturwissenschaften*, XVIII (1930)

Boumann and Grunbaum, "Experimentellpsychologische Untersuchungen zur Aphasie und Paraphasie," *Zeitschrift für das gesamte Neurologie und Psychiatrie*, XCVI (1925)

Brunschvicg, L., *L'Expérience humaine et la causalité physique*, Paris, Alcan, 1922

———, *Spinoza et ses contemporains*, 3rd ed., Paris, Alcan, 1923

Bühler, L., *Die geistige Entwickelung des Kindes*, 4th ed., Jena, Fischer, 1924

Buytendijk, F., "An Experimental Investigation into the Influence of Cortical Lesions on the Behavior of Rats," *Archives néerlandaises de physiologie*, XVII (1932)

———, "Das Verhalten von Octopus nach teilweiser Zerstörung des Gehirns," *Arch. néerl. de physiol.*, XVIII (1933)

———, "Die Bedeutung der Feldkräfte und der Intentionalität für das Verhalten des Hundes," *Arch. néerl. de physiol.*, XVII (1932)

———, "Le Cerveau et l'Intelligence," *Journal de Psychologie*, XXVIII (1931)

———, "Les Différences essentielles des fonctions psychiques de l'homme et des animaux," *Cahiers de philosophie de la nature*, Vrin, IV (1930)

———, *Psychologie des animaux*, Paris, Payot, 1928

———, Versuche über die Steuerung der Bewegungen," *Arch. néerl. de physiol.*, XVII (1932)

and Fischel, "Strukturgemäszes Verhalten von Ratten," *Arch. néerl. de physiol.*, XVI (1931)

———, "Ueber die akustische Wahrnehmung des Hundes," *Arch. néerl. de physiol.*, XVII (1933)

———, "Ueber die Reaktionen des Hundes auf menschliche Wörter," *Arch. néerl. de physiol.*, XIX (1934)

Fischel and Ter Laag, "Ueber die Zieleinstellung von Ratten und Hunden," *Arch. néerl. de physiol.*, XX (1935)

and Plessner, "Die physiologische Erklärung des Verhaltens, eine Kritik an der Theorie Pawlows," *Acta Biotheoretica*, Series A, I (1935)

Callois, R., "La Mante religieuse, recherche sur la nature et la signification du mythe," *Mesures*, April, 1937

Cassirer, E., "Geist und Leben in der Philosophie der Gegenwart," *Die neue Rundschau*, XLI

———, "Le Langage et la constitution du monde des objets," *Journal de Psychologie normale et pathologique*, January, 1934

Cassou, J., *Le Greco*, Paris, Rieder, 1931

CHEVALIER, J., *L'Habitude*, Paris, Bouvin, 1929
CLAUDEL, P., *Art poétique: Traité de la co-naissance au monde et de soi-même*, Paris, Mercure de France
DE BROGLIE, L., "Individualité et interaction dans le monde physique," *Revue de Métaphysique et de Morale*, April, 1937
———, "La Réalité physique et l'idéalisation," *Revue de Synthése*, April-October, 1934
DEJEAU, R., *Étude psychologique de la "Distance" dans la vision*, Paris, Presses Universitaires de France, 1926
DESCARTES, R., *Œuvres complètes*, ed. V. Cousin, Paris, 1824-1826
———, *Œuvres de Descartes*, ed. Adam and Tannery, Paris, Cerf, 1897-1910
———, *Œuvres et Lettres*, ed. Bridoux, Paris, Pléiade
D'ORS, EUGENIO, *L'Art de Goya*, Paris, Degrave, 1928
DRABOVITCH, W., "Les Réflexes conditionnés et la chronaxie," *Revue philosophique*, CXXIII (1937)
FINK, E., "Vergegenwärtigung und Bild," *Jahrbuch für Philosophie und phänomenologische Forschung*, XI (1930)
FUCHS, W., "Eine Pseudofovea bei Hemianopikern," *Psychologische Forschung*, I (1922)
———, "Experimentelle Entersuchungen über das simultane Hintereinander auf derselben Sehrichtung," *Zeitschrift für Psychologie*, XCI
GELB, A., and GOLDSTEIN, K. "Ueber Farbennamenamnesie," *Psychologische Forschung*, VI (1925)
———, "Zur Psychologie des optischen Wahrnehmungs und Erkennungsvorganges," in *Psychologische Analysen Hirnpathologischer Fälle*, I
———, (Ed.), *Psychologische Analysen Hirnpathologischer Fälle*, I, Leipzig, J. A. Barth, 1920
GOLDSTEIN, K., *Der Aufbau des Organismus*, The Hague: Martinus Nijhoff, 1934 (*The Organism*, New York: American Book, 1938)
———, "Die Lokalisation in der Grosshirnrinde," in *Handbuch der normalen und pathologischen Physiologie*, ed. by Bethe, X
———, "Ueber die Abhängigkeit der Bewegungen von optischen Vorgängen," *Monatschrift für Psychiatrie und Neurologie*, LIV-LV (1923-1924)
GUILLAUME, P., *La Formation des habitudes*, Paris, Alcan, 1936
———, *La Psychologie de la forme*, Paris, Flammarion, 1937
———, "Le Problème de la perception de l'espace et la psychologie de l'enfant," *Journal de Psychologie*, XXI, (1924)
———, *L'Imitation chez l'enfant*, Pairs, Alcan, 1925
———, "L'Objectivité en psychologie," *Journal de Psychologie*, November-December 1932
———, *Traité de psychologie*, Paris, Alcan, 1931
HEAD, SIR HENRY, "Speech and Cerebral Localization," *Brain*, vol. 42 (1923)
HEGEL, G., *Jenenser Logik* in *Hegels Sammtliche Werke kritische Ausgabe*, ed. G. Lasson, Leipzig: Meiner, 1905—
———, *Vorlesungen über die Philosophie der Geschichte, ibid.*
HEIDER, G., "New Studies in Transparency, Colour and Form," *Psychologische Forschung*, XVII (1933)
HOCHHEIMER, H., "Analyse eines Seelenblinden von der Sprache aus," *Psychologische Forschung*, XVI (1932)
HUSSERL, E., "Formale und transzendentale Logik," in *Jahrbuch für Philosophie und phänomenologische Forschung*, X (1929)
———, "Ideen zu einer reinen Phänomenologie und phänomenologische Philosophie," I, in *Jahrbuch für Philosophie und phänomenologische Forschung*, Halle, H. Niemeyer, I, (1913). (Critical edition: ed. W. Biemel, The Hague, Nijhoff, 1950)
———, *Méditations cartésiennes*, Paris, Colin, 1931 (Critical edition: *Cartesianische Méditationem und Pariser Vorträge*, ed. S. Strasser, The Hague, Nijhoff, 1950.

English translation: *Cartesian Meditations,* tr. D. Cairns, The Hague, Nijhoff, 1960)

———, "Vorlesungen zur Phänomenologie des inneren Zeitbewusztseins," in *Jahrbuch für Phänomenologie und phänomenologische Philosophie,* IX (1928)

HYPPOLITE, J., "Vie et prise de conscience de la vie dans la philosophie hégélienne d'Iena," *Revue de Métaphysique et de Morale,* January, 1938

JAENSCH, E. R., "Ueber die Wahrnehmung des Raumes," *Zeitschrift für Psychologie,* VI (1911)

JANET, PIERRE, *De l'angoisse à l'extase,* II, Paris, Alcan, 1928

———, "La Tension psychologique et ses oscillations," in G. Dumas, *Traité de Psychologie,* I, Paris, Presses Universitaires de France

JENNINGS, H. S., *The Behavior of the Lower Organism,* New York, Columbia University Press, 1906

JORDAN, P., "Die Quantenmechanik und die Grundprobleme der Biologie und Physiologie," *Die Naturwissenschaften,* XX (1932)

KANT, I., *Kritik der reinen Vernunft* in *Gesammelte Schriften,* Berlin, Reimer and W. De Gruyter, 1902-1942 (*Critique of Pure Reason,* tr. N. K. Smith, London, Macmillan, 1931)

———, *Kritik der Urtheilskraft* in *Gesammelte Schriften,* Berlin, Reimer and W. De Gruyter, 1902-1942 (*Critique of Judgment,* tr. J. H. Bernard, London, Macmillan, 1931)

KLAGES, L., Vom Wesen des Bewusztseins, Leipzig, J. A. Barth, 1921

KOEHLER, W., "'An Aspect of Gestalt Psychology," in *Psychologies of 1925,* ed. by C. Murchison, Worcester, Mass., Clark University Press, 1928

———, *Die physischen Gestalten in Ruhe und im stationären Zustand,* Erlangen, Braunschweig, 1920

———, *Gestalt Psychology,* London, G. Bell, 1930.

———, *Intelligenzprüfungen an Menschenaffen,* 2nd ed., Berlin, 1921 (*The Mentality of Apes,* tr. E. Winters, London, Routledge & Kegan Paul, 1925. *L'Intelligence des singes supérieurs,* Paris, Alcan, 1927)

———, "Nachweis einfacher Strukturfunktionen beim Schimpansen und beim Haushuhn," *Berliner Abhandlungen,* Jahrang 1918

———, "Optische Untersuchungen am Schimpansen und am Haushuhn," *Berliner Abhandlungen,* Jahrang 1915

KOFFKA, K., "Mental Development," in *Psychologies of 1925,* ed. by C. Murchison, Worcester, Mass., Clark University Press, 1928

———, "Perception. An Introduction to the Gestalt Theory," *Psychological Bulletin,* XIX (1922)

———, *Principles of Gestalt Psychology,* New York, Harcourt, Brace, 1935

———, "Some Problems of Space Perception," in *Psychologies of 1930,* ed. by C. Murchison, Worcester, Mass., Clark University Press, 1930

———, "Some Remarks on the Theory of Colour Constancy," *Psychologische Forschung,* XVI (1932)

———, *The Growth of the Mind,* New York, Harcourt, Brace, 1925

LALANDE, A., *Les Théories de l'induction et de l'expérimentation,* Paris, Boivin, 1929

LAPICQUE, L., "Physiologie générale du système nerveux," in G. Dumas, *Nouveau Traité de Psychologie,* I, Presses Universitaires de France

LASHLEY, K. S., *Brain Mechanisms and Intelligence,* Chicago, University of Chicago Press, 1929

———, "Cerebral Control versus Reflexology," *Journal of Genetic Psychology,* V (1931)

MALEBRANCHE, N., *Correspondance avec Mairan,* édition nouvelle, J. Moreau, ed., Paris, Vrin, 1947

MARINA, "Die Relationen des Palaeencephalon sind nicht fix," *Neurol. Centralbl.,* 1915

MILLER, N. E., "A Reply to 'Sign-Gestalt or Conditioned Reflex?'" *Psychological Review,* XLII (1935)

MOURGUE, R., *Neurobiologie de l'hallucination*, Brussels, Lamertin, 1932

NELLMAN, H. and TRENDELENBURG, W., "Ein Beitrag zur Intelligenzprüfung niederer Affen," *Zeitschrift für vergleichende Physiologie*, IV (1926)

OMBREDANE, M., "Le Langage," *Revue Philosophique*, 1931

PAINLEVÉ, *De la méthode dans les sciences*, I (1909)

PAVLOV, I. P., *Die höchste Nerventätigkeit von Tieren*, München, Bergmann, 1926

———, *Ein Beitrag zur Physiologie des hyponotischen Zustandes beim Hunde* (unter Mitarbeit von Dr. Petrova)

———, *Leçons sur l'activité du cortex cérébral*, Paris, A. Legrand, 1929

———, *Les Réflexes conditionnels*, Paris, Alcan, 1932

PIAGET, J., *La Causalité physique chez l'enfant*, Paris, Alcan, 1927

———, *La Représentation du monde chez l'enfant*, Paris, Presses Universitaires de France, 1948

PIÉRON, H., "Du rôle des réflexes localisateurs dans les perceptions spatiales," *Journal de Psychologie*, XVIII, 10 (1921)

———, *Le Cerveau et la pensée*, Paris, Alcan, 1923

———, "Les Problèmes de la perception et la psychophysiologie," *Année psychologique*, XXVII (1926)

———, "Les Réflexes conditionnés," in Dumas, *Nouveau Traité de Psychologie*, II, Paris, Presses Universitaires de France

———, "Recherches sur les lois de variation," *Année Psychologique*, XX (1913)

POLITZER, G. (see also AROUET, FRANÇOIS), *Critique des fondements de la psychologie*, Paris, Rieder, 1929

REVESZ, G., "Experiments on Animal Space Perception," *VIIth International Congress of Psychology, Proceedings and Papers*, Cambridge, 1924

RUBIN, E., *Visuell wahrgenommene Figuren*, Christiana, Gyldendalske Boghandel, 1921

RUGER, H. A., "Psychology of Efficiency," *Archives of Psychology*, XV (1910)

RUYER, R., "Un modèle méchanique de la conscience," *Journal de Psychologie*, XXIX (1932)

SARTRE, J.-P., "La Transcendence de l'Ego," *Recherches philosophiques*, 1936-1937

SCHELER, M., "Der Formalismus in der Ethik und die Materiale Werthethik," *Jahrbuch für Philosophie und phänomenologische Forschung*, I-II, Halle, M. Niemeyer, 1927

———, *Die Stellung des Menschen im Kosmos*, Darmstadt, Otto Reichl, 1928

———, *Die Wissensformen und die Gesellschaft*, Leipzig, Der Neue Geist, 1926

SCHILDER, P., *Das Körperschema*, Berlin, Springer, 1923

SCHNEIDER, KARL C., *Tierpsychologie*

SHEPHERD, W. T., "Tests on Adaptive Intelligence in Rhesus Monkeys," *American Journal of Psychology*, XXVI (1915)

SHERRINGTON, C., *The Integrative Action of the Nervous System* (new ed.), Cambridge, Cambridge University Press, 1947

SHINN, M. W., "Notes on the Development of a Child," *University of California Studies*, I (1893)

STEINFELD, "Ein Beitrag zur Analyse der Sexualfunktion," *Zeitschrift für das gesamte Neurologie und Psychiatrie*, 187 (1927)

TILQUIN, A., *Le Behaviorisme, origine et développement de la psychologie de réaction en Amérique*, Paris, Vrin, 1942

———, "Un behaviorisme téléologique," *Journal de Psychologie*, November-December, 1935

TOLMAN, E. C., *Purposive Behavior in Animals and Men*, New York, Century, 1932

———, "Sign-Gestalt or Conditioned Reflex?" *Psychological Review*, XL (1933)

TUDOR-HART, B., "Studies in Transparency, Form and Colour," *Psychologische Forschung*, X (1928)

VOLKELT, H., *Die Vorstellungen der Tiere*, 1914

VON KRIES, J., *Über die materiellen Grundlagen der Bewusztseinserscheinungen*, Tübingen u. Leipzig, 1901

VON WEIZSÄCKER, V. F., "Reflexgesetze," in *Handbuch der normalen und pathologischen Physiologie,* ed. by Bethe, X

WAHL, J., *Vers le concret,* Paris, Vrin, 1932

WALLON, H., *Stades et troubles du développement psycho-moteur et mental chez l'enfant,* Paris, Alcan, 1925 (republished under the title: *L'Enfant turbulent,* 1925)

WERTHEIMER, M., "Experimentelle Studien über das Sehen von Bewegung," *Zeitschrift für Psychologie,* LXI (1912)

———, "Ueber Gestalttheorie," *Symposion I* (1927)

WOERKOM, "Ueber Störungen im Denken bei Aphasiepatienten," *Monatschrift für Psychiatrie und Neurologie,* LIX (1925)

WOLFF, W., "Selbstbeurteilung und Fremdbeurteilung . . . ," *Psychologische Forschung,* XVI (1932)

INDEX OF AUTHORS CITED